- There is power.

- women drew a sword. pg 54

- nuns granted animal husbandry rights by women pg 74

THE NEW MIDDLE AGES

BONNIE WHEELER, *Series Editor*

The New Middle Ages is a series dedicated to pluridisciplinary studies of medieval cultures, with particular emphasis on recuperating women's history and on feminist and gender analyses. This peer-reviewed series includes both scholarly monographs and essay collections.

PUBLISHED BY PALGRAVE:

Women in the Medieval Islamic World
edited by Gavin R. G. Hambly

The Ethics of Nature in the Middle Ages: On Boccaccio's Poetaphysics
by Gregory B. Stone

Presence and Presentation: Women in the Chinese Literati Tradition
by Sherry J. Mou

The Lost Letters of Heloise and Abelard: Perceptions of Dialogue in Twelfth-Century France
by Constant J. Mews

Understanding Scholastic Thought with Foucault
by Philipp W. Rosemann

For Her Good Estate: The Life of Elizabeth de Burgh
by Frances A. Underhill

Constructions of Widowhood and Virginity in the Middle Ages
edited by Cindy L. Carlson and Angela Jane Weisl

Motherhood and Mothering in Anglo-Saxon England
by Mary Dockray-Miller

Listening to Heloise: The Voice of a Twelfth-Century Woman
edited by Bonnie Wheeler

The Postcolonial Middle Ages
edited by Jeffrey Jerome Cohen

Chaucer's Pardoner and Gender Theory: Bodies of Discourse
by Robert S. Sturges

Crossing the Bridge: Comparative Essays on Medieval European and Heian Japanese Women Writers
edited by Barbara Stevenson and Cynthia Ho

Engaging Words: The Culture of Reading in the Later Middle Ages
by Laurel Amtower

Robes and Honor: The Medieval World of Investiture
edited by Stewart Gordon

Representing Rape in Medieval and Early Modern Literature
edited by Elizabeth Robertson and Christine M. Rose

Same Sex Love and Desire among Women in the Middle Ages
edited by Francesca Canadé Sautman and Pamela Sheingorn

Sight and Embodiment in the Middle Ages: Ocular Desires
by Suzannah Biernoff

Listen, Daughter: The Speculum Virginum *and the Formation of Religious Women in the Middle Ages*
edited by Constant J. Mews

Science, the Singular, and the Question of Theology
by Richard A. Lee, Jr.

Gender in Debate from the Early Middle Ages to the Renaissance
edited by Thelma S. Fenster and Clare A. Lees

Malory's Morte Darthur: *Remaking Arthurian Tradition*
by Catherine Batt

The Vernacular Spirit: Essays on Medieval Religious Literature
edited by Renate Blumenfeld-Kosinski, Duncan Robertson, and Nancy Warren

Popular Piety and Art in the Late Middle Ages: Image Worship and Idolatry in England 1350–1500
by Kathleen Kamerick

Absent Narratives, Manuscript Textuality, and Literary Structure in Late Medieval England
by Elizabeth Scala

Creating Community with Food and Drink in Merovingian Gaul
by Bonnie Effros

Representations of Early Byzantine Empresses: Image and Empire
by Anne McClanan

Encountering Medieval Textiles and Dress: Objects, Texts, Images
edited by Désirée G. Koslin and Janet Snyder

Eleanor of Aquitaine: Lord and Lady
edited by Bonnie Wheeler and John Carmi Parsons

Isabel La Católica, Queen of Castile: Critical Essays
edited by David A. Boruchoff

Homoeroticism and Chivalry: Discourses of Male Same-Sex Desire in the Fourteenth Century
by Richard E. Zeikowitz

Portraits of Medieval Women: Family, Marriage, and Politics in England 1225–1350
by Linda E. Mitchell

Eloquent Virgins: From Thecla to Joan of Arc
by Maud Burnett McInerney

The Persistence of Medievalism: Narrative Adventures in Contemporary Culture
by Angela Jane Weisl

Capetian Women
edited by Kathleen D. Nolan

Joan of Arc and Spirituality
edited by Ann W. Astell and Bonnie Wheeler

The Texture of Society: Medieval Women in the Southern Low Countries
edited by Ellen E. Kittell and Mary A Suydam

Charlemagne's Mustache and Other Cultural Clusters of a Dark Age
by Paul Edward Dutton

Troubled Vision: Gender, Sexuality, and Sight in Medieval Text and Image
edited by Emma Campbell and Robert Mills

Queering Medieval Genres
by Tison Pugh

Sacred Place in Early Medieval Neoplatonism
by L. Michael Harrington

The Middle Ages at Work
edited by Kellie Robertson and Michael Uebel

Medieval Fabrications: Dress, Textiles, Clothwork, and Other Cultural Imaginings
edited by E. Jane Burns

Was the Bayeux Tapestry Made in France?: The Case for St. Florent of Saumur
by George Beech

Chaucer's Jobs
by David R. Carlson

Medievalism and Orientalism
by John M. Ganim

Queer Love in the Middle Ages
by Anna Klosowska

Performing Women: Sex, Gender and the Iberian Lyric
by Denise K. Filios

Necessary Conjunctions: The Social Self in Medieval England
by David Gary Shaw

Visual Culture in the German Middle Ages
edited by Kathryn Starkey and Horst Wenzel

Medieval Paradigms: Essays in Honor of Jeremy duQuesnay Adams, Volumes 1 and 2
edited by Stephanie Hayes-Healy

False Fables and Exemplary Truth in Later Middle English Literature
by Elizabeth Allen

Ecstatic Transformation: On the Uses of Alterity in the Middle Ages
by Michael Uebel

Sacred and Secular in Medieval and Early Modern Cultures: New Essays
edited by Lawrence Besserman

Tolkien's Modern Middle Ages
edited by Jane Chance and Alfred K. Siewers

Representing Righteous Heathens in Late Medieval England
by Frank Grady

Byzantine Dress: Representations of Secular Dress in Eighth-to-Twelfth Century Painting
by Jennifer L. Ball

The Laborer's Two Bodies: Labor and the 'Work' of the Text in Medieval Britain, 1350–1500
by Kellie Robertson

The Dogaressa of Venice, 1250–1500: Wife and Icon
by Holly S. Hurlburt

Logic, Theology, and Poetry in Boethius, Abelard, and Alan of Lille: Words in the Absence of Things
by Eileen Sweeney

The Theology of Work: Peter Damian and the Medieval Religious Renewal Movement
by Patricia Ranft

On the Purification of Women: Churching in Northern France, 1100–1500
by Paula Rieder

Writers of the Reign of Henry II: Twelve Essays
edited by Ruth Kennedy and Simon Meecham-Jones

Lonesome Words: The Vocal Poetic of the Old English Lament and the African American Blues Song
by M.G. McGeachy

Performing Piety: Musical Culture in Medieval English Nunneries
by Anne Bagnell Yardley

The Flight from Desire: Augustine and Ovid to Chaucer
by Robert R. Edwards

Mindful Spirit in Late Medieval Literature: Essays in Honor of Elizabeth D. Kirk
edited by Bonnie Wheeler

Women, Power, and Religious Patronage in the Middle Ages
Erin L. Jordan

WOMEN, POWER, AND RELIGIOUS PATRONAGE IN THE MIDDLE AGES

Erin L. Jordan

WOMEN, POWER, AND RELIGIOUS PATRONAGE IN THE MIDDLE AGES
© Erin L. Jordan, 2006.

All rights reserved. No part of this book may be used or reproduced in any manner whatsoever without written permission except in the case of brief quotations embodied in critical articles or reviews.

First published in 2006 by
PALGRAVE MACMILLAN™
175 Fifth Avenue, New York, N.Y. 10010 and
Houndmills, Basingstoke, Hampshire, England RG21 6XS
Companies and representatives throughout the world.

PALGRAVE MACMILLAN is the global academic imprint of the Palgrave Macmillan division of St. Martin's Press, LLC and of Palgrave Macmillan Ltd. Macmillan® is a registered trademark in the United States, United Kingdom and other countries. Palgrave is a registered trademark in the European Union and other countries.

ISBN-13: 978–1–4039–6656–8
ISBN-10: 1–4039–6656–7

Library of Congress Cataloging-in-Publication Data

Jordan, Erin L.
    Women, power, and religious patronage in the
  Middle Ages / Erin L. Jordan.
      p. cm.—(New Middle Ages)
    Includes bibliographical references and index.
    ISBN 1–4039–6656–7 (alk. paper)
    1. Women—France—History—Middle Ages, 500–1500.
    2. Women—Flanders—History—Middle Ages, 500–1500.
    3. France—History—Medieval period, 987–1515. 4. Jeanne, of Constantinople, ca. 1200–1244. 5. Marguerite, of Constantinople, 1202–1279. 6. Hainaut (County)—History—To 1500.
    7. Flanders—History—To 1500. I. Title. II. New Middle Ages (Palgrave Macmillan (Firm))
HQ1147F7 J67 2006
305.48′962109040902—dc22   2005056617

A catalogue record for this book is available from the British Library.

Design by Newgen Imaging Systems (P) Ltd., Chennai, India.

First edition: May 2006

10 9 8 7 6 5 4 3 2 1

Printed in the United States of America.

CONTENTS

Acknowledgments	vii
Introduction: Powerful Women and Religious Patronage	1
1 Accessing Authority: 1206–14	17
2 Wielding Power: 1214–80	37
3 Securing Power through Religious Patronage	61
4 Translating Secular Power into Spiritual Gains	87
Conclusion	111
Appendix 1: Monastic and Religious Foundations in Thirteenth-Century Flanders and Hainaut	117
Appendix 2: Genealogy of the Counts of Flanders and Hainaut	123
Notes	125
Bibliography	173
Index	191

ACKNOWLEDGMENTS

As historians, we are taught that an event is seldom the result of a single cause, but rather the outcome of a multiplicity of factors, which combine over time to produce an outcome. In a similar fashion, no book is exclusively the product of one individual, but it represents the collaboration of family, friends, and colleagues. This is certainly the case here.

This project was completed with the support of several institutions. The majority of the archival work was made possible by a Seashore Dissertation-year Fellowship in the Humanities from the University of Iowa. Later research was supported by the Economic History Association and several grants from the University of Northern Colorado. I would like to thank in particular Maurice Vandermaesen of the Rijksarchief Bruges for his enthusiastic reception of a timid graduate student and his interest in the project. Considerable amount of time was spent in the Archives Départmentales du Nord, Lille, where the archivists made available their vast collection of charters as well as their impressive knowledge of the region. The efforts of the Inter-Library Loan departments at the University of Iowa and the University of Northern Colorado made feasible a project that relied upon rather obscure Belgian sources.

I am deeply indebted to several Belgian scholars whose meticulous efforts provided the historical foundation on which this study relies. The works of Theo Luykx, Ludo Milis, and Walter Simons in particular made a complex and often contentious history available to a nonnative, and proved invaluable in the course of researching and writing the present work. I would also like to thank the members of the history department of the University of Northern Colorado for useful feedback and important encouragement. I am particularly indebted to Barry Rothaus, who provided the guidance and direction necessary for a junior member of any faculty. This project also benefited from many conversations with colleagues from a variety of institutions who offered insight, useful references, and ideas for additional avenues of exploration. This list includes, but is by no means limited to, Erika Lindgren, Paul Hyams, Janet Burton, Bob Berkhofer, and Russell Martin. A special thanks is due to colleagues closer to home, including Tom Bredehoft, Lisa King, Michael Kramp, Ann Little, and Ken Nivison. Their willingness to read numerous drafts of the project at various stages and offer tireless support when it was most needed will not be forgotten. The original draft was considerably improved by suggestions from the anonymous readers for Palgrave and from Bonnie Wheeler, the series' editor. Any errors remain, naturally, my own.

I feel most fortunate that Constance Berman, my dissertation director, did so much more than direct a dissertation, no mean feat in and of itself. This project, which first began under her tutelage as a Master's Thesis at the University of Iowa, morphed several times, first into a dissertation and then into the present study. Both I and the project benefited considerably from her guidance and support at every stage of the process. She continues to be a invaluable mentor, role model, and friend.

During the years since this project was first conceived, my family has provided encouragement and much-needed respites from the thirteenth-century world of women, power, and patronage. Their efforts were always appreciated. My mother in particular provided the quiet, but unrelenting confidence that was often needed to persevere. I dedicate this book to her, for her inspiration and unconditional support.

INTRODUCTION: POWERFUL WOMEN AND RELIGIOUS PATRONAGE

Johanna flandrie et hainonie comitissa omnibus presentes litteras inspecturis salutem. Quia omnis potestas a Domino Deo tribuitur, et naturale jus exigit, ut omnis potestas in ejus servitio a quo potestatem assequitur se exerceat, dignum est ut Religiosam vitam eligentibus nostro occurramus praesidio

[*Johanna, countess of Flanders and Hainaut, greetings to all who see the present letters. Because all power is bestowed by God, and justice stems from him, so that all power in his service should be exercised by him on whom he bestows it, we should protect those deemed worthy of selecting a religious life.*]

Foppens, *Diplomatum Belgicorum*

Universis presentibus et futuris presentes litteras inspecturis Margareta flandrie et haynonie comitissa salutem. Quia omnis potestas a domino deo tribuitur et naturale ius exigit ut omnis potestas in eius servicio a quo potestatem assequitur se exerceat dignum est ut religiosam vitam eligentibus nostro occurramus praesidio.

[*To all who see these letters in the present and future, greetings from Marguerite, countess of Flanders and Hainaut. Because all power is bestowed by God, and justice stems from him, so that all power in his service should be exercised by him on whom he bestows it, we should protect those deemed worthy of selecting a religious life.*]

Rijksarchief Bruges, no. bl. 7441, January 1275

In 1206, the counties of Flanders and Hainaut, comprising one of the most powerful fiefdoms in France, passed into the hands of a six-year-old girl. For the majority of the next century, the political landscape of this region would be dominated by women, first Jeanne, who ruled until 1244, and then her sister, Marguerite, who ruled as countess until 1278/1280. Even at first glance, the prominence of the two sisters in the affairs of such important counties challenges assumptions, both medieval and modern, about the position of women in thirteenth-century society and their relationship to power. We are often led to believe that after the year 1100 in particular, women were increasingly excluded from the realm of politics, relegated to the world of the personal and the domestic. Men had established a firm monopoly on power, itself increasingly associated with the public sphere that had emerged to define and confine political action.[1] However, not only were Jeanne and Marguerite considerable heiresses, but they also ruled Flanders and Hainaut alone for fifty-seven of their combined seventy-four years as countesses. As the excerpts above from two charters issued by Jeanne and Marguerite to the Cistercian abbey of Spermalie demonstrate, even the countesses themselves were cognizant of the power they wielded, both secular and spiritual, and the responsibilities that accompanied their position. This apparent discrepancy between the presence of these two women in the public sphere wielding power in a very political manner and feudal norms that professed to reserve such power for men begs further exploration and explanation.[2] It is precisely such an examination that provides the focus of this study.

In order to reconcile assumptions about the patriarchal nature of medieval society and the prominence of these two women, one might anticipate that Jeanne and Marguerite functioned as mere figureheads, feudal placeholders, and passive pawns manipulated by the men around them. However, investigation of their respective experiences proves otherwise. While neither sister can be dismissed as a passive pawn, a silent witness to a political game beyond her control, neither were they the norm in thirteenth-century society, where power remained largely the provenance of men. Their political prominence was in many ways accidental, the product of a convergence of circumstances beyond the control of those around them. In fact, it is almost certain that in the year 1200, few people would have predicted that events would unfold in such a manner to propel these two women, in succession, to positions of such importance in northern Europe. The future of Flanders and Hainaut seemed nothing but promising under the rule of their parents, Baldwin IX and Marie of Champagne, a granddaughter of Eleanor of Aquitaine. After several key victories in his ongoing struggle with Philip Augustus, Baldwin had reaffirmed the autonomy of Flanders vis-à-vis France, forcing the French king to return key territories lost under Baldwin's predecessor, Philip of Alsace. Confident in his triumph over the French king, Baldwin felt secure enough in his success to contemplate an extended absence from his domains.[3] On Easter Sunday, 1200, Baldwin and his wife Marie took the cross, pledging their support for the impending campaign intended to oust the Muslims from Jerusalem and return the Holy Land to Christian control. The ceremony took place in the newly built church of St. Donatien located in the bustling port city of Bruges, witnessed by adoring crowds who cheered on their young count and countess.

After extensive preparation, Baldwin departed for the Holy Land in 1202. Forced to delay her own departure due to the impending birth of her second child, Marie remained behind, serving as regent of the counties until her own departure in 1204. Leaving her daughters in the care of

Matilda, the widow of Philip of Alsace and dowager countess of Flanders and the administration of the counties in the hands of a regency council handpicked by Baldwin prior to his own departure, Marie headed to Jerusalem. At this stage, the countess was unaware of the events that had diverted Baldwin and the crusaders from their initial destination. Baldwin and his companions had been caught up in the intrigue consuming the troubled city of Constantinople, where Baldwin was elected emperor in 1204. Before she was able to reunite with her husband, Marie's life was abruptly cut short by illness. Her final days were spent at the port city of Acre, where she died of flu in 1205. Baldwin's own triumph proved equally short-lived. Forced to make repeated forays outside the city's walls to defend his right to the imperial throne in the face of continuing opposition, the emperor was captured by Ionnitsa, the Bulger king. Although scholars lack the evidence needed to definitively determine whether Baldwin was executed or died in captivity, most concur that he was dead within a year of his coronation. News of Baldwin's death gradually traveled north, reaching France by 1206.[4]

Although much of Europe was shocked to learn of this tragic turn of events, the two individuals most immediately affected were likely too young to fully comprehend the ramifications of their father's death. Jeanne, as the elder of the two daughters, became an heiress of considerable importance at the tender age of six, the future ruler of one of the most important fiefs of France. Marguerite, the younger of the two, was also transformed in the eyes of the adults around her, becoming extremely wealthy in her own right at the age of four. Within the year, the two girls found themselves at the center of an extremely high stakes political game, the outcome of which would determine not only their personal futures, but also the future relationship between Flanders and France. Both girls were seized by their uncle Philip of Namur as soon as news of Baldwin's death reached Flanders and transferred into the custody of the scheming Philip Augustus. The king of France clearly saw in his young charges the opportunity to curb the autonomy of the county of Flanders, securing his own position at their expense. Baldwin's demise dramatically altered the political landscape of France, and precipitated a chain of events that would have lasting consequences, for Flanders as well as for northern Europe generally.

As their lives unfolded, the premature death of their parents would not be the only tragedy experienced by the two girls. Initially treated as pawns by the powerful men who surrounded them, both girls would suffer further losses. Jeanne, married to Ferrand of Portugal in 1212, was forced to endure not only the extended incarceration and eventual death of her young husband but also the death of their only child at the age of five. In spite of a second marriage to Thomas of Savoy, Jeanne was destined to remain childless. To compound these difficulties, her position as ruler of Flanders was challenged in a dramatic fashion by an imposter, a local hermit who claimed to be the long lost Baldwin. In addition to dealing with an ensuing rebellion and the defection of many of her staunchest supporters, Jeanne was faced with accusations of parricide after orchestrating the capture and execution of the perpetrator. Marguerite experienced her own difficulties. Married for the first time at the age of ten, she was forcibly separated from her husband, Bouchard of Avesnes after eight years of marriage and three children. Although the eldest of her children did not survive his early childhood, the younger two were taken from her after her separation from Bouchard in spite of their youth, and placed in the household of her new husband's brother.[5] Although she would eventually be united with the children from her first marriage, their rivalry with her children from her second marriage to William of Dampierre would embroil Flanders and Hainaut in an extended civil war, with Marguerite at the center. Marguerite was predeceased by her second husband William of Dampierre, and she lost her eldest son from her second marriage to a fluke accident at a tournament in 1253.

As the above discussion of their experience intends to demonstrate, both Jeanne and Marguerite inherited authority in the manner more often associated with men; however, they were by no means immune to medieval notions about gender and perceived limitations about members of their sex. Until recently, much of our knowledge of the position of noblewomen in the High Middle Ages was the result of studies concerning the centuries preceding, which projected conclusions upon a slightly later, but distinct period. Such conclusions argued that during the High Middle Ages, political power had become, with a few exceptions, the provenance of men. The dramatic decline in the position of elite women was believed to have occurred in conjunction with the establishment of primogeniture as the dominant method of inheritance and the centralization of power under the French kings, which accelerated the emergence of the divide between public and private.[6] According to this understanding of society and the forces that determined one's access to power, we would hardly expect to find women in positions of real authority, acting openly in the public sphere.

Although recent scholars have convincingly made the case that women remained a continued presence in the public sphere during the twelfth and thirteenth centuries, hence challenging assumptions about marginalization, knowledge of how their presence was understood by their contemporaries remains elusive.[7] This foray into the lives of the countesses of Flanders and Hainaut is intended to build upon an ever-increasing body of work devoted to uncovering the reality of medieval noble women. Work by Theodore Evergates, Amy Livingstone, Kimberly LoPrete, Fredric Cheyette, Linda

Mitchell, Penelope Adair, and Miriam Shadis, among others has dramatically altered our view of the standing of noblewomen in medieval society after the year 1100.[8] Women wielding power in their own right after 1100 are now too numerous too be dismissed as exceptional and too prominent to be discounted as viable players in medieval politics. However, their presence alone is not sufficient to counter current beliefs about the tendency of feudal society to prefer men. In fact, their very position as heiresses is the product of attempts by families to privilege the male line that first resulted in the adoption of such practices as primogeniture and patrilineal descent. In many ways, women like Jeanne and Marguerite represent a malfunction in a patriarchal system specifically designed to promote men.

Although a number of women occupying positions similar to those of Jeanne and Marguerite have been identified, they have yet to be integrated more fully into our general understanding of the feudal system. Since they are too numerous to be dismissed as anomalous, it is necessary to reconcile their presence with the patriarchal nature of medieval society. This study seeks to situate such women more firmly within the wider political context of thirteenth-century France and to identify the social conditions that conferred authority and power on individuals.[9] Under what circumstances and by what means were women able to access power, and how was their ability to wield it affected by prevailing gender norms? To what end was such power employed by women? Feudal practice dictated that women inherit in the absence of men, but to what extent were they able to actually exercise the authority they inherited? Once they had entered the realm of the political, were the rules that governed participation the same regardless of sex, or did they differ for men and women?

Jeanne and Marguerite, two extremely visible women who ruled for a considerable period of time, provide an ideal opportunity to explore such questions about the political as it functioned in the High Middle Ages and its particular meaning for women. Since their visibility in the historical record is due in no small part to their religious patronage, their actions as patrons will be central to this discussion, shedding additional light on their experiences as political actors. In modern society, gaining and maintaining power is often deemed success in and of itself in the political game. Although undoubtedly true for the medieval period, securing secular power would have also been viewed as a means by which an individual could obtain spiritual power, hence ensuring salvation. The discussion here will examine the ability of both countesses to extend their power, both secular and spiritual, through religious patronage. The connection between power and patronage was very real in the Middle Ages, as the charter quoted in the beginning of the chapter suggests. The argument here is predicated upon the belief that religious patronage in the Middle Ages was both public and political.[10] Hence, exploring the actions of the countesses as patrons furthers our ability to appreciate how power operated and was understood during this period. Ultimately, this examination of Jeanne and Marguerite as women, political players, and religious patrons furthers our knowledge of female experience and broadens our understanding of what constituted the political in the thirteenth century.

While, as the example of Jeanne and Marguerite demonstrates, the possibility of female rulers existed well into the thirteenth century, attitudes toward them were extremely ambivalent. Characterizations of both countesses in narrative sources demonstrate the myriad of responses prompted by these presence in politics, further complicating our attempts to accurately understand their position and evaluate their experience. The historiographical tradition surrounding the two countesses of Flanders and Hainaut is particularly polemical. Whether they were targets of scorn, pity, or praise, Jeanne and Marguerite were unilaterally presented as controversial figures, The tension prompted by female rulers was exacerbated by the fact that thirteenth-century Flanders was situated in a maelstrom of political conflict, itself a pawn in the power struggle between France and England that ultimately transformed northern Europe. While the origins of this struggle were located prior to the period when the countesses exercised power, many of the events that moved Flanders more securely into the orbit of France occurred during their respective rules. The role played by the countesses in such developments explains in part why they have proven to be extremely contentious figures in narrative sources.[11]

While historians are fortunate in the number of medieval texts devoted to the history of Flanders, these texts are extremely difficult to navigate due to the discrepancies that pepper them. In addition, the majority of narrative sources are quite subjective, the portrait painted of Jeanne and Marguerite filtered through the lens of the authors' respective agendas, both personal and professional.[12] Narrative sources tend to fall into three categories. The first contains texts produced by individuals who enjoyed the patronage of Philip of France, who viewed the countesses and Flanders as important only in their ability to demonstrate the political savvy and military prowess of their king. Since Flanders functioned as a stepping stone used to elevate the French monarchy to unprecedented heights of power, events in which the countesses were involved are mined by royal chroniclers for evidence of French superiority. The countesses are either praised for their complicity in French attempts to control Flanders, or critiqued for their attempt to act autonomously; resistance to French royal policy or demonstrations of opposition to the monarch are condemned accordingly. This category includes the chronicles of Guillaume le Breton, most notably the *Philippide* and *De Rebus gesti Philippi-Augusti*, and the rhymed history of Philippe Mouskes, known as the "Chronique Rimée" of France. Mouskes was particularly negative in his characterization of Marguerite. While Mouskes attributed Jeanne's troubles to her rebellious husband, he held Marguerite personally responsible for the problems experienced by Flanders during her rule, as reflected in his reference to her as "la dame noire" [the black lady].[13] Both of these men were attached to the court of France, and wrote from a perspective intent on praising the king and his accomplishments.[14]

The second category of narrative texts includes chronicles originating in Flanders or Hainaut. In these, the countesses are typically excoriated by the authors for what is perceived as their complicity in French attempts to curb the autonomy of Flanders. These texts, such as the chronicle attributed to Bauduin d'Avesnes and that apparently authored by Bauduin Ninove, condemn the countesses for their apparent pro-French stance and their increasing subordination to the king.[15] In addition, several chronicles of Flemish origin produced by members of various religious orders exist. These texts capture the full spectrum of attitudes toward the countesses, ranging from laudatory to derisive, condescending to dismissive. The most visible example of this category would be the history of Jacques de Guyse, a Franciscan friar from Valenciennes. While de Guyse, who composed his narrative toward the end of the fourteenth century, claimed to be copying earlier chronicles verbatim, most scholars agree that his text is rife with errors, incorporating fact as well as fable.[16]

A third, significantly smaller category, is composed of authors of neither French nor Flemish origin. This category includes pro-English chronicles, such as those produced by Matthew Paris and Alberic of Troisfontaines.[17] According to Matthew Paris in his *Chronica Majora*, while Jeanne "rendered herself infamous in the eyes of all men...by the parricide which she committed," Marguerite was a "second Medea," bringing shame on all women for the role she played in the civil war raging amongst her sons.[18] These texts not only present scathing portraits of the two countesses, but are rife with errors that result from anti-Flemish bias. English views of Flanders were particularly clouded by the detrimental effects of the extended trade war waged by Marguerite in the later thirteenth century.[19] Although their colorful language and considerable detail prove compelling for modern scholars, the accuracy of such sources is often suspect, and they must be very carefully navigated.

The inconstancies that abound in medieval chronicles are compounded by a series of nineteenth-century studies, which add additional confusion and ultimately fuel the modern debate that tends to obscure the reality of the countesses' experiences. While Jeanne frequently appears as a helpless pawn, a victim of circumstances behind her control, Marguerite is almost uniformly condemned by modern historians, particularly those who base the bulk of their conclusions on narrative sources of French origin, especially that of Philippe Mouskes. These two extremes are reflected in the competing works of Édouard Le Glay and J. de Mersseman.[20] While Le Glay praises Jeanne profusely for her attempt to rule justly, attributing all difficulties to the fact that her feminine nature was simply not suited to wielding power, de Mersseman characterizes her as arrogant, ambitious, and cruel, willing to inflict considerable harm in order to preserve her autonomy and authority. J. de Mersseman explains the difficulties encountered by Jeanne as the product of her own personal ambition and ruthlessness, exacerbated by the irrational nature of women generally. While drawing extensively from the corpus of medieval chronicles, neither author provides a clear assessment of the available sources, but rather both seem to confer reliability upon the texts that best corroborate their own view of events. Such sources serve only to confuse the situation, revealing more about the personal agenda of the two modern authors than they do about the lives of their medieval subjects.

Other nineteenth-century studies, such as that produced by Kervyn de Lettenhove, are not as transparent in terms of their own agenda but lack consistent citation and often fail to indicate sources, particularly problematic considering the numerous discrepancies present in the thirteenth-century accounts.[21] Perhaps the most reliable nineteenth-century history is that of Léopold Warnkoenig, which explicitly addresses the polemical nature of medieval sources and includes an extremely detailed bibliography. However, Warnkoenig undertakes a sweeping study of the history of Flanders, from the period of Roman settlement on, and analyzes numerous aspects of Flemish society, ranging from the political to the economic to the religious. The thirteenth century and the countesses comprise merely one section of a much larger work.[22]

More recent examinations of the countesses that alternate between reliance upon narrative sources and documents of practice achieve a greater degree of accuracy. The monumental studies by Theo Luykx are informed by an impressive knowledge of the archival material and an extremely careful use of narrative sources. Unfortunately, the work of Luykx is yet to be made available to a non-Flemish audience.[23] The biography of Jeanne and Marguerite by Geneviève de Cant attempts to remedy past neglect of these two women by adding a full account of their accomplishments to the historical record.[24] In addition, there are several studies of medieval Flanders more generally that include a brief discussion of Jeanne and Marguerite, including Henri Pirenne's *Histoire de Belgique*, David Nicholas's *Medieval Flanders*, and Gabrielle Spiegel's *Romancing the Past*.[25] Karen Nicholas has studied countesses of Flanders and Hainaut generally over the course of several centuries, including both Jeanne

INTRODUCTION

and Marguerite in her discussions. While extremely useful in creating a l historical narrative of Flanders, which includes the contributions of the two countesses, her work is fairly limited in focus, providing only a brief sketch of Jeanne and Marguerite's lives.[26]

In spite of the range of opinions expressed by medieval authors regarding these two women and their role in Flemish affairs, the one consistent element in all narrative depictions is the presence of gender bias. It is in no small part because of the importance of Flanders and the role played by its rulers during the transformative thirteenth century that the countesses appear as such contentious figures in the historical record. However, this was undoubtedly exacerbated by the fact that they were women occupying a position usually associated with men. Gender bias is particularly acute in medieval narrative sources, which are informed by beliefs and attitudes about members of the female sex that were prevalent in the thirteenth century. Both Jeanne's failings and Marguerite's flaws are often explained as the natural product of their feminine nature, which made them weaker, more emotionally unstable, and more susceptible to influence and extremes than their male counterparts.[27] However, their right to rule a principality as powerful as Flanders is accepted without hesitation in all of these texts, hinting at the complexity of attitudes about powerful women in thirteenth-century society.

In exploring the various questions about the position of noblewomen, their relationship to power and the role of religious patronage as they pertain to the countesses of Flanders and Hainaut, this study attempts to move beyond the assumptions about these two women that first appeared in medieval sources and were incorporated without question into modern accounts. To that end, it privileges proscriptive sources, most notably charters issued by the countesses themselves. Unlike narrative sources, such charters provide a record of their actions themselves, rather than medieval perceptions of their actions. This distinction is particularly useful in regards to the presentation of women. Not only is our understanding of their position impeded by ideological views of medieval authors, but it is often equally clouded by modern assumptions about the appropriate position of women in the High Middle Ages. In attempting to identify a normative view of society in medieval chronicles, modern scholars often ignore potentially dissenting views and silence discordant voices. The result of such efforts is to emphasize similarities at the expense of difference, establishing a monolithic view of women that fails to appreciate the diversity of experience that clearly existed. Although they certainly pose their own set of challenges and limitations, charters make it possible to construct an understanding of female experience that is free from assumptions about the inherently destructive nature of women or the incapacity of the female sex to rule.[28] As this study will demonstrate, such attitudes, though prevalent in thirteenth-century narrative sources, have yet to be definitively established as uniformly present in the mind of the medieval male. They seem even more out of place in the mind of the modern scholar, yet are often encountered in assessments of Jeanne and Marguerite and their political legacy for the county of Flanders. Although such studies will be referenced when the conclusions presented here differ considerably from those advanced in past studies or in moments where the historical record lacks consensus, the purpose of this exploration of the countesses is not to engage in exhaustive historiographical debate; it is rather to offer a new approach to the study of medieval noblewomen and religious patronage, which can further discussions about these topics and provide insights into often asked questions to which the answers remain elusive.

Such reliance on proscriptive sources is possible due to the extremely rich archival collections and the numerous extant charters which document the actions of Jeanne and Marguerite, both as religious patrons and as political actors. Examination of the experience of these two sisters as it is reflected in charter evidence provides a foil to the depiction of them found in narrative sources produced in the period. This study considers over 1,000 charters issued by Jeanne and Marguerite to approximately 180 religious and monastic communities within their domains. This corpus is supplemented by hundreds of charters issued by them in a strictly secular capacity in conjunction with political and diplomatic affairs.[29] This approach also makes it possible to incorporate both quantitative as well as qualitative analysis, further strengthening conclusions. Ultimately, examination of these proscriptive sources suggests that the reality of the countesses' experience challenges assumptions about male power and encourages the formulation of a more complex understanding of the position of women in thirteenth-century politics.

While this study does not argue that female power was either intended or the norm in the thirteenth century, it attempts to identify the conditions that made it possible. It also assesses how women like Jeanne and Marguerite were perceived by their contemporaries, and the range of options available to them in their attempt to exercise the authority they inherited. The tendency among some scholars has been to understand heiresses as mere figureheads, objects of exchange among men who ruled in their stead or placeholders for future male offspring.[30] However, investigation into the lives of Jeanne and Marguerite challenges such expectations, and it calls to question a variety of assumptions, both medieval and modern, about the position of women and their relationship to power. As the discussion in the first two chapters here intends to demonstrate, examining the actual experience of Jeanne and Marguerite complicates existing notions of what comprised the public sphere in the thirteenth century and how the political functioned during this period.

Chapter 1 traces the experience of the girls from the death of Count Baldwin in 1206 to the pivotal battle of Bouvines in 1214. It examines the custom of primogeniture and the preference for patrilineal descent as they affected the position of noblewomen generally and addresses how such factors influenced the situation in Flanders and Hainaut. As the case of Jeanne and Marguerite illustrates, in thirteenth-century French society, status ultimately trumped gender and feudal practice prevailed over negative attitudes about the female sex in determining the ability of women to inherit fiefs. The discussion in chapter 1 outlines this relationship between status and gender as it existed in the thirteenth century, ultimately demonstrating the complexity of medieval attitudes. Not only is this approach intended to provide a more accurate view of women in this pivotal century, but it also contributes to our understanding of feudal society. Women like Jeanne and Marguerite were not isolated examples, aberrations in a society that otherwise reserved authority for men. Understanding their experience requires a more in-depth investigation into the fabric of medieval society and an assessment of how certain beliefs translated into practices capable of producing powerful women like the countesses of Flanders and Hainaut.

While chapter 1 examines the features of society that ultimately established the criteria that determined one's eligibility to participate in the political game of the thirteenth century, chapter 2 identifies the rules that governed play. Through tracing their lives from 1214 until 1280, it is possible to identify and appreciate the full spectrum of factors that shaped the experience of noblewomen during this period. It is important to caution that the presence of women in the political sphere does not automatically imply that their exercise of power was never impeded by perceptions about gender. This section will explore the various ways these women would have been regarded by their male counterparts, assessing the extent to which the strategies they employed to further their power conformed to a non-gendered norm, or differed as a result of their sex. In particular, it will examine their understanding of the office of countess, and the various ways they deployed the resources at their disposal to affirm their legitimacy as rulers and secure their secular power.

Together, the first two chapters identify the range of factors such as status, gender, personality, marital circumstance, and age, which would have exerted the most influence on the position of women and affected their individual experience. However, rather than attempting to isolate any of these factors or identify one as the most significant, the discussion in these chapters will focus on the interplay of all of them, tracing the push and pull that always exists in any complex society, medieval as well as modern. As the discussion in these chapters demonstrates, an accurate appreciation for the complexity of their experience cannot be achieved through reliance on models that posit a rigid divide between the public and the private in medieval society. Nor can we continue to underestimate the diversity of attitudes that undoubtedly existed in the Middle Ages by insisting upon the presence of a single, uniform view of women.

Chapters 3 and 4 continue to investigate questions about power and the various strategies employed by medieval rulers regardless of their sex to secure that power, both secular and spiritual. By focusing specifically on religious patronage, it is possible to assess the extent to which individuals were able to enlist monastic and religious communities in their secular agendas, ultimately increasing their wealth and prestige and enhancing their image as rulers. In addition, such communities were keys to obtaining spiritual power, understood in the thirteenth century as necessary to guarantee salvation. Scholars have discussed the role of patronage in the Middle Ages at length, demonstrating the importance of donations to monastic communities in the medieval Christian belief system. In a world where it was almost unanimously accepted that one's actions on earth directly translated into one's experience in the afterlife, generosity on behalf of monastic communities was a key element of piety.[31] However, while the general role of patronage in medieval society has been well documented and adequately discussed, the actions of the countesses of Flanders and Hainaut make it possible to employ a comparative approach to patronage, examining why certain monastic or religious communities appealed to certain patrons. Such an approach proves especially fruitful for the High Middle Ages, when religious patrons were presented with an array of choices when it came to choosing a recipient for their donations.[32] Like most areas in Europe during this period, Flanders and Hainaut boasted a wide variety of monastic and religious communities for donors to consider. And like most medieval rulers, the countesses of Flanders and Hainaut were ideally positioned to impact the spiritual landscape of the region. Both women commanded vast resources in terms of land and money, resources that they generously dispensed on behalf of hundreds of communities within their domains. By identifying patterns in their patronage, which point to clear preferences exhibited by Jeanne and Marguerite, it is possible to explore the appeal of certain orders or communities in an attempt to identify the more specific concerns that motivated patrons. To this end, chapters 3 and 4 assess the extent to which Jeanne and Marguerite, as countesses and as women, were able to translate the wealth and prestige at their command into power, both secular and sacred.

While modern, Western society tends to view activity deemed religious as private and personal, such an association did not exist in the medieval world, where distinctions between public and private were hard to determine and religion pervaded all aspects of society. Patronage of monastic communities was both public and political, intended to be witnessed and acknowledged by as many people as possible. Furthermore, although the modern mind tends to equate power with the secular, rather than the sacred realm, such a distinction would have been meaningless in the Middle Ages. The medieval patron would have had no qualms about enlisting monastic or religious communities to further their own secular power on earth. A combination of motives prompting donations, ranging from the secular to the sacred, would have been accepted without hesitation by the medieval donor and recipient alike.[33] Monastic communities in Flanders and Hainaut were often enlisted by the countesses as political, economic, judicial, and even military agents, providing their savvy patrons with numerous opportunities to simultaneously secure their position on earth while furthering their salvation.

In the medieval world, property equaled power. Although this equation became increasingly more complex as the Middle Ages progressed, most scholars would concur that in the thirteenth century, the ability to control property was a key indicator of one's power.[34] Alienating land, granting exemptions, and confirming the rights of others in regards to property were key elements in legitimating feudal authority. Nowhere are such actions more visible than in the realm of religious patronage, particularly in a climate that increasingly discouraged the alienation of feudal land for secular purposes in the interest of maintaining the integrity of the patrimony. Hence, tracing the actions of the countesses in conjunction with patronage in chapter 3 allows us to gauge their ability to maneuver in the political sphere.

In a similar fashion, to women like Jeanne and Marguerite, it was entirely appropriate, if not expected, to use their secular wealth to secure religious power in the guise of a patron, securing the prayers of monks and nuns necessary to secure their position in the afterlife.[35] Earthly power would not have been viewed as an end in and of itself but rather as the means by which the astute individual could secure the ultimate goal, salvation. Donations to religious communities were surely viewed as material investments in a spiritual future. Chapter 4 will explore Jeanne and Marguerite's preferences as patrons in order to determine what factors or considerations guided their decisions, ultimately identifying the orders or communities viewed by the countesses as offering the most return on their investment.

Since religious patronage was central to their experience, both as women and as rulers, this exploration also sheds light on the role of patronage during this period, revealing its meaning to patrons as well as its wider function in society. The extent of their activity on behalf of the monks and nuns in Flanders and Hainaut prompts a certain degree of curiosity about their motives. What prompted the actions of these two women? Were they just particularly pious, or where they, on some level, more concerned than their contemporaries about their salvation, motivated by spiritual desperation and the desire to secure the prayers of the truly pious on their behalf? Was their support of the monasteries within their domains merely the manifestation of a generous spirit, or a reflection of the tragedy and violence that marred their lives, both as children and as grown women? It would not be beyond the realm of reason to suppose that for Jeanne and Marguerite, surrounded by intrigue and struck by tragedy on numerous occasions during the course of their lives, the one accused of parricide and the other of bigamy, donations to religious communities and requests for prayers were not merely a routine gesture, but rather a necessity. Both chapters assess whether or not the motives that prompted the patronage of Jeanne and Marguerite, both secular and spiritual, were influenced by concerns important to women generally and to female rulers more specifically. Did their approach to patronage differ as a result of their sex, suggesting that female rulers were forced to operate differently than their male counterparts, or was patronage merely one component of the larger political game, employed by men and women alike? While many of their actions on behalf of monastic or religious communities reveal concerns specific to women, they challenge the tendency among some scholars to suggest that patronage was essentially a gendered activity. By renegotiating our understanding of how religious patronage functioned in society and how it was used by women in particular, we can further revise our expectations about the limitations placed upon female activity during the thirteenth century.

Although both the position of women and the role of religious patronage are areas that have been frequently investigated by scholars, many questions remain unanswered. The distance that divides modern from medieval society is more than chronological, it is conceptual as well. It is often difficult to understand the beliefs and practices that provided the warp and weave of the fabric of medieval society from our modern perspective. This is particularly true of Western society, where secularization of culture and the establishment of relative equality among men and women are professed, if not completely realized, elements of our society. It is often difficult to fully appreciate the experience of men and women in the Middle Ages, and the beliefs and ideas that shaped that experience. The difficulty encountered by modern scholars is exacerbated by the scarcity of self-reflective texts produced during this period, in which men and women explain the motives or concerns that prompted their actions in life. Although problematic in their own right, such sources would certainly help bridge the gap between the modern and medieval mindset. Medieval scholars instead have recourse to much sparser texts, forced to tease out understanding of the medieval experience from cryptic accounts or myopic chronicles. The charters consulted here reveal both women acting in a variety of capacities, as rulers and lords, as well as

INTRODUCTION

mothers, sisters, and wives. This abundance of documentation assess the actions of Jeanne and Marguerite as they occurred, through a third party's perception of those actions.

The countesses' actions as patrons certainly reflect upon the both as women and as powerful rulers. The divide between the medieval and the modern world and the limitations of the extant sources have proven particularly challenging in regards to the two topics discussed here, the position of women and the practice of religious patronage. This study benefits methodologically from examining these two topics in tandem. The charters generated by religious patronage are, in many cases, the most abundant source documenting the actions of medieval women. While this is not true for the countesses of Flanders and Hainaut, records of their actions on behalf of monastic communities remain a key source of their activity and experience generally, and they provide an invaluable supplement to the secular charters issued strictly in their capacity as countesses. The thousands of charters issued by Jeanne and Marguerite provide an incredible body of evidence, making it possible to avoid reliance on narrative sources, which, as discussed previously, have proven rather problematic in the past.

As the ensuing discussion will demonstrate, Jeanne and Marguerite were able to transform themselves from pawns to successful players in a powerful political game, negotiating the myriad of rules that dictated play, overcoming obstacles and not infrequent challenges to secure and even strengthen their position as rulers of Flanders and Hainaut. Both women effectively employed the resources at their disposal to increase their secular power, which they then deployed at their advantage to obtain the ultimate end, salvation. However, in order to fully appreciate their experience, and explore the beliefs and practices that influenced their relationship to power, it is necessary to return to the year 1206, the death of Count Baldwin, and the moment that marked the transformation of their lives and beginning of this story.

CHAPTER 1

ACCESSING AUTHORITY: 1206–14

Once the news of Baldwin's death reached northern Europe, Philip of Namur seized the reigns of government from the regency council previously appointed by the count. He also seized physical control of his two nieces, Jeanne and Marguerite, who had been transformed into extremely powerful heiresses seemingly overnight. Philip Augustus acted with similar urgency, hearing the news while laying siege to Chinon. The king immediately dispatched Barthélemy de Roye to offer an alliance to Philip of Namur.[1] The two Philips concluded the treaty of Pont de l'Arche in 1206, which granted Philip of Namur immediate control of the county in return for the concession of key cities along the border, reversing key gains made by Baldwin IX. The treaty also granted Philip Augustus custody of both girls and control over their eventual marriages, a significant concession in light of the current state of relations between France and Flanders.[2] As a reward for his complicity, Philip of Namur was engaged to Marie, the daughter of Philip Augustus. A second charter detailing the terms of this marriage was signed in August 1206, and the fate of the two young orphans was permanently sealed.[3] In September, 1208, Jeanne and Marguerite were officially placed under Philip's personal custody as wards of the crown, and transferred to the royal court in Paris where they remained until Jeanne's marriage in January, 1212.[4]

As a result of the events that transpired in 1206, Jeanne and Marguerite, ages six and four respectively, had been propelled from relative obscurity to the forefront of the political stage, becoming pawns in an intense power struggle between the nobles of Flanders and the king of France. Most members of the Flemish nobility objected, claiming that the Holy Roman emperor's rights had been abrogated by the treaty of Pont de l'Arche, since the county of Flanders north of the Scheldt river was held in fief from him. The acts of both Philips were denounced by the Flemish nobility, and the claims by Philip of France to the two heiresses were rejected as illegitimate and only possible because of their uncle's desire for personal aggrandizement, achieved at the expense of his family and his country. The response of the two young girls, those most affected by this turn of events, remains unclear. It is impossible to determine the exact whereabouts of Jeanne and Marguerite during this process of negotiation, a pivotal moment in the history of Flanders. However, it is obvious that as minors, the preferences of the heiresses were neither considered nor consulted. They are present only as silent witnesses to the political manipulation that would not only impact their personal lives, but would transform the political landscape of northern Europe.[5]

Although the rights of Philip of France regarding the heiresses of Flanders and Hainaut were widely discussed and disputed by his contemporaries, Jeanne's right to inherit the counties following the death of her father Baldwin IX was never challenged. In the absence of a male heir, the expectation was that Baldwin's patrimony, and all of the prerogatives and responsibilities that accompanied it, would pass intact to his eldest daughter. In a similar fashion, Marguerite's right to succeed her elder sister as countess following Jeanne's death in 1244 was never contested. She immediately occupied the vacant office even though five of her sons had attained their majority. Unlike her sister, she never expressed a desire to wed during her thirty-four-year rule as countess of Flanders and Hainaut. Such clear evidence of female succession to a fiefdom as powerful as the county of Flanders raises important questions about how political space was configured in thirteenth-century society. In terms of inheritance, neither woman was hampered by attitudes about the female sex or expectations of male privilege. The experience of Jeanne and Marguerite begs further explanation of the position of women and their potential to access and wield power. In this world where men were typically considered the dominant sex and expected to monopolize governance accordingly, how can we explain the persistence of female inheritance and the continued presence of women in the political sphere? Under what circumstances would medieval society accept women in such space otherwise reserved for men? This chapter will explore the fabric of society in thirteenth-century France in order to provide answers to these questions, focusing in particular on the impact of primogeniture and patrilineage, and the gender perceptions that informed such practices. It seeks to broaden our understanding of power by examining its social and political conditions, specifically in regards to women. After identifying the various avenues by which women could access power it will then examine the experiences of Jeanne and Marguerite from the death of Baldwin in 1206 to the battle of Bouvines in 1214 in order to assess the extent to which they could wield it.

By the thirteenth century, primogeniture had become the dominant inheritance practice in northern Europe, replacing the division of land, goods, and offices equally among all heirs. While movable goods remained subject to division, it was widely understood that fiefs were to remain intact as an essential component of aristocratic family strategies to maximize power and importance, and should pass to the eldest son.[6] Primogeniture was adopted in response to increasing fears about the impact of partible inheritance and the resulting fragmentation of the patrimony, which threatened to weaken the power of families. Georges Duby argues that such changes in inheritance practice were visible by the beginning of the eleventh century, as reflected in the "tendency of family lineages to adhere to a single branch, an axis by which, so it appears, the eldest son succeeded."[7] Philippe Godding concurs with Duby's chronology, concluding that by the beginning of the eleventh century, fiefs in the Pays-Bas and northern France were kept intact and passed, ideally, to the eldest son of the senior branch of the family.[8] Jane Martindale dates such changes slightly later to the twelfth century, transforming family structures when fluid dynastic strategies were replaced with much more rigid guidelines that emphasized the consolidation of resources and their transmission to future generations along the masculine line, preferably to the eldest son.[9] Although the timing and nature of such shifts concerning inheritance continues to be the subject of debate among scholars, there is little doubt that they did occur and primogeniture had become a standard practice among noble families in northern Europe well by the thirteenth century.

Furthermore, prevailing feudal custom in Flanders, as elsewhere in France, not only prevented the division of the land and offices that comprised the patrimony, but also excluded collateral branches of the family from inheritance.[10] In the interest of passing fiefs intact from one generation to the next, families choose to privilege the descendents of the eldest child, forcing the offspring of younger sons and daughters into less favorable positions. When combined with the practice of primogeniture, the impact of patrilineage was considerable, and it provided the fortunate branch of the family the opportunity to control a patrimony that was potentially strengthened, rather than diminished, over time.[11] Scholars have often viewed the adoption of primogeniture and patrilineage as detrimental to members of the female sex, who were subsequently denied control of land and further removed from proximity to the main source of power in medieval society. In accordance with the ideals that informed such inheritance practices, the exclusion of younger sons and daughters was a necessary sacrifice, their individual futures outweighed by concern for the family. Once the fluid, collateral family practicing partible inheritance was replaced with a more conservative one that preferred a system of feudal tenure under which indivisible fiefs passed intact to eldest sons, "wives, daughters, and younger sons forfeited rights to their share in inheritance and extended kin were effectively pruned from the family tree."[12] Privileging the masculine line of the family, some scholars suggest, reduced daughters to mere objects of exchange among powerful families. According to Pauline Stafford, such changes "were inimical to the idea of female rule and power." Stafford argues that by the eleventh century, the rights of women regarding property "were curtailed as part of general attempts to preserve family property."[13] Many younger daughters, no longer dowered with a portion of the patrimony, were deemed unmarriageable and consigned to convents.

However, examination of the experience of noble families in the twelfth and thirteenth centuries reveals how the ideal of reserving inheritance for men only and unilaterally excluding women failed at times to translate into reality. A variety of factors, including the popularity of the Crusades, the dangers to which participants in tournaments were exposed, and the violence endemic in society generally, converged to produce a disproportional number of families lacking male heirs. While the practice of primogeniture in theory privileged men, in the absence of sons, the same ideals that informed this inheritance practice dictated that the patrimony pass to the eldest daughter. The manner in which a fief could devolve to a female is described by Scott Waugh, who concludes that "feudal custom preferred male heirs to female, yet because it also preferred the nearest blood relative to distant relations, women inherited in the absence of a direct male heir."[14] Duby identifies a range of variables that could potentially result in female inheritance, suggesting that "the superiority of direct descendants over collaterals, combined with the effects of restricted marriages, frequently resulted in a daughter who had no brothers inheriting her father's possessions. . ."[15] Instead of dividing the wealth, prestige, and prerogatives of the patrimony, feudal law in France dictated that it pass intact to the eldest daughter. The continental preference for preserving the integrity of the patrimony maximized the power of eldest daughters, at times producing women with considerable authority. Furthermore, if the inheritance in question was a powerful fief, like the county of Flanders, marriage did not result in the relocation of the woman. Rather, the husband was expected to change his residence, adopting the family, titles, and responsibilities of his wife. Such women did not function as objects of exchange among families, but rather remained in their own homes, which undoubtedly provided them with a considerable advantage in terms of networks of support and securing access to power.

While it cannot be argued that the adoption of primogeniture as the dominant inheritance practice among the medieval nobility improved the position of women generally, the case of the countesses does demonstrate that on occasion it offered some women the opportunity to access authority that far exceeded that enjoyed by their predecessors in the Early Middle Ages. In the absence of male heirs, the ambitions of individual aristocratic families triumphed over prevailing notions of gender that otherwise limited female power, producing women who exercised authority in their own right as heiresses, not according to male whim as consorts. Ultimately, in certain cases, the demands of the feudal system required the subordination of the ideals privileging males to the practicalities of ensuring stable rule. While medieval norms professed to reserve power for men, female heirs were the inevitable result of family strategies that privileged the senior branch and preferred patrimonies to pass intact to the next generation. Hence, the same principles that resulted in an extremely powerful eldest son applied in the instance of female inheritance; the eldest daughter inherited the entire patrimony and the authority that accompanied it.

Examination of France during the late twelfth and thirteenth centuries reveals at least eleven such occasions when women inherited considerable fiefs. In addition to Jeanne and Marguerite, this list includes the countesses of Auxerre, Nevers, and Tonnerre, Agnes, her daughter Matilda, and granddaughter Agnes; Constance and Alix, who inherited the county of Brittany in succession. The counties of Blois and Chartres were also ruled by several generations of women. In 1218, Marguerite, the granddaughter of Eleanor of Aquitaine and King Louis XII, succeeded to the county of Blois. Her daughter Marie inherited the county from her in the 1230s. Marguerite's sister Isabelle succeeded to Chartres, ruling until her death in 1248 when the county passed to her daughter Mathilde.[16] The county of Boulogne devolved to a woman following the death of King Stephen's only remaining son William in 1159. Stephen's eldest daughter Mary was removed from her position as abbess of Ramsey Abbey, becoming countess of Boulogne in 1160 and forcibly married to Mathieu of Alsace. Mary was allowed to return to her abbey in 1170, when Mathieu had the marriage annulled in order to wed an even wealthier heiress, Aliénor of Vermandois. Mary's eldest daughter Ida succeeded as countess of Boulogne, eventually marrying the infamous Renaud of Dammartin.[17]

Although these women inherited authority, understood here as the legitimate right to act, the extent to which they could impose their will on those around them requires assessment. While the combination of the violence endemic in medieval society and the prevalence of primogeniture frequently resulted in female heiresses, these women would not have been expected to actually exercise power due to gender perceptions and expectations about the natural limitations of the female sex.[18] By allowing women to inherit, but arranging for power to be exercised in their stead by men, noble families provided a solution for their predicament, ensuring the transmission of fiefs from generation to generation while diminishing the possibility of women in positions of actual power. They were intended to serve as vehicles to transmit feudal offices from one generation to the next, the authority they inherited passing first to their husbands, who would act in their stead, and then to their male offspring. This understanding made it possible for medieval society to reconcile the reality of female authority with the accepted norm of male superiority in the public sphere. According to Linda Mitchell, such an arrangement ensured that the presence of women in the realm of the political did not corrupt the feudal structure, since heiresses were expected to relinquish control over their inheritance to men.[19] Hence, in serving only as the repository of feudal authority, but never personally exercising power, women played an important role in securing the transmission of the patrimony from one generation to the next, without disrupting social norms adverse to powerful women.[20] Since a woman wielding power would have been perceived by many as subverting the natural order of society, the provision of husbands and sons to restrict her activities and ensure that public action remained the sole provenance of men was necessary, and made the presence of females in the ruling order palatable.

Such expectations were predicated upon a distinction between authority and power in the medieval understanding of political agency. While they are often used interchangeably by modern authors, these two terms referred to two very distinct forms of action in the Middle Ages. The difference between these two terms requires further exploration in order to achieve an accurate understanding of the position of women in the thirteenth century and their ability to act in ways that would have been categorized by people in the Middle Ages as political. Since examples of women wielding power in the manner more typically associated with men clearly exist, failure to factor them into the feudal system results in a view of medieval governance that is both inaccurate and insufficiently complex. Rather than dismissing them as anomalous and rejecting them as legitimate political actors, it is necessary to revise and refine our understanding of how the political operated in the transformative thirteenth century by more clearly demarcating medieval conceptions of authority and power.

While authority typically connotes a hierarchical chain of command, a control exercised by right, power is significantly more abstract, often defined as the "ability to act effectively on persons or things, to make or secure favorable decisions which are not of right allocated to the individuals or their roles."[21] According to this definition, while authority connotes a hierarchy, power is much more elusive, based on personal effectiveness rather than on sanctioned right to command. This distinction clearly operated in the feudal order of the Middle Ages, where the two concepts were related, but certainly not synonymous. In his discussion of the position of women in thirteenth-century England, Douglas C. Jansen defines public authori "the legitimate and sanctioned use of power in the public sphere."--- Authority, or the legitimate right to rule, was associated with feudal offices, which granted individual office holders the legitimate right to rule in a certain region and according to certain prescribed regulations. This distinction between authority and power as they are discussed here to a large degree hinges on the question of legality. Authority denoted actions that were legally sanctioned by the current political system. While legality was not necessarily a condition of power, actions taken without it would not have been deemed legitimate, legal, or officially sanctioned.[23]

An example that illustrates the difference between these two terms in their nature and application in medieval society more widely is the position of the monarchy in France during the late twelfth and early thirteenth centuries. Although possessing the feudal authority to impose their will on their vassals within the kingdom of France, few French monarchs prior to Philip Augustus were able to effectively command the counts of Flanders. While the de jure ruler of Flanders as the legitimate feudal lord, the young Philip Augustus was de facto ruled by Flanders, forced to accede to Flemish demands and follow the advice, although often unsolicited, of the count. Even after he had freed himself from the tutelage of Philip of Alsace, his struggles with Flanders continued, as the discussion of his feud with Baldwin IX that appears later in this chapter demonstrates. Eventually, Philip was able to assert his own will, but only after he was able to merge his feudal authority with power, bolstering his position by increasing the resources at his disposal and employing military action when necessary to enforce his laws.[24]

The confusion that results from conflating these two terms obscures our ability to discern the range of actions available to men and women during the High Middle Ages. To suggest that authority and power were synonymous actions is to elide the very real differences that existed between activity that stemmed from one or the other. Equally problematic are interpretative models that position the two as a binary and then equate each action with notions of gender. For example, anthropologists first discussing such distinctions tended to associate authority, or legally sanctioned activity, with the public sphere, and hence with men. According to this interpretive view, women, as a result of their confinement to the private, domestic sphere, were forced to resort to subversive tactics in their attempt to exercise influence, actions that were assigned the term power.[25] This binary equation was appropriated by medieval historians, who, in their attempt to situate female action within a wider context, located women exercising agency through a variety of means that they characterized as "power."[26] When women wielding authority in the public sphere did appear, their presence was explained as anomalous. Their experience was consequently dismissed as unrepresentative of their sex and not factored into general discussions of political action or feudal governance.

However, such rigid categorization not only presupposes a distinction between personal and political activity, which may not have been present in the medieval mind, but it posits the existence of clearly differentiated public and private spheres of action. The extent to which such spheres existed in the twelfth and thirteenth century has been the focus of much recent scholarly debate.[27] As the argument here suggests, the lines between the personal and the political, although sharpening considerably during the course of the thirteenth century, remained much more blurred than previously assumed. If a boundary separating public and private realms did exist, it was at times extremely fluid, proving quite permeable to women like the countesses of Flanders and Hainaut. However, acknowledging their ability to penetrate both spheres does not imply that the women occupying such positions of authority enjoyed unlimited agency and were free from the constraints imposed by perceptions of gender. These women can neither be dismissed as anomalous nor accepted without reservation as having as much agency as men. In order to produce a more inclusive understanding of how the political functioned during this period, it is necessary to examine medieval expectations about such women and integrate their experience into existing notions of feudal governance.[28]

Medieval scholars would nearly unanimously agree that such noblewomen occupied a unique position. Even if women never exercised any actual agency, merely serving as vehicles that transmitted authority and legitimated the activity of the males around them, they nevertheless were viewed as the source of feudal rights and prerogatives. Interpretive models that associate women with power and men with authority fail to account for this feature of feudal governance, and ensuing attempts to explore the position of women fail to engage their role in this respect. Ultimately, as is reflected in the experience of Jeanne and Marguerite, when women became heiresses of the family's patrimony, they automatically inherited the office associated with that patrimony and the legitimate authority that the office conferred.[29] However, according to the definition of terms offered above, inheriting authority did not imply that they automatically inherited power. Since the two concepts (authority and power) were distinct in the medieval mind, it would have been possible to possess authority without simultaneously possessing power. In a similar manner, individuals could exercise power, but unless such power was derived from authority, it would not have been officially sanctioned.[30] In other words, women could inherit authority, but, for a variety of reasons ranging from age to sex to personality to marital status, they could have been prevented from exercising power. Such women would have merely functioned as feudal placeholders, that is, objects of exchange among the men who retained control of them, both physically and politically. Ideally, women like Jeanne and Marguerite were expected to serve as pawns in a very high stakes political game. Repositories of feudal authority, their importance would have been derived from their ability to sanction the actions of the men who wielded power in their stead. Distinguishing between authority and power in this manner made it possible for medieval society to reconcile notions of male precedence with the reality of female inheritance.

Tracing events as they unfolded in Flanders following Baldwin's death clearly illustrates this perception of female heiresses and the role they were expected to play in medieval politics. Examination of Jeanne's early years suggests that initially, her experience conformed to such expectations. While she inherited authority as Baldwin's rightful heir to the counties of Flanders and Hainaut, arrangements were made to ensure that power was exercised in her stead by men. She and her sister were placed under the personal custody of Philip Augustus as wards of the crown in 1208 after being transferred to the royal court in Paris. While the two young girls were raised at the French court, Philip of Namur exercised power in Flanders and Hainaut in their name.

They remained in King Philip's custody until they attained the age of majority, when appropriate marriages were arranged for them. Jeanne could only return to Flanders when the king of France found a husband considered suited to wield power in her stead. Philip Augustus was clearly aware of what he stood to gain both personally and politically from the glitch in the feudal system that had produced a female ruler. The power vacuum that prevailed in Flanders and Hainaut as a result of an heiress offered him the opportunity to extend the authority of the monarchy at the expense of his once-powerful, and often rebellious, vassal.

In essence, the treaty of Pont de l'Arche, in ceding control of the two girls to the king of France, significantly curbed the future autonomy of the counts of Flanders and Hainaut, and it ultimately reduced the previously powerful principality to a docile and dependent vassal of the French crown.[31] Although feudal law dictated the subordination of the counts of Flanders to the king of France, the reality of the situation had been considerably different prior to the thirteenth century. The counts of Flanders were extremely powerful in their own right through the majority of the twelfth century, manipulating their strategic location to their advantage and often challenging the king of France for political and military supremacy in the region.[32] The combination of its pivotal location and extreme wealth made Flanders a powerful force in medieval Europe.[33] The prestige and authority commanded by the counts of Flanders during the twelfth and early thirteenth centuries was not derived from the size of their domain but rather from its exceptional prosperity, based primarily on commerce and industry. In addition, Flanders was uniquely situated geographically, juxtaposed between the kingdom of France and the Holy Roman empire, and marked by extensive coastline, which provided easy access to the realm of England. Since the mid-twelfth century the Flemish count was universally acknowledged as an active participant in the ongoing battle for dominance of northern Europe.[34] Accordingly, counts of Flanders and their subjects were courted by the kings of both England and France, who recognized the principality's potential to decisively shift the balance of power in Europe.[35]

During the last decade of the thirteenth century, it appeared that this balance had shifted in favor of England and Flanders. Due in no small part to his alliance with Richard I, Baldwin IX was able to challenge the power of King Philip, dealing his feudal lord several costly military defeats. However, although arguably more successful in his endeavors than his predecessors, Baldwin was not the first count of Flanders to challenge the authority of the French crown. The last decades of the twelfth century and the opening decades of the thirteenth witnessed a series of hostile encounters between Philip Augustus and the counts of Flanders.[36] In the late twelfth century, the frontier that divided the kingdom of France from its frequently recalcitrant vassal, the count of Flanders, consisted primarily of the Vermandois territory, which included the Amienois and Valois. This land first became a point of contention between France and Flanders in 1182, following the death of Elizabeth, countess of Vermandois, the wife of Philip of Alsace, who was the count of Flanders at that point of time. During the course of their marriage, Elizabeth had conceded control of the territory to her husband Philip, and this transfer of authority was confirmed by both Louis VII and Philip Augustus, successive kings of France, in 1179 and 1180 respectively.[37]

After securing control of the Vermandois territory, Philip of Alsace attempted to further his political position and solidify control of the young French king by arranging the marriage of Philip to his niece, Isabelle of Hainaut, in 1180. Isabelle was granted the territory of the Artois as dowry, which included the key Flemish cities of Arras, Aire, Bapaume, and Saint-Omer and conferred suzerainty over the territories of Hesdin, Béthune, Boulogne, Lens, Guines, Saint-Pol, Lilliers, Ardres, and Richebourg. Philip's decision to endow his niece with such valuable territory was not prompted by a generous spirit. Rather, his action was more likely a calculated maneuver, intended to force the king to reaffirm Flemish control of the Vermandois. Although this maneuver was initially successful, Philip Augustus withdrew his confirmation of the claim by Philip of Alsace in 1182, following the death of Elizabeth. With the aid of a papal legate, King and count reached a new agreement at La Grange that guaranteed Philip of Alsace control of the land for the present but stipulated that it pass to Elizabeth's sister Aliénor following count of Philip's death.[38]

While Philip of Alsace initially enjoyed a position of preeminence at the French royal court as the regent of the young king, his position deteriorated with each passing year. The king's ambition grew in proportion to his resentment of Count Philip's continued attempts to maintain his influence over French affairs. Philip of Alsace, seemingly oblivious to King Philip's increasing hostility, doggedly pursued his claims to the Artois in open defiance of the settlement reached at La Grange. In 1184, Count Philip openly provoked Philip Augustus by his decision to include portions of the Artois, previously granted to Isabelle, in the dower lands he conferred on his second wife, Matilda of Portugal.[39] The dispute between the King and Philip of Alsace erupted into a protracted series of military conflicts. Much to Count Philip's chagrin, he was resoundingly defeated by Philip Augustus and forced to concede to particularly unfavorable terms in the Peace of Amiens in 1186, which stipulated that he permanently relinquish all claims to the Vermandois.[40] Philip of Alsace's schemes regarding the Artois were permanently foiled in 1187, when the birth of Isabelle and Philip's son signaled the passage of this territory from Flemish to French control, which officially occurred in 1190.[41] According to one French chronicler, the acquisition of the Vermandois was the event that earned Philip the sobriquet "Augustus" as a reflection of his considerable contributions to the growth of the French royal domain.[42]

Although the king of France was the immediate victor in the struggle for control of the Franco-Flemish frontier in 1191, his success was short-lived. When the county of Flanders passed to Baldwin IX, the ambitious young count severed ties to France, formed an alliance with King Richard of England, and resurrected his uncle's claims to the Artois.[43] His alliance with England provided Baldwin with the military means and financial support necessary to openly rebel against his feudal lord, the king of France, and Baldwin promptly invaded and occupied the border towns of Douai, Péronne, Roye, Bapaume, Hesdin, and Arras. Baldwin's bold maneuver caught the French king off guard, and the count of Flanders soon gained the advantage over the considerably larger forces of Philip. Although the capture of his brother, Philip of Namur, forced Baldwin to call a temporary cessation of hostilities and agree to a truce, he was nevertheless able to dictate the terms of the treaty of Péronne, concluded in 1200. Baldwin was granted control of the cities of Aire and Saint-Omer, He was also granted the lordship of Guines, Ardres, Lilliers, Richebourg, and Béthune, recovering the majority of the land lost by his predecessor, Philip of Alsace.[44] To Philip Augustus, Baldwin's decision to take the cross in 1204 and his ensuing death were welcome events, providing the king with an opportunity to reestablish French control of the region and bring the recalcitrant county to heel. Baldwin's unexpected death proved even more opportune. It seems clear that Philip fully intended to use the remaining years of Jeanne's minority wisely and efficiently, furthering French interests at the expense of the young countess and her counties.

Ultimately, the policies pursued by Philip when Jeanne was a minor were part of a broader strategy employed by the king to consolidate control of potentially wayward vassals like the counts of Flanders and centralize royal authority within France. While the reconstitution of official modes of governing had begun centuries earlier across Europe, the process culminated in France during the late twelfth and early thirteenth centuries under the aegis of Philip Augustus.[45] Scholars have examined the policies implemented by Philip, acknowledging not only his success in conclusively establishing Capetian dominance in France, but also his contribution to the transformation of medieval governance more generally. The processes of centralization of power and consolidation of feudal authority as they evolved are discussed in greatest detail by John Baldwin, who traces the implementation of policies that strengthened the position of the monarch vis-à-vis his vassals, often accomplished in conjunction with increased production of documents and record keeping. Philip's success was due in no small part to his masterful exploitation of the feudal prerogatives that the king traditionally enjoyed, but was previously unable to enforce, including the rights of wardship, feudal relief, and legal appeals, bringing previously autonomous vassals under royal control over the course of his extended reign.[46] By augmenting royal authority at the expense of his vassals, and introducing governance that relied primarily on paid officials, Philip Augustus facilitated the transformation of French government and freed the king from dependence upon often unreliable vassals.

The tension that marked relations between France and Flanders during the late twelfth century comprised a legacy of dispute and discord inherited by the countesses in the thirteenth century, and it explains Philip's determination to exploit the power vacuum created by the premature death of Baldwin IX and the minority of his heir. Philip Augustus was able to influence policy initially through the regent Philip of Namur, establishing a pro-French party among the Flemish nobility that seriously jeopardized the traditional Anglo-Flemish alliance.[47] Philip of Namur's complicity earned him the scorn of many of the Flemish people, as reflected in a contemporary account of his final days. Caesarius of Heisterbach states that after experiencing a premonition that his death was near, Philip tied a cord around his neck and paraded through the streets of Valenciennes crying "I lived like a dog, it is just that I die like a dog.'"[48] The charter evidence confirms the perception of Philip's actions presented by Caesarius. When Philip of Namur finalized the terms of his proposed marriage to the king's daughter, only five Flemish nobles agreed to serve as witnesses to what would have otherwise been considered an auspicious occasion.[49]

While Philip of Namur's actions regarding his nieces incurred the rancor of the staunchest members of the pro-English party in Flanders, Philip Augustus was able to woo many nobles to his side through his generous dispensation of fief rents during Jeanne's minority. In the years following Baldwin's death, nearly 1,219 *livres* were paid out to Flemish nobles in the form of money rents. While only one leading noble of Flanders was on the French payroll in 1206, that number had increased to six in 1210. By 1212, 49 percent of all the fief rents dispensed by Philip were directed toward Flanders. Philip's largesse was made possible in no small part by his successful campaign in Normandy, and the additional revenues and resources he acquired as a result. Although King John tried to counter the actions of the French king, his dispute with Arthur, the young count of Brittany and claimant to the English throne, diverted his attention from the situation in Flanders long enough for Philip to establish a considerable base of support among the county's leading nobles.[50]

As he wooed nobles away from their traditional ally, England, Philip simultaneously moved to curb Flemish autonomy by choosing a husband for Jeanne certain to harbor French sympathies. His ability to personally designate a future count for Flanders and Hainaut significantly bolstered Philip's chances to establish permanent control of the region. The man chosen by the king would presumably be loyal to lord who had bestowed a prize as lucrative as the heiress of Flanders and Hainaut.[51] While the suit of the first candidate, Engeurrand of Coucy, was rejected, the second, Ferrand of Portugal, was accepted.[52] Ferrand was related to Matilda, the widow of Philip of Alsace, dowager countess of Flanders, who was willing to pay the exorbitant sum of 50,000 *livres* demanded by the king of France in order to secure the hand of the young countess for her nephew. Philip undoubtedly expected the twenty-four-year-old Ferrand, a stranger to Flemish politics, to be malleable and easily manipulated, certain to adhere to French policies.[53] Following the marriage of Ferrand and Jeanne in the royal chapel in Paris on January 22, 1212, the young count performed homage to the French king, and then departed for Flanders with his young wife. Philip's confidence in his power over the young count was displayed almost immediately following the ceremony, when the newlyweds were intercepted en route to Flanders, militarily detained by the dauphin, and forced to sign the treaty of Pont-à-Vendun on February 25, ceding the much-coveted towns of Saint-Omer and Aire to France.[54]

Lacking allies in Flanders and Hainaut, Count Ferrand was forced to submit at Pont-à-Vendun in 1212. Although he would never forgive the king for the humiliation he suffered, his first priority was securing control of the county and quelling the opposition he encountered among the anti-French Flemish nobles. Ferrand, conducting a solo tour of his newly acquired possessions, found the gates of the city of Ghent barred to him. The residents of this powerful city demanded that he provide proof of his marriage to the countess, the heir of Baldwin and legitimate ruler of the county.[55] Ferrand and his small entourage fled the city, returning to Douai to fetch the countess, who was prominently positioned at the side of the count on their return to Ghent. It is no surprise that the most serious opposition encountered by Ferrand was centered on the northern city of Ghent, the heart of the Flemish cloth trade and hence the region with the closest financial ties to England. Such resistance to Ferrand's assumption of power was clearly prompted by fears that as count he would function as a pawn of the French king, facilitating French attempts to reduce the autonomy of Flanders.

Not only does this episode illustrate the myriad of competing political and economic interests that animated Flemish society during the thirteenth century, but it also reveals the attitudes of individuals during this period toward authority. The nobles of Flanders unequivocally accepted Jeanne as the heir to Baldwin IX, hence the repository of legitimate feudal authority. Ferrand ruled only as an extension of her person, in her stead and as her representative.[56] The nobles refused to accept Ferrand as their count without evidence that he was, in fact, the legitimate husband of their countess, the true source of authority in Flanders. However, while Jeanne was clearly perceived as the repository of feudal authority, once the validity of their marriage was established, it was expected that Ferrand wield power in her name, participating actively in the public sphere while she remained confined to the margins of Flemish affairs. In this manner, Jeanne and Ferrand conformed to societal expectations for the first few years of their marriage, she conferring legitimacy and authority and he actively ruling in her stead.

This depiction of Jeanne's role in governing Flanders during the years between 1212 and 1214 is supported both by the silence of contemporary narratives regarding her activity as well as extant charter evidence. Examination of their activity regarding religious patronage illustrates her marginalization. From 1212 to the battle of Bouvines in July, 1214, Jeanne's name appears in only six charters, of which five were issued jointly with Ferrand.[57] The only charter issued solely by Jeanne was concerned with a promise made jointly by the couple in May 1212 to the community of Saint-Jean of Jerusalem. In the charter issued by Jeanne in April 1214, she affirmed their earlier agreement to pay the hospitalers of Saint Jean the 700 *livres* owed for the ransom of Gerard of Mons within one year.[58] It was probably not a coincidence that this action occurred in the months just preceding the outbreak of hostilities between France and Flanders. During the spring of 1214, Ferrand was consumed by his quarrel with Philip thereby forcing Jeanne to deal with an affair internal to the county.

Documents dealing with secular matters issued by the countess between her marriage in 1212 and the battle of Bouvines in 1214 were even scarcer, attesting to her limited role in political affairs. Her name seldom appears in charters issued by Ferrand during this period, indicating that Ferrand's decisions as count did not require his wife's consent. Ferrand alone performed homage to Philip following his marriage to Jeanne in 1212. Her name is never mentioned in the charter recording this act, and only his seal was attached. Although several Flemish nobles, including Siger of Ghent, Jean of Nesle, Jean, castellan of Lens, and Matilda, the dowager countess of Flanders, pledged security for the young count, the young countess was not among the witnesses.[59] While Jeanne did consent to the transfer of Saint-Omer and Aire, this was needed because it was a situation where land was being alienated from the patrimony of Flanders.[60] Ferrand could not act in her stead; Jeanne's assent was needed in such instances for transactions to be legitimate.

With the exception of the transaction at Pont-à-Vendun and a charter confirming the alliance between Ferrand and John I of England, only one other act issued by Ferrand in 1212 mentions the countess. In 1214, Ferrand and Jeanne jointly issued a charter that stated their intention to investigate the circumstances surrounding the marriage of Marguerite to the bailiff of Hainaut, Bouchard of Avesnes.[61] It seems quite likely that Jeanne's inclusion in this charter was a result of its more personal nature, pertaining to the sudden, and probably unexpected, marriage of her younger sister, who was only ten years old at the time. The absence of Jeanne's name from the majority of charters issued by the count during this early period is an indication of Ferrand's supremacy in Flanders and Hainaut and his ability to act in her stead. In fact, the full extent of Jeanne's marginalization is reflected in a charter issued by Philip Augustus to the échevins of the city of Douai in June 1213, during the military hostilities that preceded the battle at Bouvines. While Philip prohibited the city's leaders from expressly signing a peace treaty with Count Ferrand or with the dowager Countess Matilda, he made no mention of his wife, the current countess, clearly discounting her as a viable political player in events.[62]

The relative absence of Jeanne's name in the written record is indicative of her relegation to the margins of political activity from 1212 to 1214, space that one would expect her to occupy in accordance with thirteenth-century expectations regarding female rulers. The text of the charters demonstrate that Ferrand's actions did not require Jeanne's consent, and there is no indication that Jeanne exerted any influence on the affairs of the county or on her twenty-four-year-old husband during the first few years of their marriage. Clearly, Jeanne inherited authority as countess, but Ferrand wielded power in her stead, dictating policy in Flanders and Hainaut. Marguerite was even more restricted in her activity than her older sister between their return to Flanders in 1212 and the battle of Bouvines. She too conformed to expectations, proving to be almost as valuable a pawn as her older sister. After Philip's attempts to arrange a marriage for Marguerite in 1212 had failed, she was placed under the tutelage of the pro-French Bouchard of Avesnes, who had recently been appointed bailiff of Hainaut. In spite of narrative accounts that accuse Marguerite of seducing Bouchard, at least thirty years her senior, it is unlikely given her age and the circumstances surrounding the marriage that the ten-year old girl was responsible for instigating the union. Marguerite remains completely silent in charter evidence during this period, and proves an equally elusive figure in narrative sources. While the contention surrounding her marriage will be addressed at length in chapter 2, it is important to note her apparent conformity to social norms. To Bouchard, Marguerite's value lay primarily in the wealth and comital connections she brought to her marriage. For a younger son of a lesser noble, marriage to the sister of the countess, a not insignificant heiress in her own right, was a stroke of extreme fortune, elevating his position considerably.

While the age of both women undoubtedly played a role in restricting their activity in the years following their return to Flanders in 1212, the impact of gender perceptions cannot be discounted. In fact, the very mechanism of feudal succession that allowed women to inherit yet assumed males would act in their stead was predicated upon perceptions about the abilities, or lack thereof, of members of the female sex.[63] In attempting to discern the medieval view of gender, scholars have been forced to rely primarily on theological texts, in which views about men and women were filtered through not only a patriarchal but also a Christian world view. Ensuing notions about perceived differences in biological function of medieval men and women have been described in detail by scholars and do not need to be reiterated here. This discussion will focus on how the medieval understanding of gender, or basic differences between men and women, informed attitudes about power, particularly in conjunction with women. In "Women and Power," Georges Duby provides a synopsis of the male view of women in the Middle Ages. This view was informed primarily by assumptions about the female nature, positing both biological and moral differences between the sexes. According to Duby, "All the men whose thought's we can know were convinced that woman by nature is weak, that she is dangerous. . .and that she must therefore be subjected to the man."[64] It is clear from this statement that Duby assumes that a sing uniform view of gender existed in medieval society. If "all" the men who committed their views to writing ascribed to this view, it was not only the normative view in Duby's interpretation, but the only view. However, not only does this type of consensus about any topic seldom exist in a society, but examination of the texts that formed the basis of such conclusions reveals not only the probability of a dissenting view toward gender, but it also reveals the possibility of a different interpretation altogether.[65]

Beliefs about the nature of women would have had obvious implications for their perceived ability to wield power, as illustrated in a letter sent by Bernard of Clairvaux to Melisende, the queen of Jerusalem. In the words of Bernard, perhaps the most authoritative voice of the twelfth century in terms of normative Christian views of female power, "It is not normal for a woman to wield *potestas*: if, by lineage, by what she owes to her ancestors, she is endowed with power, it falls to the man to whom she has been entrusted to exercise it. When the man is gone, then the woman must overcome her nature, must be a man's equal."[66] In his letter to one who would be considered a "powerful women," Bernard provides revealing insight into the mindset of some medieval men concerning female rulers. Clearly, Bernard assumed the norm of male power, a norm that was based upon the medieval understanding of differences between men and women. However, not only does Bernard accept that in certain situations, women can inherit authority, the final sentence of the quote above raises some provocative questions about his attitude toward women and power generally. Clearly, he was able to envision a possible scenario in which women ruled, a clear divergence from the norm. While he viewed such female rule as an aberration, he nonetheless accepted it as a potential reality in medieval society. In exhorting Melisende to overcome her nature and "be a man's equal," he essentially acknowledged that she could, indicating that even Bernard did not categorically dismiss women as incapable of ruling, supporting the use of an interpretive model that attempts to understand such realities as based upon a continuum. Although the norm associated men with power, society accepted that at times, the position of women along the continuum could shift, until they occupied space typically equated with men. It is equally important to note that Bernard did not suggest that Melisende "be a man," hence accepting the potential conflation of such normative categories as men and women, power and authority, but rather he exhorted her to essentially "be like a man," a very real difference.[67]

In the Middle Ages, just like today, notions of gender were predicated upon a biological understanding of men and women and the perceptions of difference which resulted. However, as a cultural construct, notions of gender obviously vary over time and across space. Any analysis of gender must incorporate the peculiar features of a society. As recent studies have very successfully demonstrated, it is impossible to impose a monolithic view of gender upon the Middle Ages.[68] Such studies demonstrate the need to account for the full range of factors that may have influenced a particular group's understanding of what it meant to be masculine or feminine, and how such an understanding would have translated into activities deemed appropriate for men and women. It is necessary to acknowledge that women could exhibit behavior deemed masculine; such would be the case of female rulers. Any attempt to understand the influence of gender on an individual's relationship to power in the Middle Ages must account for the extremely rigid social stratification of society. Adopting a monolithic view of "woman" that fails to incorporate the importance of status can only result in an inaccurate understanding of the position of many women. Just as the meaning and experience of "woman" differs among races and classes in the modern world, the meaning and experience of "woman" differed among social categories in the medieval world. This sentiment is conveyed by Carol Clover, who poses the question "was femaleness any more decisive in setting parameters on individual behavior than were wealth, prestige, marital status or just plain personality and ambition?"[69] For women like the countesses of Flanders and Hainaut, elevated social status was a key determinant of experience, position, and proximity to power.

However, in spite of this divergence in experience among women in such a socially stratified society, it is important to acknowledge the presence of certain commonalities that would have transcended social status. Certainly there are similarities that seem to uniformly affect individual actions and experiences among men and women. For example, no matter what their social status, women were generally associated more directly than men with reproduction and child rearing. Even powerful women like the countesses would still be regarded as women, and consequently subject on occasion to polemical diatribes about the inherent weaknesses of their sex. In spite of the very overt demonstrations of their personal authority and the power they wielded in the office of countess, the actions of Jeanne and Marguerite were on occasion circumscribed by notions of gender. Such views could manifest themselves in attempts to perpetuate their political marginalization or as challenges to their ability to exercise power.

While Jeanne continued to hover along the periphery of Flemish affairs, Ferrand became increasingly assertive. After successfully establishing his position as count and overcoming any remaining opposition among the nobility of Flanders, Ferrand lost no time in demonstrating his continued resentment of Philip's treatment of him and his determination to rule independently of France. He dispelled all suspicion of subservience to Philip Augustus in 1213 when he refused to participate in the king's proposed invasion of England unless the cities of Saint-Omer and Aire were returned to Flanders. Philip responded disdainfully to Ferrand's claims, dismissing him from the French royal assembly of nobles at Soissons and ordering his army, assembled at Gravelines, to invade Flanders instead of England.[70] By June, Philip's army had surrounded the city of Lille. From Spring 1213 until Summer 1214, Flanders was the main theater of war. Fields were destroyed and villages were razed by the competing troops.

Following Philip's declaration of war, Jean of Nesle and Siger of Ghent, pro-French nobles who had been ejected from Flanders by Ferrand following his breach with the king, led Philip's army on a rampage through the county, seizing control of the major cities of Lille, Ypres, and Bruges.[71] Ferrand, once informed of the destruction wrought by the French army, appealed to the English king, who dispatched a fleet under the command of the count of Salisbury. Salisbury and the English fleet reached Flanders on May 30, and were joined by Ferrand and his troops the following day. The English fleet then proceeded to the Flemish city of Damme, surprising the French and destroying at least half of the king's ships, which had been moored in the port pending the imminent invasion of England. Although the Flemish troops rallied around their count, immediately reversing French gains and proceeding as far south as Tournai, hostilities continued into 1214, devastating the towns and countryside of Flanders.[72] Ferrand traveled to England in January, 1214, formalizing his alliance with King John and participating in the formation of an anti-French coalition under the direction of Philip's former ally, Renaud of Dammartin, the count of Boulogne. The coalition planned a two-pronged invasion, designed to attack France simultaneously from the south and the northwest, thus forcing the French to divide the king's army and significantly diluting the strength of his troops. While John led the English in Poitou, the armies of Ferrand, Otto of Brunswick, Henry of Brabant, and Renaud assembled in Flanders, attacking the French on July 27, 1214, at Bouvines.[73]

Ferrand's defiance of Philip and the latter's ensuing campaign to subdue his recalcitrant vassal set in motion the chain of events that ultimately culminated in the encounter at Bouvines, a moment that was to irrevocably alter relations between France and Flanders for the duration of the Middle Ages and, more immediately, drastically alter the position Countess Jeanne. In spite of a slight numerical advantage, the anti-French coalition suffered a crushing defeat at Bouvines. One hundred and thirty knights were taken hostage, among them the leading nobles of Flanders, including Count Ferrand.[74] Ferrand was led in chains through the streets of Paris to the newly constructed Louvre prison, a dramatic demonstration of the king's response to recalcitrant vassals.[75] Once notified of the defeat of Ferrand's forces at Bouvines, Jeanne left immediately for Paris. The young countess petitioned Philip Augustus to spare the life of her husband and refrain from confiscating the county, the king's prerogative as liege lord of Flanders.[76] Although Philip appeared to heed the pleas of his niece, sparing Ferrand's life and allowing Jeanne to remain in nominal control of Flanders, the terms of the treaty of Paris, signed on October 24, 1214, imposed a more subtle, but no less devastating, penalty upon the young countess and her husband. Philip refrained from executing Ferrand, but he failed to stipulate a prospective date for his release from prison. Unlike the majority of the captured nobles, ransomed and returned to Flanders in the years immediately following Bouvines, Ferrand would remain in prison for twelve years.[77] Philip demanded that Jeanne forfeit the son of the duke of Brabant as a hostage, raze the fortresses of Valenciennes, Ypres, Audenarde, and Cassel, and refrain indefinitely from any new defensive constructions without first securing his assent. In addition, Jeanne was required to restore Jean of Nesles and Siger of Ghent, nobles who had fought alongside the king, to their Flemish possessions.[78]

Once the terms had been dictated and the treaty sealed, the fourteen-year-old countess returned to Flanders and Hainaut alone. Vulnerable and inexperienced, she was now surrounded by men who intended to use her youth and perhaps her sex to their own advantage. Jeanne was isolated from her sister Marguerite, who remained in the custody of her husband Bouchard of Avesnes in his family's castle in Hainaut. At this moment, Jeanne seemed to be even more powerless than before, subject to men who had no stake in the continued independence of Flanders, and whose interests were vested in promoting their own advantage at her expense. The degree to which they would succeed would depend upon a myriad of factors, not the least of which was the countesses' own determination to transform herself from a pawn, a silent witness to the manipulations of the men around her, into an active political player in her own right. Jeanne's experience from the death of her father in 1206 to the imprisonment of Ferrand in 1214, recounted here, illustrates how status continued to precede gender in importance among individuals of elevated social conditions, providing women with access to authority. However, the extent to which she was able to translate such authority into power was quite limited during this period. Yet, the dramatic shift in circumstances after the battle of Bouvines offered her an opportunity to alter her position and begin to actively wield power. She, along with her sister Marguerite, would become increasingly assertive over time, effectively transforming themselves from pawns to players in the political arena.

CHAPTER 2

WIELDING POWER: 1214–80

When Jeanne returned to Flanders after her failed attempt to ransom Ferrand, she found herself in a unique position. Faced with the disastrous outcome of her husband's role in the battle of Bouvines, the young countess was forced to accept the harsh terms dictated by Philip Augustus. Although there is no evidence to suggest that the fourteen-year-old countess had played any part in her husband's revolt, the burden of negotiating the political and economic ramifications of his failed rebellion fell to her. While Philip would exact a steep penalty from the count, who would spend the next decade in prison, it was Jeanne and the county of Flanders that would truly pay the price. In keeping Ferrand incarcerated, Philip Augustus forced Jeanne into a relationship of dependence upon the French monarchy, attempting to utilize a pro-French council of nobles which he personally chose to serve as an extension of royal control into Flanders. It was expected that Jeanne would continue to function as a pawn, conferring authority upon those who acted in her name. While her role was to remain relatively unchanged, the cast of male characters around her was altered. Philip intended to be certain that those acting in her name and wielding power would be supporters of France and would dictate Flemish policy according to French interests.

Since status took precedence over gender in determining the ability to inherit authority, the possibility of female power continued to exist in the thirteenth century.[1] While it was anticipated that such women would serve to legitimate the actions of men, at times this ideal of female authority/ male power failed to translate into reality, as the experience of Jeanne and Marguerite will demonstrate. From the death of their father to the battle of Bouvines in 1214, both women seemed to conform to expectations. However, circumstances converged to produce an opportunity for both Jeanne and Marguerite to transform themselves from pawns to active players, challenging not only the men around them but also the very ideological rules that governed access to power during this period. Although she initially remained a pawn post-Bouvines, manipulated by the king of France and his pro-French council, Jeanne gradually matured both physically and politically, playing an increasing role in comital affairs and learning how to assert her authority as countess. Marguerite's political learning curve was considerably less steep than that of her sister and predecessor. Although she too was initially reduced to a pawn, first by her husband and later by her own sister, her right to succeed in 1244 was never challenged. Marguerite ruled Flanders and Hainaut until her death in 1280. This difference in experience will be explored throughout the course of this chapter, examined for what it reveals about the various factors that determined the ability of women to wield power. While both women would eventually establish themselves as active participants in the political game alongside their male peers, neither was immune to the gender expectations that pervaded medieval society. Both faced challenges that seemed to stem expressly from the uniqueness of their position as female rulers. These moments will be discussed here in order to more accurately understand how such women who inherited authority and exercised power were understood by their contemporaries and factored into the feudal mode of governance.

In the aftermath of Bouvines Philip Augustus intended to take full advantage of Ferrand's absence and Jeanne's inexperience by appointing the pro-French Jean of Nesle as bailiff of Flanders in order to exert royal control on Flemish affairs and influence comital policy. It is clear that the presence of Jean of Nesle was intended to provide the young countess, still the legitimate authority in Flanders and Hainaut, with a male who could wield power in her stead. Unlike Ferrand, or a potential new husband, Jean of Nesle had proven his loyalty to France on numerous occasions, aligning his own political and financial interests with French royal policy and proving his loyalty to King Philip.[2] The anti-French nobles, impoverished as a result of the enormous ransoms exacted after Bouvines, were hardly in a position to challenge this direct imposition on Flemish autonomy. Neither was their fourteen-year-old countess, who had occupied the periphery of political affairs since her marriage and lacked the experience and the resources to assert her independence at this juncture of events.

While Philip's refusal to ransom his prisoner may be viewed as merely typical treatment meted out to recalcitrant and rebellious nobles in thirteenth-century France, it lacks precedent, both in terms of the severity of the sentence and in its political implications. Philip's decision to keep Ferrand in prison indefinitely significantly complicated Flemish affairs, and it contributed to the precariousness of Jeanne's position as ruler of Flanders and Hainaut.[3] As this chapter will demonstrate, closer examination of Philip's actions suggests that his refusal to liberate Ferrand may have been part of a broader plan intended to consolidate his position and establish his authority over his more powerful vassals. As long as Ferrand lived, the countess was unable to marry and replace him with another male who could exercise power in her stead. Not only did this force the countess into a position of dependence on her liege lord, the king of France, but it also neutralized the potential threat of this once powerful county. While Flanders was without a count, Philip could be certain that there would be no repeat of Bouvines. In other words, it was actually in his best interest to have a woman in charge.

Jeanne's continued liminal status in the years immediately following her husband's imprisonment is illustrated by the number of charters issued in the first few years following Ferrand's revolt. In 1214, the year of Bouvines, Jeanne issued three charters to monastic or religous communities in her domains, all pertaining to administrative matters. This number increased slightly over the next few years, reaching a total of ten by 1217, and began to involve donations of land and grants of privileges.[4] While becoming more active as a patron of monastic foundations, Jeanne's personal involvement in comital affairs remained limited during this period in spite of the absence of Ferrand, suggesting that the situation conformed to Philip's expectations. Jeanne continued to function as the source of feudal authority in the county, yet in reality she was merely a figurehead, and politics were dictated from Paris and executed in the two counties by the various members of the pro-French council installed by the king and led by Jean of Nesle. As long as the situation continued in this fashion, it was in Philip's best interest to keep Ferrand in prison, which explains his indifference to Jeanne's repeated requests for her husband's liberation.

While Jeanne's ability to exercise power post-Bouvines was initially circumscribed by the regency council imposed by Philip Augustus, as she gained in age and experience, she began to increasingly assert her own will in Flanders and Hainaut. Between the battle of Bouvines and the return of Ferrand in 1223, Philip's plans to maintain control of Flanders were foiled by factors beyond his control, including the maturation of its countess. She proved increasingly unwilling to remain a pawn, gradually establishing her autonomy and asserting control in her domains. Although she had proven unsuccessful in her bid to secure the release of Ferrand from Philip's prison, she could force the return of Marguerite to the comital court. Separating her younger sister from her husband, Bouchard of Avesnes, seems to have been Jeanne's first priority, and she proved more than willing to appeal her case to the highest authorities in Europe, including the pope.

In spite of a lack of scholarly consensus regarding Marguerite's marriage to Bouchard of Avesnes, which occurred some time in 1212, the sources unanimously agree that Ferrand and Jeanne were not present at the ceremony.[5] Moreover, the wedding may have even occurred without their consent, as there is not a single document that testifies to Jeanne or Ferrand's complicity in the affair. A charter issued in April 1214 from Ghent is the first concrete indication that Jeanne and Ferrand were even aware of the union. Ferrand and Jeanne promised to appoint a commission composed of Gerard of Jauce, Guillaume "the uncle", the castellan of Beaumont, Arnould of Audenarde, Bauduin of Comines, and Gilbert of Berghelles to decide "what was owed to Bouchard on account of his marriage to Marguerite."[6] Specific details about the affair do not appear in any charters until 1246, when questions about the legitimacy of the marriage reemerged following Marguerite's ascendence to the office of countess. According to one account, the wedding was celebrated in July 1212 at Quesnoy, and it was witnessed by approximately thirty guests. Marguerite was described as more than willing and, in spite of her age (ten), the marriage was consummated that same evening.[7]

The absence of documentation prior to that produced by the inquest of 1246 is surprising in light of Marguerite's position. Not only was she the sister of the countess of Flanders and Hainaut but she was also a wealthy heiress in her own right.[8] As long as her sister remained childless, Marguerite was next in line as ruler of Flanders and Hainaut. In fact, according to Charles Duvivier, at the time of the wedding, Ferrand was engaged in negotiations with the count of Salisbury concerning the marriage of his sister-in-law.[9] The circumstances surrounding the marriage, and Jeanne's later reaction to it, suggest that Bouchard, appointed bailiff of the county of Hainaut by Ferrand shortly after 1212 at the instigation of Philip Augustus, took advantage of his position as custodian of Marguerite to attempt to further his own ambitions.[10] Marguerite's youth at the time of the marriage would have required the consent of her formal guardian. In this case, such consent would have been provided by Ferrand and Jeanne or perhaps by the king, who still stood to profit from her marriage. Yet, none of the extant documents related to the affair record an attempt by Bouchard to secure permission to marry Marguerite from anyone who would have been in position to grant it. The historical record is equally silent in terms of official statements regarding the union or terms of the dowry. Both of these omissions are surprising in light of Marguerite's age as well her importance as sister (and successor in the absence of children) to Jeanne. Although official opposition was not expressed until 1215, when Jeanne appealed to the Fourth Lateran Council, Ferrand had replaced Bouchard as bailiff of Hainaut prior to November 22, 1213. His decision may be interpreted as retribution against Bouchard, who had the temerity to marry his sister-in-law without his consent.[11]

Whether or not the marriage occurred with the consent of Marguerite, it was clearly opposed by Jeanne. On the basis of the latter's complaint to the Fourth Lateran Council, the marriage was declared invalid and Bouchard was excommunicated by Archbishop Alberic of Rheims on January 17, 1216. The accusations levied against Bouchard included abduction of Marguerite, marriage without first securing the papal dispensation necessary for relations within the fourth degree of consanguinity, and above all, failing to reveal his status as a subdeacon and cantor of Notre-Dame of Laon.[12] Bouchard's excommunication was to be publicly announced, and the residence where Marguerite was detained to be placed under interdict until he complied with the archbishop's demands. The excommunication was confirmed by Innocent III in a bull issued on January 19, 1216, in which he referred to the "execrable crime" committed by Bouchard at the expense of Marguerite.[13] Innocent, "moved by pity for the young girl, and wishing to fulfill the mandate of his pastoral office" ordered that Bouchard be publicly denounced as excommunicate and his crime revealed to all every Sunday and feast day, when the church bells rang and the candles were lit. He ordered Bouchard to restore Marguerite to her sister and return without delay to the clerical life to which he had previously committed himself.[14]

Following Bouchard's failure to respond to Innocent's commands, Jeanne reiterated her appeal to the papacy, prompting the issuance of another bull and a second sentence of excommunication, levied by Honorius III in July 1217.[15] In April 1219, Honorius reaffirmed the excommunication of Bouchard and extended the sentence to include Marguerite, Guy, Bouchard's brother, and several other supporters who had been aiding and abetting the couple, including Waleram and Thierry of Houffalize.[16] In his statement, Honorius revealed the extent of the anguish experienced by Jeanne as well as growing suspicions of Marguerite's complicity. Unfortunately, the last few years of Marguerite's marriage to Bouchard remain shrouded in mystery. The French chronicler Philippe Mouskes reported that Jeanne resorted to military force in order to separate the couple, capturing Bouchard in 1219 and imprisoning him first at the Gravensteen in Ghent and later at her stronghold in Rupelmonde.[17] Honorius's sentence of excommunication against Marguerite was lifted on November 16, 1221, indicating that she had complied with papal demands, separating from Bouchard by this date. She returned to Jeanne's court, where she resided until her eventual remarriage in 1223.[18] Jeanne's campaign to separate Marguerite from Bouchard lasted nearly a decade, involving three different popes and numerous ecclesiastical officials. In spite of her initial lack of success, Jeanne ultimately prevailed, securing an annulment, reclaiming custody of her sister and arranging her marriage to William of Dampierre in 1223.[19]

Jeanne's actions in conjunction with the episode of her sister's first marriage demonstrate her determination to achieve her goal. Jeanne successfully exercised power as countess, imposing her will on Bouchard and his supporters, and making clear to her nobles the consequences of thwarting her will. Her direct appeals to successive popes on Marguerite's behalf demonstrate a gradual recognition of the power and prestige at her command. Their repeated intervention reveals papal recognition of her importance as countess of Flanders and Hainaut, and perhaps even an acknowledgment of her generosity as a monastic patron. It is clear from the ecclesiastical documents issued concerning the affair that Jeanne was acting alone in this endeavor. Philip Augustus did not lend his voice to her appeals, and the majority of the leading nobles of Flanders remained distanced from the entire process. In part, it is possible to read her opposition to Bouchard as more than a response to his personal affront in marrying Marguerite without her consent. The Avesnes family was traditionally pro-French, one of the few to be on Philip's payroll from the late eleventh century. Bouchard's appointment as bailiff of Hainaut in 1212 was almost certainly orchestrated by Philip, as it occurred right after Ferrand's arrival on the Flemish scene. It seems quite plausible that Jeanne viewed the separation as both in the best interest of her sister as well as part of a wider policy to assert her own authority by distancing herself from Philip and pro-French Flemish nobles.

However, Jeanne's success in securing the separation of Marguerite and Bouchard may have been one of the only moments of triumph the young countess experienced in the first few years of her rule. In the decade or so following Bouvines, Jeanne was forced to fend off several challenges to her authority, both external and internal. Jeanne's first battle occurred in conjunction with portions of Flanders located east of the Scheldt, which were held in fief of the Holy Roman emperor. After her return to Flanders in 1214, Jeanne was dismayed to discover that Frederick, the Holy Roman emperor, had transfered authority over the region to William, the count of Holland, claiming that Jeanne had failed to render homage for it. After repeated appeals, Jeanne was able to force the Holy Roman emperor to reverse his decision. In the charter reinstating her, issued in 1220, Frederick accepted Jeanne's explanation for her failure to perform the necessary acts, citing the danger of the roads and the recent imprisonment of her husband Ferrand.[20] It is very likely that the Holy Roman emperor planned to use the countess's youth and inexperience to deprive her of her traditional rights over this territory. However, his plans were foiled by her assertiveness and insistence that the customary prerogatives of the counts of Flanders be observed.

In addition to the external challenge to her authority posed by Frederick, Jeanne expended a considerable amount of effort in the years between 1214 and 1223 fending off challenges from her own nobles, particularly members of the pro-French party in Flanders. In 1221, Jeanne designated Jean of Nesle as arbitor of a dispute with Arnould of Audenarde concerning the collection of a tax on wine at Yseel. Jean of Nesle ruled in Jeanne's favor, concluding that the countess, rather than Arnould, should receive the payment. The two were also involved in a dispute concerning a vineyard at Ath. Again, arbitration ruled in favor of the countess.[21] In 1224, Jeanne forced Arnoul of Landas to return territory that he had seized from her in the previous year. He agreed to renounce all further claims to land at Fratrelos once it was returned to the countess.

Jeanne acted decisively to establish her authority in 1218, when she purchased the castellany of Cassel from Michel of Boulers, the hereditary constable of Flanders. Through this purchase, she gained control of extensive territory within the county.[22] In return for his concession of the castellany, which conferred considerable authority on the individual who controlled it, Jeanne granted Michel of Boulers land in northern Flanders, along with several rents in coin and in kind.[23] She would later secure another victory in her dispute with her former constable, forcing him to return land he claimed in Alost that, according to Jeanne and her arbiters, was not part of the original exchange.[24]

By 1222, Jeanne considered her position secure enough to target Jean of Nesle, Philip Augustus's staunchest ally among her council. As a constant advocate for pro-French policies, Jean would have proven a significant opponent to Flemish independence, serving as a daily reminder of the humiliation of Bouvines. While details concerning Jean's ejection from her council remain elusive, charter evidence clearly indicates that he resigned his position as baillif of Flanders and Hainaut by 1222.[25] In 1226, Jeanne moved to further neutralize his impact on Flemish politics by purchasing the castellany of Bruges from him. By appealing to the king of France, Jean of Nesle was able to exact the enormous sum of 23,546 *livres parisis, 6 sous, 8 deniers* from the countess. Although the cost was considerable, Jeanne was permanently freed of his influence on comital policy.[26] After the sale was concluded and formally approved by the King, Jean left the county of Flanders, withdrawing to his lands in France. Within a decade of Bouvines, Jeanne's household was comprised of a completely different cast of characters all selected by the countess herself. This list included Franco of Mallenguien, the prévôt of Bruges and chancellor of Flanders, Robert of Wavrin, who had become her seneschal, and Gérard of Oudenbourg, her chamberlain.[27]

The countess also appears to have courted the support of the urban centers of Flanders, possibly as an attempt to counter the challenges posed by her own nobles. Set against the relief of her repeated battles with members of the nobility, Jeanne's actions on behalf of Flemish towns can be viewed as deliberate attempts to secure their favor. During the High Middle Ages, the towns of Flanders and the nobles of the county found themselves increasingly at odds.

traditional tensions were exacerbated by developments in the thirteenth century that benefited urban centers and their inhabitants but failed to reverse the declining fortunes of the nobility. The interests of the towns of Flanders had traditionally been aligned with those of England due to the ties of dependency created by the woolen industry. Jeanne overtly demonstrated her desire to foster such connections by offering valuable exemptions to members of the industry. In 1216, she issued a charter from Audenarde that encouraged settlement in the city of Courtrai, promising newcomers life exemption from the tax levied on the city's residents.[28] In 1224, Jeanne extended this exemption to include taxes owed to the count by fifty men who had migrated to the city for the specific purpose of participating in the wool trade.[29] In 1216, the city of Ghent was granted the right to levy their own taxes on inhabitants who resided within the city's walls, and in 1218, Jeanne granted the residents of the city of Seclin the right to follow the laws, privileges, and customs enjoyed by the nearby city of Lille.[30] In 1225, the burghers of Biervliet were granted the right to elect their own aldermen every year, furthering their ability to establish internal governance independent of the traditional feudal system.[31] These acts were most likely intended to garner support for the countess among the cities of her domains, key players in Flemish politics throughout the thirteenth century.[32] In championing towns in their struggles against local nobles and offering urban centers expanded opportunity for self government, Jeanne revealed her desire to further distance the county from France and French control.

Jeanne also secured the support of the numerous monastic communities that dominated the landscape of Flanders and Hainaut. The number of charters issued by the countess to foundations within her domains rose steadily over the period between Ferrand's imprisonment and his return reflecting Jeanne's increasing assertiveness. The countess issued an average of fourteen charters each year from 1214 to 1225, reaching a high of twenty-two in 1219. On the eve of the count's return in 1223, Jeanne issued a total of twenty charters in conjunction with patronage, conveying a range of donations and privileges. Her activity as a founder also intensified in the years preceding Ferrand's return in 1226, as the discussion in chapters 3 and 4 will demonstrate. Her actions as a patron were not only intended to secure prayers for herself and her incarcerated husband, but they were also intended to garner the goodwill of the monasteries in her domains. Many of these abbeys, particularly those affiliated to the Benedictine and Cistercian orders, controlled large patrimonies and could potentially be powerful political agents. Repeated demonstrations of generosity and material benevolence were certainly an effective way for the countess to gain their support.

While Jeanne's attempts to court the urban centers and rural monasteries so crucial to the prosperity of Flanders and the position of its countess were largely successful, control of her nobles, particularly those from the predominantly rural, less commercial county of Hainaut, proved elusive. Her success in removing most of the staunchest members of the pro-French party from her inner circle was overshadowed by the affair of the false Baldwin. The challenge posed by this imposter, who first surfaced in 1224, would prove to be the most serious of Jeanne's rule, illustrating the continued precariousness of her position. The hermit named Bertrand of Rains was able to pose as Jeanne's father for over a year.[33] The mysterious circumstances surrounding Baldwin's death facilitated the hermit's ability to persuade the common people that he was their chivalrous and charismatic count, transformed into a mythical figure by the popular imagination of the people of Flanders and Hainaut within a mere two decades of his death.[34] The impostor's appearance coincided with one of the worst famines to impact the region during the Middle Ages, which explains his appeal to the people in the predominantly rural county of Hainaut, more dependent on agriculture than their more urban, commercial counterparts in Flanders. While people in the countryside were seduced by the romance of the returning count, disenchanted members of the nobility seized upon the hermit as a means to dislodge their countess from power.[35] The success of Bertrand, albeit short-lived, was due in part to deep-seated resentment among several nobles for their countess. The imposter found his staunchest allies among a group of nobles from Hainaut, led by Bouchard of Avesnes, whose support prolonged the farce. The false Baldwin, followed by his entourage, toured the cities of Valenciennes, Lille, Courtrai, Bruges, and Ghent, issuing charters and commissioning his own seal.[36] He even received a letter from Henry III of England celebrating his safe return and proposing an alliance against their mutual enemy, King Louis of France.[37] Abandoned by many of the nobles of Hainaut, and faced with widespread rebellion amongst the towns of Flanders, Jeanne was forced to enlist the support of Louis VIII, agreeing to his terms unconditionally. After successfully unmasking the impostor during a personal encounter at Peronne in 1225, King Louis proceeded to intervene militarily in order to subdue the cities that refused to submit to their countess.

After quelling the rebellion of the false Baldwin, Jeanne re-established her authority in Flanders and Hainaut, issuing pardons to the towns which had betrayed her by supporting the impostor.[38] Although she was able to eliminate the imposter and resume control of her domains, the episode proved to be extremely costly, both in terms of the monetary compensation Louis demanded in return for his intervention, and for future Flemish independence. Louis demanded 10,000 *livres parisis*, and forced the countess to raze several fortresses, including that at Ypres.[39] Gabrielle Spiegel identifies the episode of false Baldwin as the culmination of decades of French attempts to subjugate Flanders. According to Spiegel, by definitively establishing her dependence upon the king of France the revolt resulted in the loss of any autonomy that Jeanne could still claim as countess.[40]

Furthermore, this episode illustrates the unique predicament faced by female rulers who lacked a husband or a representative equivalent. Faced with the rebellion of her subjects, Jeanne was unable to provide a successful military defense. In the absence of a male representative she enlisted the support of her cousin, the king. Ferrand's incarceration had left her in an unusual situation. In spite of her success in ejecting the pro-French council installed by Philip Augustus and her increasing assertiveness as countess, she remained vulnerable, a target of potential revolt. The scholarly consensus suggests that most Flemish nobles were aware that Bertrand was not, in fact, Baldwin IX, which raises an interesting question about their motives. While the absence of reliable sources makes it difficult to ascertain the reason for their discontent, it is possible that some of the nobles who supported the impostor would have preferred a male to rule in her stead. It is equally possible that the impostor provided them with justification for a rebellion predicated upon general resentment of being forced to submit to any central authority, and Jeanne's sex was not a factor. However, the unusual nature of the rebellion, the ludicrousness of Bertrand's claims, and willingness of the leading nobles of Flanders and Hainaut to play along with the charade illustrates a general recognition of Jeanne's vulnerability as countess and, as a result, the likelihood that such a rebellion could succeed.

One is forced to wonder whether or not the rebellion would have occurred if Ferrand had been acting alongside Jeanne as count of Flanders. However, he continued to languish in prison in spite of his wife's efforts to secure his release. While a steady stream of nobles had been returning to Flanders and Hainaut since Bouvines, culminating with Rasse of Gavre in 1217, Ferrand remained in captivity.[41] Jeanne had been lobbying for his release since 1214, to no avail. By 1219, it had become clear that Philip Augustus had no intention of honoring the terms of the treaty of Paris and releasing the count. Jeanne had been soliciting donations from various individuals, towns, and religious communities in order to raise the ransom required to free her husband. In addition to these donations, she borrowed vast sums of money from local lenders, as evidenced by a charter issued in 1221, which included a list of loans secured by the countess from a variety of individuals.[42] Jeanne's appeal to Honorius III had even elicited papal intervention on her behalf; the pope had promised the king that he would excommunicate Ferrand if, after his release, he failed to observe the terms of the treaty.[43] Despite these efforts, Philip Augustus remained intransigent, refusing to negotiate Ferrand's release right up to his own death in July 1223. Even in light of Philip's anger in the immediate aftermath of Bouvines, it is difficult to explain why the king continued to refuse to liberate the count, particularly after the rest of the Flemish captives had been ransomed and returned to Flanders. Jeanne's success in raising the funds demanded by the king proves that a considerable ransom was within her grasp. Clearly the king stood to profit handsomely from Ferrand's liberation. However, he remained obstinate, refusing to grant Jeanne's request.[44]

Philip's son and successor, Louis VIII, initially adopted his father's stance toward the liberation of the count. Although Louis willingly began the necessary negotiations in 1225, his death in November 1226 halted the process, which was not resumed until after the coronation of Louis IX in November 1226.[45] Negotiations between Jeanne, the king, and Blanche of Castile as regent, eventually culminated in the treaty of Melun, signed in April 1226. Louis and Blanche demanded new concessions regarding Flemish autonomy and extorted an enormous ransom of 50,000 *livres parisis*.[46] Jeanne spent most of December gathering signatures from the towns and nobles of Flanders to guarantee the terms of the treaty.[47] After raising the required sum, Jeanne traveled to Paris, where she and Ferrand pledged homage to Louis in December 1226. Unlike the previous occasion on which the couple appeared before the king of France in 1214, Jeanne's name was included in this charter, which was issued jointly by "*Ego Fernandus, Flandrie et Hanonie comes, et ego Johanna uxor mea, Flandrie comitissa. . .*"[48] [I Ferrand, count of Flanders and Hainaut, and I Jeanne, his wife, countess of Flanders. . .]. Following these formalities, Ferrand was officially released from the king's custody. His liberation on January 6, 1227, ended a confinement that had lasted for twelve years, five months, and nine days. It was precisely Jeanne's sex, and societal reservations about the ability of women to rule, that drove French policy and prompted the king to maintain her in a position of real power. Clearly, Jeanne was not viewed by her contemporaries as a man, but rather remained a woman occupying a position typically associated with men. While status enabled her to access authority, gender continued to restrict her actions.

A number of scholars view the episode of the false Baldwin as the catalyst for Ferrand's release from prison, tangible proof that a woman could not effectively rule without a man. The reversal of policy resulting in the count's liberation has been interpreted as the French reluctantly accepting that the count's return was the only way to provide stability in the region.[49] However, consideration of the terms of Melun, along with an understanding of French policy more broadly speaking, suggests that the episode of the false Baldwin was not the primary consideration prompting Ferrand's release. In addition to requiring that Jeanne pay all of the expenses he incurred in the process of quelling the rebellion, which were considerable, the king demanded that she raze several key fortresses in Flanders. Such demands were not only unrelated to the challenge posed by the false Baldwin, but would have made her position even more precarious, and the county even more vulnerable to external threats. When viewed in this manner, the episode of the false Baldwin provided the king of France with yet another opportunity to weaken Flanders to French advantage. Releasing Ferrand hardly seems consistent with French policy since it could only serve to limit such opportunities in the future.

In addition to specifying the enormous ransom required by the king, and demanding that the countess secure the guarantee of the nobles and leading burghers of Flanders and Hainaut, the treaty of Melun also required that Jeanne and Ferrand restate their wedding vows. Apparently, rumors circulating in France suggested a possible marriage between Jeanne and Pierre Mauclerc, the duke of Brittany.[50] Faced with the possible alliance of Flanders and Brittany, Louis was forced to free the count, perhaps hoping that Ferrand's extended incarceration would be sufficient to guarantee future obedience and compliance. According to Jean Richard, the news circulating about Jeanne's marriage to Pierre were more than rumors. Richard argues that Jeanne had secured an annulment from the pope, and it was only the intervention of the papal legate Romanus Frangipani that prevented the marriage from occurring. At the request of Louis, Frangipani was able to secure the revocation of the annulment and a dispensation confirming the legitimacy of Jeanne's marriage to Ferrand.[51] It was the possibility of marriage to an even stronger opponent of France, rather than the episode of the false Baldwin, that forced the king's hand and secured the liberation of the count.

Examined together, these factors suggest that French determination to undermine Flemish autonomy was, in fact, served by the episode of the false Baldwin. In the process of the revolt, French authority was increased at the expense of the countess and Flanders, consistent with the policy pursued by Philip Augustus. As discussed earlier, the circumstances surrounding the episode, including the complete lack of proof offered by the imposter and the tenuous nature of his claims, reveal a level of dissatisfaction with the countess that may have been predicated upon resistance to female rule. Clearly such a challenge would have proved less threatening to a male ruler, who would have been able to face the imposter with an army, rather than forced to flee in fear and humiliation. It was precisely the vulnerability of the countess and the opposition to her rule that fostered a climate in which such a revolt was possible, ultimately serving French interests at the expense of Flanders. It was precisely Jeanne's sex, and societal reservations about the ability of women to rule, that drove French policy and prompted the king to maintain her in a position of real power. Clearly, Jeanne was not viewed by her contemporaries as a man but rather remained a woman occupying a position typically associated with men. While status enabled her to access authority, gender continued to restrict her actions.

Other examples suggest that French reluctance to liberate the count may have been an integral component of their policy to consolidate control of their most powerful, and therefore most threatening, vassals. While the circumstances that resulted in Jeanne's ability to wield power independently of a husband from 1214 to Ferrand's release from prison in 1226 are unusual, a number of women can be seen in France during the thirteenth century ruling without a consort in a more conventional fashion. In return for his support of her regency for her unborn son, Philip required Blanche of Navarre to submit any future marriage plans for royal approval. Similar promises were elicited from Alix de Vergy in 1218, the widow of the duke of Burgundy and regent for their son during his minority.[52] Apparently, Philip was content to let these women remain unmarried, concerned only that, if a marriage were to occur, he would retain the right to approve it. It seems quite possible that the revolt of two of his vassals who had come to power as a result of marriage to heiresses (Ferrand and Renaud of Dammartin) led Philip to seriously consider the advantages of female rulers.

Tracing the situation as it occurred in Flanders may perhaps shed light on the rationale that informed such a policy. After the debacle of Jeanne's marriage to Ferrand, Philip seems to have recognized the potential danger that accompanied the marriage of an heiress and the corresponding transfer of power to a husband. He also seems to have been aware of the potential advantages derived from independent female rulers, as evidenced by his determination to keep Ferrand in prison. Ferrand's extended absence left Jeanne bereft of a male relative to exercise authority in her name, thus forcing her, when challenged, to seek the aid of the king, a situation that could only benefit France.[53] French reluctance to provide the countess with a male representative can be seen again in 1235. After Ferrand's death in 1233, Jeanne began to explore her options for a second marriage, entering negotiations with Simon de Montfort. Fearing a union between the countess and this extremely powerful noble, the king of France was forced to act. Jeanne was summoned to Peronne in April 1237, where she pledged homage to "mon signor la roi de France Loois, ki est mi sires liges devant toz" ["My seigneur the king of France Louis, who is my liege sire before all"]. In the charter documenting her pledge, Jeanne described herself as the king's "feme lige" ["liege woman"]. In second charter issued by the countess on the same occasion, Jeanne promised to break off negotiations with de Montfort immediately.[54] In return for the countess's concessions, the king arranged for a second marriage to Thomas of Savoy, the queen's uncle and a considerably more dependable ally as count of Flanders than Simon de Montfort. Although reluctant, the king of France was forced to acquiesce in response to Jeanne's desire for a second marriage. Rather than allowing a potential rival to marry the countess, possibly foiling royal attempts to consolidate control over Flanders, the king clearly preferred to choose a husband whose interests were aligned with those of France.

Following Jeanne's death in 1244, Marguerite immediately assumed authority as countess, her right to inherit in the absence of heirs from Jeanne's marriages unchallenged. Rather than risking the possibility of introducing an uncertain element into Flemish affairs in the guise of a third husband, or witnessing as power passed to one of Marguerite's sons, who could return to the anti-French policies of his predecessors and renew hostilities against France, the king allowed Marguerite to wield power in her domains from 1244 to 1280. His decision is consistent with French policy generally regarding the consolidation of royal authority over vassals. Female rulers, perceived by their contemporaries as more vulnerable than men, were less capable of resisting French demands, and more conducive to furthering French interests. As a result of French policy, Marguerite provides yet another example of an heiress who failed to conform to societal expectations concerning the appropriate relationship between women and power.

Marguerite was a widow throughout her rule as countess, choosing to remain unmarried after the death of her second husband, William of Dampierre, in 1232. Although her two marriages had produced a combined total of eight children, of whom four were males who survived to adulthood, Marguerite did not merely act as a regent, controlling the counties until her eldest son was sufficiently mature to take the reigns of government. Rather, she acted autonomously as countess of her domains, conferring the title of count on her eldest son at the appropriate moment and sharing some power but remaining firmly in control of political affairs until her abdication as countess of Flanders at the age of seventy-six in 1278. She retained direct control of the county of Hainaut until her death in 1280.[55] Rather than serving as a vehicle, transmitting authority and power to a husband who acted in her stead, or ruling the counties of Flanders and Hainaut until her male sons came of age, Marguerite ruled autonomously from 1244 to 1280. Such differences in the actual experiences of Jeanne and Marguerite illustrate the various factors that would have influenced the actual relationship between women and power, most notably marital status, age, and personality.

Although Marguerite was more effective than her sister in asserting her power from the beginning of her rule and her decision to remain a widow meant that she never shared power with a husband, she did face challenges specific to female rulers. Such challenges were not posed immediately upon her succession, but they emerged a decade after she succeeded her sister, the product of extended disputes amongst her sons and potential heirs to Flanders and Hainaut. The process of determining Marguerite's heir was complicated by the contention surrounding her marriage to Bouchard of Avesnes, discussed earlier. The question of succession ultimately centered on the validity of Marguerite's first marriage and the subsequent legitimacy of her children through that marriage.[56] In January, 1234, ten years prior to the death of Jeanne, Marguerite, Bouchard, and her seven children had amicably agreed to divide her inheritance equally among all of her offspring.[57] Although Pope Gregory IX declared the Avesnes children legitimate in 1237, his declaration did not affect the inheritance settlement.[58] However, once Marguerite became countess in 1244, the prospective inheritance increased considerably, precipitating a period of open hostility between the children of her two marriages. Marguerite's plans for the succession were challenged by her Avesnes children, who appealed to Louis IX before he could accept the homage of her eldest son from her second marriage, William of Dampierre, for the county of Flanders.[59] Louis IX agreed to arbitrate the dispute, and the outcome of his deliberations was announced on July 1246. The king divided Marguerite's possessions between the sons of her two marriages, confirming William of Dampierre's right to inherit the county of Flanders but designating Jean of Avesnes as the heir to the county of Hainaut.[60] In October 1246, William of Dampierre payed homage to crown Flanders, the portion of his domains held in fief of the king of France.

Despite his pledge to abide by the king's arbitration, Jean of Avesnes protested the verdict on the grounds that Louis, as king of France, lacked the jurisdiction necessary to designate an heir for the county of Hainaut, held in fief of the bishop of Liége and ultimately of the Holy Roman emperor. Jean appealed to William II of Holland, already an enemy of the countess of Flanders, securing an alliance through marriage to William's daughter Alix. With the aid of his brother Baldwin, Jean seized the castle of Ruplemonde, located along the northern border of Flanders near Antwerp, signaling the beginning of overt hostilities between the two factions. The revolt of the Avesnes was significantly bolstered by the election of Jean's new father-in-law, William II, as Holy Roman emperor in October 1247. Marguerite and her Dampierre sons immediately recognized the seriousness of the situation posed by Jean's alliance with the Holy Roman emperor, and they responded to the challenge with political savvy rather than military might. In August 1247, Marguerite arranged the marriage of her eldest son William to Beatrice, the daughter of the duke of

Brabant, thus gaining a powerful new ally. The following year, William took the cross, embarking for the Holy Land on August 25.[61] During the year of William's absence, the county of Flanders was granted papal protection. Any military attack would immediately elicit divine punishment in the form of the excommunication of the guilty party. As long as William was on crusade, Flanders was protected from military harm, and the hostilities between Marguerite and her Avesnes children ceased.

Although successful in avoiding hostilities, such maneuvers were only a temporary solution. In 1249, the matter of succession was again appealed to papal jurisdiction. Innocent IV agreed to a second inquest and demanded that all relevant witnesses assemble at the Cathedral of Soissons on November 5, 1249. After hearing testimony from a variety of individuals concerning the marriage ceremony of Bouchard and Marguerite and details of their ensuing relationship, the arbiters of the dispute, the bishop of Châlons and the abbot of Liesses, pronounced Marguerite's first marriage valid and the children born from it legitimate. However, despite the pronouncement of the bishops and the later confirmation by Innocent IV, the legitimacy ruling was valid only in an ecclesiastical court. In order to alter the terms of succession, the Avesnes would need to secure recognition of their legitimacy in a feudal court as well. At this juncture, the Avesnes seemed satisfied with their anticipated inheritance of Hainaut and papal confirmation of their legitimacy. The countess had actually favored the inquest and seemed fairly amenable to the outcome and the rift between Marguerite and her Avesnes children was temporarily mended. However, the situation was altered again in 1251 when William of Dampierre was killed at a tournament in Trazegnies. The prospect of the imminent reordering of the succession prompted the Avesnes to reiterate their initial claims to the county of Flanders and Hainaut, forcing Marguerite to contest the verdict pronounced by Innocent IV in 1249. While Jean of Avesnes argued that his legitimate status nullified any previous barriers to his succession, Marguerite countered with claims that the inquest of 1249 was biased by the participation of the bishop of Châlons, a noted Avesnes supporter, and occurred during the absence of William of Dampierre, who was on crusade.[62]

In February 1252, Guy, Marguerite's second eldest Dampierre son, performed homage for the county of Flanders to Blanche of Castile, Louis IX's representative during his absence on crusade. William II of Holland responded by confiscating Marguerite's possessions in imperial Flanders, which he then granted to Jean of Avesnes.[63] The following April, Pope Innocent confirmed the ruling of 1249, reiterating the validity of Marguerite's first marriage and the legitimacy of her Avesnes children. Both factions began mobilizing their armies, and open hostilities between the two seemed imminent. However,

Innocent successfully placed a temporary halt to events by agreeing to dismiss the results of 1249 and by arranging another inquest that would guarantee neutral arbiters and ensure equal representation for all parties.

In an attempt to prevent the further escalation of military hostilities, Henry, the duke of Brabant offered to serve as a mediator for the dispute.[64] Even though both sides publicly accepted the duke's offer, and agreed to meet at Antwerp, Marguerite deliberately violated the truce, orchestrating a surprise attack on her enemies by attempting to land troops at the isle of Walcheren. The Dampierres apparently viewed the peace as an ideal opportunity to surprise their enemies, quell the revolt, and permanently quash the ambitions of the Avesnes. However, Marguerite's strategic maneuver failed miserably, resulting in the resounding defeat of her army at the battle of Westkappelle on July 4, 1253. The Avesnes had been alerted of Marguerite's intentions, appearing on the scene while her troops were disembarking from their ships. The combination of the marshy land and the receding tide effectively trapped the soldiers in the shallow water, leaving them at the mercy of their enemies. The battle resulted in massive causalities, and numerous nobles of Flanders and Hainaut were taken captive by the army of the Avesnes.[65] Guy and Jean of Dampierre were among the captives.

The devastation of her army and the loss of its commanders, Guy and Jean, left Marguerite with few options. In order to assert control in Flanders and secure the freedom of her sons, Marguerite enlisted the support of Charles of Anjou, the younger, opportunistic brother of Louis IX. In a treaty signed in October 31, 1253, Marguerite promised Charles the county of Hainaut in return for the decisive defeat of the Avesnes and the liberation of her Dampierre sons. However, fate intervened before Marguerite actually relinquished control of Hainaut. The sudden death of William of Holland in January 1256 undermined the strength of the Avesnes, and after his return from the Crusades, Louis IX immediately acted. By September 1256, the king had restored order, orchestrating the peace of Peronne, which confirmed his earlier arbitration of 1246, assigning Flanders to the Dampierres and Hainaut to the Avesnes.[66] The peace also stipulated that the two Dampierres be released from prison, and arranged for appropriate monetary compensation for Charles of Anjou. Guy and Jean of Dampierre were released on October 15, 1256. Peace was permanently restored in December of the following year after the death of Jean of Avesnes.[67]

This protracted battle between Marguerite and her sons reveals the one area in which the countess was most vulnerable. Clearly, her adult male children provided her with a means to militarily defend her domains. Unlike her sister, who completely lacked a male representative after the incarceration of Ferrand, Marguerite could rely on her Dampierre sons if necessary to serve in the one capacity denied to her, leading an army. Perhaps the presence of adult male children explains the difference in the sisters' attitudes toward marriage. While Jeanne actively sought the return of her absent husband, and orchestrated her own second marriage after his death, Marguerite demonstrated no inclination to remarry after becoming countess. However, in the absence of her sons after the debacle at Westkappelle, Marguerite was as impotent as her sister, and she was forced to enlist the aid of her cousin, Charles of Anjou. It seems unlikely that anything but the most dire of circumstances would prompt Marguerite to relinquish the entire county of Hainaut. Fortunately for Marguerite, Louis IX was less ambitious than his brother. While he secured what compensation he deemed appropriate for his brother's services, he annulled the agreement regarding the county, restoring it to Marguerite, who continued to rule as countess until her death in 1280, when it passed to her grandson, Jean II of Avesnes.[68]

As these examples demonstrate, both Jeanne and Marguerite were faced with a difficult predicament, stemming undoubtedly from medieval gender norms regarding the ability of women to exert physical force on each of the occasions discussed here. Their inability to personally provide for the defense of their domains when necessary seems to be the direct result of their inability to command an army. According to Georges Duby, it was precisely the ability to wield a sword that differentiated between men and women when it came to questions about power.[69] Duby suggests that the restrictions which prohibited women from wielding a sword translated into their inability to wield political power. While the discussion here demonstrates the inaccuracy of this equation overall, Duby is correct in positing certain limitations to a woman's ability to rule. While participation in military conflict was hardly the only limitation encountered by women, in the case of the countesses, it proved to be particularly costly.[70] It certainly demonstrates one way that perceptions of gender and behavior deemed appropriate for women and men could directly impact the experience of a female ruler.

As illustrated by the experiences of Jeanne and Marguerite, the benefits the kings of France derived from situations in which women wielded power clearly prompted them on numerous occasions to indirectly, and perhaps subconsciously, promote the autonomous exercise of authority by women. Philip in particular seemed aware of the basic belief in thirteenth-century society that, while accepted as the source of feudal authority, women seldom directly exercised power but rather intended to confer it on men. When faced with the occasional, opportunity to wield power independently of men, their actions were constrained by prevailing views about the limitations of their gender and the supposed incompatibility of the feminine nature and political activity.[71] Hence, women like Jeanne who lacked the male who typically wielded power in her stead would have been in an undoubtedly disadvantageous position. Not only did the resulting precariousness of her position as a woman attempting to rule in a male-dominated world virtually guarantee the king a complacent vassal, but the vulnerability of her situation forced her into a unique position of dependence upon him as feudal lord. If her ability to assert her authority was questioned or her rule challenged, an appeal to the king of France as feudal lord would have presented itself as the logical, and potentially even the only, solution to her predicament. Such recourse would have provided the king with the opportunity to strengthen his hold on the county, reaffirming his position of preeminence and emphasizing the subordinate status of his vassals. The liminal position of these women is illustrated by the experiences of the two countesses. Each time they requested support from the king, they were forced to relinquish more of their independence, further curtailing the autonomy of Flanders and Hainaut. While their inability to act militarily would have been viewed by female rulers like Jeanne and Marguerite as a liability, it may have appeared in a different light to Philip Augustus. Ultimately, such female rulers would be forced at times into moments of dependence, moments that he could then exploit to his own advantage.

The transformation of government initiated by Philip Augustus may have inadvertly benefited female rulers in another respect as well. Philip's attempt to bureaucratize government and create mechanisms for governing in a manner distinct from the feudal system fostered new attitudes about the relationship between individuals and their official function. A much more rigid distinction between one's person and the office one occupied had emerged, replacing the previous belief that authority stemmed from the individual himself. In other words, the count's authority did not derive from his person but rather from the office he inherited and occupied. In addition, it was not possession of the land per se that conveyed authority, but rather it was the office associated with the land and the rights and obligations that the office conferred on the holder. Scholars who have considered the impact of the transformation of French government on women have concluded that it exacerbated their already tenuous position. First marginalized by the adoption of primogeniture and patrilineage, they were further relegated to a position of inconsequence by the centralization of power and bureaucratization of government. Developments such as the revival of instruments of governing that shifted authority away from powerful aristocratic families to salaried officials are discussed in order to assess their contribution to the relegation of women to the private sphere. As with the establishment of primogeniture, the outcome of this shift is often purported to disadvantage women. Scholars argue that their earlier access to authority and power was predicated upon their membership in powerful families. Since public power was no longer invested in noble families, it was no longer accessible to women.[72] The duties, responsibilities, and opportunities to exercise power that accompanied fiefs as offices shifted to salaried officials in a paid bureaucracy, eliminating avenues to power previously available to females and compounding inheritance practices already disadvantageous to women.[73]

Contrary to these views, the countesses of Flanders and Hainaut appeared to have benefited from this transformation in the medieval conception of government.[74] Both Jeanne and Marguerite were aware of the very public nature of their authority, which they deliberately manifested in visible symbols of power. This first tangible expression of this recognition can be seen in Jeanne's decision to commission a new seal in the first few years following Ferrand's imprisonment, most likely created shortly before 1219. Her original seal, used as early as 1212, presented Jeanne in a standing position, with her head slightly bowed, resting one hand on her hip and supporting a falcon with the other. In the second seal, Jeanne is seated on horseback, a presentation typically preferred by males. Her right hand is held over her heart, while her left supports a falcon. Although the first seal is shaped in the form of an oval, with pointed ends, and the second is round, both are identified as "Sigillum Johanne, comitisse Flandriae et Hanoniae." Her decision to commission a new seal can be interpreted as an indication of her own recognition of the shift in her position since Bouvines. It is possible that Jeanne deliberately chose its design, which would be more reflective of her position of power and authority within Flanders and Hainaut.[75]

The centrality of the seal in conferring authority and as a symbol of the power of the countess is revealed in an extended dispute between Jeanne and the chancellor of Saint-Donatien, who initially enjoyed the right to carry the countess's seal. His determination in forcing Jeanne to continue to permit this privilege is a reflection of the importance of the office, and of the function of the seal in establishing authority and imposing one's will.[76] The right to carry Jeanne's seal later passed to Franco de Maldeghem, also prévôte of Bruges and chancellor of Flanders in 1233. The charter documenting this transfer of power includes detailed instructions for the chancellor, who was to receive in Jeanne's stead all the revenues that accompanied the seal, along with a personal stipend of fifteen *solidis*, wine, candles, and the promise of lodging. If forced to absent himself from Jeanne's itinerant court, Franco was directed to leave the seal with master Philippe, most likely the countesses' chamberlain.[77] The presence of such detailed instructions regarding the duties associated with the seal and the privileges that accompanied possession of it reflect the importance of the seal, both as a practical device to convey comital consent and as an important emblem of the countesses' authority, a visible symbol of the power of her office. Such careful attempts to determine rights regarding the comital seal reflect the perception in medieval society that the countess' person was distinct from her office, both physically and conceptually.

In a similar recognition of the distinction between personal authority and public office, Marguerite commissioned a seal immediately after her sister's death to reflect her new status as countess.[78] Two charters issued by Marguerite following the official elevation of her position in 1244 demonstrate the importance of the seal in conferring legitimacy on individual acts. Marguerite paid homage to Louis IX in 1245 at Pontoise, promising fealty and loyalty and adherence to earlier agreements made by her sister as countess. She confirmed the authenticity of this act with her current seal, the legend of which described her as "Lady of Dampierre," her official title before she became countess. In a charter issued on the same day, also at Pontoise, Marguerite stated her intention to confirm the previous charter once her new seal, in which she was described as countess, had been commissioned and completed.[79] In stating her intention to reseal the document after the new seal was completed, Marguerite revealed her recognition of the fact that in giving her consent to the transaction, her authority was not derived from her person but from the office that she occupied as countess.[80] Marguerite's recognition that the legitimacy of her action did not derive solely from her person but when she operated in an official capacity as countess is also illustrated in her right to mint coins. Coins issued in her name as countess of Flanders and Hainaut functioned as physical manifestations of her authority and power. According to Alan Stahl, "The extent to which women were able to get their names on coins is an important index of the extent to which their right to political power was recognized by contemporaries of all classes."[81] These examples suggest that Jeanne and Marguerite harbored an understanding that while authority may lie with the individual person, real power rested in the office they occupied as countesses, and it could be bolstered through such visible symbols of authority.

Literary patronage would also have provided the countesses with an opportunity to receive public recognition, further affirmation of their authority. Jeanne seemed to be particularly active in this realm, as evidenced by the poet Manessier's dedication of his conclusion to Chrétien de Troye's *Perceval* to the countess. Lori Walters suggests that Jeanne's importance as a patron was sufficient to influence the presentation of Blanchefleur, who is portrayed as a "sympathetic and powerful character" ruling her kingdom capably and effectively.[82] The parallels between the countess and the character of

Blanchefleur would have been obvious to the members of Manessier's audience and reflect, if nothing else, the existence of positive attitudes about female rulers. Jeanne was also acknowledged by Wauchier de Denain, who was commissioned by the countess to compose a *Life of Saint Martha* in the first few decades of the thirteenth century, and he dedicated his work to her.[83] These examples suggest that the countesses were as aware as their contemporaries of the distinction often drawn between authority and power, a distinction frequently predicated along gender lines. Their deliberate manipulation of these various components of comital office illustrates an attempt to control the symbols of their office, hence translating their personal authority into actual power and establishing a visible presence in the public realm. Perhaps the most compelling example of the attempt by the countesses to exert their authority in a very public manner occurred in conjunction with the coronation of Louis VIII in 1223. Jeanne insisted that handing the sword to the newly crowned king was a traditional privilege of the counts of Flanders, a visible demonstration of their position in the feudal hierarchy, and as such should fall to her. Unfortunately for the countess, Blanche of Champagne demanded the same right, and in resolving the dispute both women were passed over in favor of the young king's uncle, Philip Hurepel.[84]

Contrary to past scholarship, which has argued that primogeniture and the centralization of feudal authority as they emerged in the twelfth and thirteenth centuries resulted in the increasing marginalization of noble women, the experience of the countesses of Flanders and Hainaut proves that some female rulers were actually propelled by those very forces into positions of power. As discussed previously, the ability of women to inherit authority was uncontested primarily because of the expectation that a male would wield power in their stead, acting as their representative in the public domain. This solution allowed noble families to continue the practice of primogeniture even in the absence of male heirs without having to confront the reality of a powerful woman, a term perhaps viewed as an oxymoron by the majority of people in the thirteenth century. It has been suggested that women who inherited fiefs were essentially powerless pawns, serving only as vehicles necessary to ensure the transmission of the patrimonies from one generation to another. Real authority was to be vested in feudal lords during their minorities and transferred immediately to husbands upon marriage. However, even preliminary examination has indicated that the reality of these women's experience differs dramatically from the ideal posited by scholars in the past.

For the countesses, perceptions based upon a basic understanding of the nature of the female sex did not prevent their ability to inherit, nor did it deny their access to feudal authority. In fact, certain beliefs about gender may have actually propelled them into positions of actual power. Neither countess functioned solely as a figurehead or a placeholder for their male descendents. In the thirteenth century, status took precedence over gender in determining an individual's relationship to authority. However, as this chapter demonstrates, their ability to wield power was, at certain junctures in their lives, constrained by societal perceptions based on gender norms. While status can be considered the primary determinant in their access to power, gender remained an important factor in influencing the extent to which they could wield it. In the case of the countesses, challenges were predicated upon accepted gender norms, and the resolution to their predicaments was provided by men.

While shifts in the way power was construed are evident in this period, and would have clearly impacted men as well as women, the extent to which these shifts resulted in the marginalization of women requires further consideration. This examination of Philip's policies in conjunction with individual women within France suggests that while these procedural changes in administration and the ensuing transformation in government was ultimately detrimental to women, in the short term, while such institutions were emerging and coalescing, the frequency with which women wielded power actually increased. If the experiences of the countesses of Flanders can be viewed as common to Philip's female vassals, it will be possible to explain the relatively high incidence of women rulers in France during the first half of the thirteenth century. Although their rise to power was accidental, circumstances frequently converged to provide these women with the opportunity to wield power, as reflected in the experience of Jeanne and Marguerite. Furthermore, both countesses were very much aware of the opportunities afforded them, as the discussion of their use of religious patronage to consolidate their authority and expand their power in chapters 3 and 4 demonstrates.

CHAPTER 3

SECURING POWER THROUGH
RELIGIOUS PATRONAGE

The sentiments expressed in the charter issued by Jeanne to the Cistercian abbey of Spermalie in 1239, presented in the introduction, illustrate the medieval understanding of the relationship between power as it pertained to rulers and religious patronage. In articulating her belief that the secular power she wielded stemmed from God, Jeanne acknowledged her obligation to use that power on behalf of others. In a sense, she viewed her position as a divine mandate to use the resources at her disposal as countess on behalf of those who sought a religious life.[1] While she would have been prompted primarily by spiritual concerns, religious patronage was a complex act that could have a variety of outcomes, secular as well as sacred. Many of the monastic and religious foundations that dominated the landscape of thirteenth-century Flanders and Hainaut were the direct result of comitial patronage. As such, they would have functioned as visible symbols of the countesses' power as well as their piety.

The argument here is predicated upon the notion that patrons like Jeanne and Marguerite were well aware that the foundation and support of a monastic community could, in addition to furthering one's salvation, achieve a variety of other ends. Although the modern inclination is to categorize actions directed toward religious foundations as personal, people in the Middle Ages would not have shared this sentiment. Such distinctions are anachronistic, and would not have been recognized by members of medieval society, who accepted the coexistence of the secular and the sacred as not only natural but inevitable. These two impulses (pragmatic and pious) were not mutually exclusive in the medieval mind, but were often present simultaneously in donations on behalf of foundations.[2] While all actions on behalf of religious or monastic foundations would have been deemed pious by medieval patrons, some of them were directed specifically at securing salvation, while others were intended for a more secular outcome. Such a diversity of medieval motives, as well as the modern tendency to posit a rigid distinction between the secular and the sacred generally, has presented historians with an interpretative challenge in assessing the meaning of religious patronage as it was understood in the Middle Ages. In their attempt to avoid constructs that demarcate between the pious and pragmatic, some scholars have proffered an alternative model, one that conflates the secular and the sacred. While such a conflation acknowledges that pragmatic and pious motives are often present simultaneously in the patron's mind, they tend to obscure difference.[3] To suggest that a single donation may have been prompted simultaneously by both pious and pragmatic concerns is not to say that these concerns weighed equally in the mind of the patron.

This study suggests that secular and sacred motives should be viewed neither as synonymous nor mutually exclusive. The actions of medieval patrons were most likely prompted by varying degrees of the combination of the two. Examination of the actions of Jeanne and Marguerite on behalf of foundations within their domains demonstrates the various ways that individuals could use patronage to assert their authority, promote their prestige, or impose their power upon subordinates.[4] Since many monastic communities amassed considerable patrimonies, they could serve political as well as spiritual functions, securing contested regions and consolidating comital control of land.[5] In addition, an assessment of the countesses' patronage reveals the myriad of economic benefits a patron could enjoy in return for their material and administrative support of communities. Monasteries in particular were large, complex institutions, ideally positioned to contribute to the agricultural and commercial development of the region in which they were located. In Flanders, where commerce and urbanization were particularly advanced, such abbeys often acted as comital agents in the countryside, stimulating commerce and facilitating the extraction of profits from the industry of the county. Perhaps most notable is their contribution to the reclamation project initiated by the countesses, which contributed to the internal transformation of Flanders by expanding the arable, creating new areas of settlement, and constructing canals, which provided effective methods of irrigation as well as convenient modes of transportation of goods. Furthermore, a discussion of their support of communities which adhered to the ideals of the *vita apostolica* [apostolic life] demonstrates the countesses' understanding of the social function of monastic and religious foundations. Comital support for such orders frequently translated directly into an improvement in the general welfare of the secular community.

While the volume of charters incorporated in this study prevents an exhaustive list of comital involvement in all foundations in Flanders and

Hainaut, the discussion that follows is intended to be representative of larger patterns deduced in their patronage. One will note a direct correlation between the orders mentioned with the most frequency in this chapter and those identified as preferred by the countesses in chapter 4. This correlation is far from accidental. Clearly, the countesses chose to direct support to those foundations deemed the most pious. However, requests for prayers could just as easily accompany donations to communities that offered more practical benefits as well. For the countesses, pious and practical benefits were not viewed as mutually exclusive in their calculations concerning which communities to patronize. Religious patronage provided rulers with an ideal way to kill two birds with one stone, simultaneously securing their political position in the present and their spiritual position in the future.

Closer examination of the pattern of foundation associated with Cistercian abbeys in thirteenth-century Flanders illustrates the diversity of interests that prompted patronage. Marguerite, as Lady of Dampierre, founded the abbey of Flines in 1234.[6] Over the course of her lifetime, Marguerite proved to be an extremely generous patron, arranging for the abbey's transfer to a more favorable location and directing numerous donations, which resulted in the emergence of Flines as one of the largest and wealthiest Cistercian abbeys for women in Europe.[7] In the official act of foundation, Marguerite granted the nuns an endowment that comprised a sizeable amount of land near the town of Orchies, located along the southern periphery of the county. Over the course of the next forty-four years, Marguerite personally orchestrated the creation of a particularly impressive patrimony for this Cistercian abbey. The countess alone was responsible for 22 donations of land, comprising a total of 449 *bonniers* (roughly the equivalent of 112 acres), and including three entire *manses*.

While Marguerite's actions on behalf of the abbey of Flines were undoubtedly motivated by her piety and religious convictions, the extent of her generosity seems surprising in light of sentiments she expressed elsewhere regarding the alienation of land by Flemish nobles. In the mid-thirteenth century, the Flemish nobility was experiencing an economic crisis of dramatic proportions. Although the county of Flanders, perhaps the most urbanized region in western Europe at that time, experienced an intense economic boom in the twelfth and thirteenth centuries, stimulated in part by the emergence of the cloth industry and large-scale textile production, the nobility failed to benefit from such commercial expansion.[8] Aristocratic families were frequently forced to stand idle and watch their traditional prerogatives challenged by the emerging urban middle classes. Increasingly impoverished and sinking further into debt, many of the leading families of Flanders began to alienate land and liquidate property at a rate that alarmed the countess.⁹ As the feudal lord of much of the land being alienated, Marguerite clearly feared that the sale of such land to monasteries, the most frequent consumers, would ultimately jeopardize her ability to exact the dues, services, and rents owed to her. In a charter issued in 1255, Marguerite condemned the current impoverished state of the Flemish nobility, characterizing the economic crisis forcing so many men and women to alienate so much property as a "voracious plague upon the land."¹⁰ In the same year, Marguerite expressed her opposition to the nobility's favorite solution to their financial woes in an ordinance that prohibited the sale of comital fiefs to churches, monasteries, or other non-nobles. Marguerite declared that "no abbey, church, religious house, priest, cleric, non-noble" may "acquire in our land of Flanders fief, rents, lands, inheritances or anything of the like."¹¹

Yet, despite her vehement and vocal opposition to this practice generally, Marguerite's own actions on behalf of certain abbeys resulted in the alienation of significant amounts of land that comprised the feudal domain of the counts of Flanders. She and her sister repeatedly approved the sale of land held in fief of the count by Flemish nobles to a number of Cistercian abbeys in Flanders. This apparent contradiction in comital policy is, at first glance, quite perplexing. However, examination of the wider patterns of comital patronage in this area and a consideration of the history of the region reveals how Cistercian abbeys were employed by the countesses to serve a very secular, political purpose.

As discussed at length in chapters 1 and 2, the reversal of Flemish fortunes in the first two decades of the thirteenth century had serious implications on Franco-Flemish relations, weakening the countesses' position vis-à-vis their stronger neighbors. The repeated attempts of both France and Flanders to establish control of the lands that comprised the Artois in the twelfth century, as outlined in chapter 2, attest to the importance of this territory. Historians have frequently identified the loss of Artois in 1190 as a pivotal moment in Flemish history, the first in a series of setbacks experienced by the counts of Flanders, which culminated in their absolute subordination to French authority. According to Gabrielle Spiegel, the Artois "represented that borderland of uncertainty about whether the king of France would succeed in subduing a powerful and independent barony and make it obedient to his will."¹² While the loss of the Vermandois in the late twelfth century foiled an ambitious attempt to establish a Flemish frontier a mere twenty-five miles from Paris, the loss of the Artois had significantly greater implications, forcing the counts of Flanders into a defensive position and facilitating further French incursions into Flemish territory. Baldwin IX had been successful in securing strategic towns in key territories in this region, the buffer zone between France and Flanders. Yet, much of what he gained had been returned to the French by the treaties of Peronne and Aire, signed in 1206 and 1214.

Remaining Flemish control of this territory was further eroded following the battle of Bouvines in 1214, when Jeanne was forced to make significant concessions to king Philip to prevent him from confiscating the counties in response to her husband's treason. Jeanne, as countess, was forced to submit to the terms imposed by Philip in the treaty of Paris, which firmly established French control of the Artois and demanded the destruction of all Flemish fortresses along the newly established southern border, including those of Ypres, Cassel, and Audenarde.[13] Marguerite inherited this legacy of an increasingly impoverished nobility and the menacing specter of France, which threatened to absorb the county directly into the royal domain when she became countess in 1244, finding herself in a rather disadvantageous position regarding the southern periphery of her domains.

While the countesses were unable to militarily combat French attempts to assert control of Flanders, an examination of their religious patronage suggests that they were able to employ other, less overt, means to challenge French ambitions in this regard. The treaty of Paris explicitly forbade the construction of any armed fortresses along the Franco-Flemish frontier. However, it did not prevent them from securing control of that region by constructing fortresses of a different nature in the form of Cistercian monasteries. Although certainly less menacing than a military fortress, these religious communities would have provided a means of consolidating control of much of the land along their southern frontier without provoking the ire, or retribution, of the French king. By initiating and supporting the foundation of Cistercian abbeys located nearly parallel to the frontier with France, Jeanne and Marguerite were able to amass a line of defense that would stymie future French attempts to encroach on Flemish territory.

Their attempt to establish a permanent border and provide some type of fortification for this area is illustrated by the extent of comital participation in the foundation of these abbeys and the location of the patrimonies they subsequently accumulated, often the product of the countesses' efforts. The abbey of Flines was not the only monastic community established along the southern periphery of Flanders, but rather the last in a series of foundations which began around 1214. By the middle of the thirteenth century, nine Cistercian abbeys for women had been founded in this particular region, including Épinlieu (1216), Woestine (1217), Notre-Dame-des-Près (1218), Vivier (1219), Bonham (1223), Marquette (1224), Verger (1227), Beaupré-sur-la-lys (1233), and Flines (1234).[14] The high concentration of abbeys in this region of the county is quite unusual, particularly in light of the fact that the remaining nineteen Cistercian abbeys for women in Flanders were almost exclusively located in the northern half of the county, most notably in the areas of dense population around the cities of Ghent and Bruges. This difference suggests that the location of these abbeys was not the result of random chance, but rather the product of deliberate comital policy. Of the nine Cistercian abbeys for women located in this southern region, the countesses of Flanders were founders of three and active patrons of at least two others.

Jeanne was instrumental in the foundation of the abbeys of Épinlieu (1216), providing the land on which it was established along with an additional seven donations. The abbey of Notre-Dame-des-Près (1218), located near the city of Douai, was the recipient of seven donations from the countesses, and its patrimony benefited from twenty-nine transfers of land, all approved by either Jeanne or Marguerite in their capacity as feudal lord. Jeanne and Marguerite together made thirty-seven donations to the abbey of Marquette (1224), and confirmed fifty-one donations and sales. The abbey of Beaupré (1233), located along the river Lys, received two donations from the countesses, who also confirmed three transactions involving feudal land.

Their intentions are further revealed in tracing the location of the land involved in these donations, as illustrated by a discussion of the patrimony amassed by Flines. Nearly all of the land involved in transactions to this abbey was located just south of the city of Lille, along the border that separated the kingdom of France from the county of Flanders. The majority of these donations involved land situated between Orchies and Flines, primarily in the parishes of Raches, Pevele, Auchy, and Namaing, all parallel to the border that divided Flanders from the kingdom of France. After becoming countess in 1244, Marguerite approved at least fifteen additional transfers of land to the abbey, made by a variety of Flemish nobles. Included among the transactions approved by Marguerite was the sale of an entire fief near Hellignies, the sale of a *manse* near Flines, and the donation of a *manse* located at Anich, all contributing considerably to the size of the abbey's patrimony.[15] Since all of the land involved in these sales and donations was ultimately held in fief of the count of Flanders, Marguerite's approval was required to confirm the legitimacy of these transactions. Jeanne shared her sister's commitment to the abbey, personally directing eighteen donations of land to the abbey in addition to the twenty-two made by Marguerite. The success of their efforts is reflected in a charter issued by Philippe, abbot of Clairvaux, in 1270, who deemed the patrimony of the abbey sufficient for the support of 100 nuns and up to 18 lay brothers and sisters.[16] All of these transactions were duly recorded by scribes in the employment of the nuns of Flines, who, through meticulous and deliberate documentation, effectively transformed these pious gifts and spiritual gestures into binding, legal property transfers.

The significant number of new communities in this region, combined with the countesses' extensive contribution to their foundation and support, provides compelling evidence that these abbeys were deliberately placed in an attempt to secure the Flemish border. Although the counts of Flanders would have relinquished possession of the land transferred to the patrimonies of these abbeys, their involvement as donors and protectors would have guaranteed their ability to maintain control of the land in the guise of preferred patrons. The presence of family members in these abbeys, as was the case with Flines, where Marguerite's daughter and granddaughter served as abbesses, would have further consolidated comital control of these communities and the land that comprised their patrimonies. The location of these abbeys and the extent of the support they received from the countesses reveal their intended role in a broad comital strategy to secure this contested region. Cistercian abbeys would serve as alternatives to traditional fortifications, compensating for the loss of the Artois and Vermandois and circumventing the royal restrictions placed on the countesses after the battle of Bouvines in 1214.

Jeanne and Marguerite's attempts to use religious patronage as a vehicle to further their political ambitions were certainly not without precedent. Patrick Geary discusses a similar use of monasteries to prevent land from falling into the hands of his enemies by Hugo of Arles. Geary suggests that by donating contested land to monastic foundations, Hugo established a "monastic trust fund," neutralizing the land in question.[17] The tendency of Cistercian foundations to play a role in establishing control of contested territory is addressed specifically by Janet Burton in regards to communities in Yorkshire. Since Cistercian abbeys were often located in peripheral areas as a result of the Order's emphasis on isolation, they seemed ideally suited to occupy contested regions.[18] The correlation between disputed territory and foundation activity suggests the presence of a deliberate comital policy designed to consolidate control of land along the Franco-Flemish frontier without openly provoking the hostility of France. By the thirteenth century, the balance of power had decisively shifted in favor of the French king, and open military provocation was never an option for either countess. However, a policy designed to cloak political strategy behind a mantle of religious piety would have allowed them to achieve their ambitions while escaping the wrath of French retribution, the perfect marriage of practical and pious concerns.

Religious patronage also offered the countesses repeated and public opportunities to demonstrate their authority over the nobles of their domains, regulating the feudal hierarchy and strengthening the office of count. The countesses appeared in charters issued to monastic and religious foundations on dozens of occasions, confirming donations made by a third party to the community in question. Historians agree that the presence of one's name in any charter can be interpreted as an indication of that individual's right over the land involved.[19] The countesses are present in a variety of charters in this capacity, confirming donations of land or rents made by others in a very public and visible demonstration of their authority. In 1241, Jeanne, along with her second husband, Thomas of Savoy, listed and confirmed the possessions and privileges of the Augustinian abbey of Saint-Nicholas in Furnes.[20] In June 1246, Marguerite confirmed a transaction between the Augustinian canons of Saint-Aubert and Pierre de Sohier and his wife Marguerite concerning the sale of land made by the couple to the canons.[21] Five charters were issued by the countesses on behalf of the Augustinian abbey of Zonnebeke, first founded in 1072 as a college of secular canons but reformed and affiliated to the congregation of Arrouaise in 1142.[22] In three of the charters, issued in 1218, 1219, and 1222, the abbey of Zonnebeke arranged exchanges of various tracts of land that was held in fief of Jeanne, who approved each transaction.[23] The abbey of Cysoing, affiliated to the order of Arrouaise in 1132, also provided the countesses numerous opportunities to assert their position as feudal lords. Of the seven charters issued to the abbey by the countesses, two confirmed sales of land.[24] In a charter issued in 1251, Marguerite confirmed the abbey's right to claim possession of land donated and later contested by the daughter of Caeserius de Harteing.[25] Presumably the individuals involved in transactions such as those described above were present when the outcome was determined, suggesting that those named in the charter would have served not only as participants but as public witnesses to these demonstrations of comital authority.

Monastic foundations were often linked to occasions on which the countesses exercised justice in their domains. In April of that year, she issued an order to the bailiffs and échevins of Flanders to aid the canons of Saint-Nicolas in their efforts to collect outstanding debts.[26] In June and July of 1241, Jeanne issued charters pertaining to the military obligations of the dependents of the abbey, granting them freedom from service.[27] In a charter issued to the Cistercian abbey of Oostekloo in 1265, Marguerite granted the nuns possession of ten mesures of arable land located in the district of Bouchout. The land had reverted to her as feudal lord after it was confiscated from Hughes Corcalboenceuf who had been banished for committing murder.[28] In a similar transaction in 1266 the countess granted the nuns of Hemelsdale a house and land just outside the city walls of Ypres so that they could relocate their community. The grant included two *mesures* fifty three *verges* of land that comprised the immediate household and an additional twenty *mesures* of adjacent garden. The land had reverted to Marguerite due to the murder of Michel de Trehout, described as a "bourgeois of Ypres," by his wife Marguerite le Meide. As punishment, Marguerite le Meide forfeited all her possessions to the feudal lord of Ypres (Countess Marguerite), and was executed. Marguerite's decision to use the forfeited land to provide a new location for the nuns of Hemelsdale seems especially appropriate considering the circumstances by which she had acquired it.[29]

While the presence of their name in such charters is in and of itself significant, as an indication of their control over the land or rents exchanged in the transaction, the rhetoric of many of these charters is also revealing. On many occasions, the countesses are explicitly identified as acting in their capacity as feudal lords, and their right as such over the land in question is overtly asserted. For example, in a charter issued by Jeanne confirming the donation of fifty-seven and one-half measures of land to the abbey of Zonnebeke, the land in question is described by the countess as "that which is held of me in fief."[30] In 1220 Jeanne issued stern orders to her bailiff of Ypres to allow the abbess of Nonnenbossche to govern her vassals in the parish of Gheluvelt in peace, and she forbade him to exercise any jurisdiction or claim any rights that had been held by the nuns "in the time of Baldwin of good memory, count of Flanders and Hainaut and after emperor of Constantinople, my father."[31] A charter issued in July 1220, recorded Jeanne's approval of an exchange made between the abbey of Loo and Lippin Beier. The land in question in this charter, located at Galghille, was described as held in fief of Jeanne; thus her consent as feudal lord was required in order for both transactions to be legitimate.[32] Of sixteen total charters issued by the countesses on behalf of the Augustinian abbey of Saint-Martin of Ypres, thirteen record confirmations of donations. Three of these charters, all issued in 1255, involved the sale of a tithe to Saint-Martin's by Johannes de Ghistella and his wife.[33] The remaining six transactions involved the transfer of various tracts of land or tithes to the abbey, all ultimately held in fief of the countesses, hence necessitating their consent.[34]

In an arbitration settled by Marguerite on behalf of the Benedictine abbey of Marchiennes in 1240, she was identified explicitly as "Lady of Dampierre" and the land in question as "held in fief of her." The charter was witnessed by nine individuals, including Arnould of Audenarde, Jeanne's chancellor, and Wago, the bailiff of Hainaut. A later arbitration concerning a fishpond claimed by both the abbey of Marchiennes and the nearby village of Bouvegnies was resolved in favor of the monks, the outcome of the dispute confirmed by Marguerite as "lady of the land."[35] Any doubts about their right to act in such a capacity as countesses would have been dispelled by the constant reiteration of their position over time in front of an accumulation of witnesses. Furthermore, in asserting their rights as feudal lords to confirm transactions, the countesses were repeatedly asserting their authority over their vassals, ultimately regularizing the feudal hierarchy as it existed in the counties of Flanders and Hainaut.

The arbitration of disputes among existing communities also provided repeated opportunities for the countesses to translate their authority into overt power. By petitioning the countesses to intervene, and then agreeing to adhere to the verdict rendered in the dispute, the communities involved were implicitly, and often explicitly, acknowledging their authority. Jeanne or Marguerite appear as arbiters on eleven total occasions. They appear in the charters of the abbey of Cambron alone on six occasions, three involving disputes regarding rights to various mills claimed by the abbey and the remaining three regarding ownership of land.[36] Such arbitrations often involved local lords or town officials, the countesses' key rivals for authority in their domains. Jeanne was called to intervene in a dispute between the Benedictine nuns of Nonnenbossche and the local bailiff of Ypres in 1220, mentioned earlier.[37] In July, 1236, Jeanne ended a dispute between the chapter of Sainte-Walburga of Furnes and the people of nearby Nieuport regarding rights to a tithe on fish. According to the charter, the dispute had turned violent, resulting in the death of two priests.[38] Marguerite, as countess, was also called to intervene in disputes involving foundations. In 1260, she confirmed the terms of a settlement between Gilles, the abbot of the Benedictine abbey of Marchiennes and the town of Bouvegnies regarding a fishery.[39] At the request of the monks of Anchin, Marguerite appointed a "sergent" to guard the gate of the abbey, involved in an ongoing dispute with Anselme de Rikemont, a local noble who contested their right to an allod donated in 1265.[40] Submission of such disputes to the countesses' jurisdiction allowed them to firmly establish their authority as feudal lords by forcing public recognition of their position.

Their authority as countesses was further bolstered by their ability to successfully intervene on behalf of new communities that encountered resistance from existing foundations. The countesses can be seen acting in this capacity on numerous occasions, either arbitrating disputes, securing concessions, or forcing existing communities to consent to the presence of new ones, often resented as potential rivals for alms or donations. Both Jeanne and Marguerite were involved in affairs in the town of Ypres on numerous occasions, most often securing consent from the powerful canons of Saint-Martin to the presence of new foundations. In June 1240, the canons, at the request of Jeanne, agreed to grant the beguines of that town land located adjacent to their abbey, in return for an annual rent of sixty *solidorum alborum*.[41] The Cistercian abbey of Hemelsdale also benefited from the support of Marguerite, who arranged for its transfer in 1270 into the town walls of Ypres. Marguerite granted the chapter of Saint-Martin a rent of ten *livres* in order to compensate the canons for any loss of revenue incurred as a result of the relocation of the nuns.[42]

The countesses were particularly active in this capacity on behalf of Dominican foundations in their domains, which often encountered the resistance, and on occasion, the hostility, of local clergy or canonical foundations. In her will, Jeanne donated 100 *solidi* to the local clergy of Bergues to compensate them for any loss of revenue incurred because of the presence of a Dominican convent, most likely established four years earlier in 1240 by her sister Marguerite.[43] In a donation made after Jeanne's death in 1244, but prior to the convent's official acceptance by the General Chapter on Pentecost, 1245, Marguerite orchestrated an exchange with city officials in order to secure property located outside of the city walls.[44] In a similar fashion, Jeanne was instrumental in the secular community's acceptance of the Dominican convent in Valenciennes. In May 1233, the friars of Valenciennes were granted temporary residence in a house owned by Jacques de Champagne, as well as permission to erect a chapel on adjacent land, purchased by Jeanne on their behalf.[45] Jeanne arranged for several prominent members of the clergy to arbitrate a dispute that resulted from the resistance of secular clergy to Dominican intrusion into the community. The arbiters ordered the town of Valenciennes to cede four *bonniers* of public pasture to the chapter of Saint-Saulve, who in turn paid an annual rent of twenty *solidi* to the curé of Saint-Marie de la Chausée.[46] In return for these concessions, the Dominicans were granted permission to build a chapel and a cemetery, to receive oblations, and to fulfill the pastoral mandate of their Order, which included the celebration of mass, preaching, administering the sacraments, and burying the dead.[47] Marguerite provided the Dominicans of Ypres the political authority necessary to overcome the opposition of the local secular clergy. In September 1268, Marguerite granted the friars a meadow and portions of the garden located behind the chateau of Zaalhof, which was formerly a comital residence.[48] The countess most likely chose this particular site in order to overcome the opposition of the canons of Saint-Martin, who had attempted to prevent mendicant incursion into the two parishes they controlled.[49] Marguerite issued two charters in 1275 concerning disputes between the Dominicans of Lille and the canons of Saint-Pierre. In the first instance, Marguerite affirmed an exchange of land, and in the second, less than a month later, she intervened in order to regulate relations between these two foundations, compensating the canons for goods and rights forfeited to the Dominicans.[50] Marguerite was particularly active on behalf of the Dominican nuns of the Abbiette. The community, whose foundation was initiated by Jeanne and completed by Marguerite, encountered some opposition from the chapter of Saint-Pierre of Lille. Marguerite arbitrated the dispute which ensued in 1277 and arranged for a level of compensation acceptable to the canons.[51]

In 1250, Marguerite was granted permission by the General Chapter to establish an abbey following the customs of Val-des-Écoliers in the village of Marly, near the city of Valenciennes. Marguerite developed an admiration for the canons of this Order as a result of several visits to their priory in Paris, which was located near the residence of the counts of Flanders. Seven canons were sent from the priory of Sainte-Catherine in Paris. Marguerite intended to provide the canons with a donation of a rather large tract of land, which she had purchased on their behalf.[52] However, opposition from local religious communities, including the Augustinian canons of Saint-Jean Baptiste, prompted Marguerite to transfer the community to the city of Mons. Once again, Marguerite purchased land on their behalf, and confirmed an additional donation of several buildings located at Cantimpré, near Mons.[53] In addition to providing the initial endowment, Marguerite also secured the approbation of Nicholas, the bishop of Cambrai, in August 1252.[54] A more complicated arrangement was required to elicit the consent of the canonesses of Saint-Waudru, who possessed a charter issued by Baldwin IV in the twelfth century that prohibited the foundation of any other religious community in Mons. In a charter issued in November 1252, Marguerite announced the approval of the canonesses, which she secured in return for the promise of an annual payment of sixteen *solidi* to be made by her on the canons' behalf.[55]

In addition to overcoming the opposition of existing foundations, the countesses also championed proposed foundations who desired admission into various monastic orders, most frequently the Cistercian. In petitioning the General Chapter on behalf of individual foundations, and successfully securing their official incorporation, the countesses demonstrated their prestige and importance. In 1236, Jeanne directly requested the Order's acceptance of the abbey of Soleilmont, originally founded as a Benedictine community in 1088.[56] In response to Jeanne's request, the General Chapter ordered the necessary inquest that resulted in the official incorporation of Soleilmont in 1237. The first contingent of nuns was sent from the abbey of Flines.[57] In 1241, the General Chapter, in response to Jeanne's petition on behalf of the abbey of Hemelsdale and upon the recommendation of the abbots of the abbeys of Ter Duinen and Loos, agreed to incorporate the house of nuns into the Order.[58] The countesses' vocal support of new abbeys was particularly crucial in regards to the Cistercian Order, due to their expressed reluctance to admit new foundations during the thirteenth century. It is unlikely that the Order would have been willing to grant their approval if the patron in question was not as generous or as powerful as the countess of Flanders and Hainaut.

In general, medieval patrons were often aware that the extent of their patronage would be perceived as a reflection of their wealth and political power. Few individuals would have been in a position to direct such extensive support to various monastic and religious communities as the countesses of Flanders and Hainaut. In contributing to the foundation and success of so many abbeys and convents, the countesses presented their contemporaries with an overt demonstration of their munificence and importance. Surely the cumulative effect of the actions described above would not have gone unnoticed by Jeanne and Marguerite nor by their contemporaries. As is the case with any type of patronage, monastic and religious communities would serve as a physical manifestation of the generosity and prestige of their founder. The litany of their actions mentioned here, which represent only a small percentage of their overall activity, would have made quite an impression, allowing the countesses to cultivate a reputation of extreme piety among their contemporaries. In addition, they would undoubtedly have been perceived not only as generous in their desire to assist monastic and religious foundations, but also as having the means and the authority nearly unrivalled amongst their peers. Although their intentions can accurately be described as pious, their actions on behalf of monastic and religious foundations would have had profound political repercussions. As the numerous examples presented above demonstrate, they frequently galvanized the resources at their disposal and used the authority conferred upon them by their office as countess on behalf of favored communities.[59] The end result of their actions was not only the transformation of the spiritual landscape of Flanders and Hainaut but also personal and political aggrandizement in a very public manner. In all of these examples, the countesses were exercising power in a way that would have been quite recognizable in thirteenth-century society.

The record of their actions on behalf of monastic and religious communities suggests that the countesses were equally aware of the potential economic advantages derived from religious patronage. Jeanne and Marguerite, like all medieval patrons, were clearly cognizant of the opportunity to employ monastic foundations in various ways to improve their financial situation, ultimately bolstering their own political positions by augmenting the material resources at their disposal. As fairly large complexes with access to considerable agricultural and industrial resources, abbeys were ideally positioned to aid the countesses in the exploitation of the natural wealth of Flanders and Hainaut. Abbeys located in the countryside were especially well placed in terms of assisting in the attempts by the countesses to maximize the profits generated by the thriving commercial activity of Flanders, centered on the production of wool for the burgeoning cloth industry. As a result of the widespread demand for wool, the key resource in the cloth-making industry that emerged in northern Europe during this period, pastoralism became one of the dominant economic practices of medieval Flanders.[60] Pastoralism was not only conducive to the natural topography of the Flemish countryside, but it proved to be extremely profitable for the individual abbeys. Pastoralism was particularly suited to the newly reclaimed land that comprised such large portions of the patrimonies of many new monastic foundations. Much of this land, first drained in the last decades of the twelfth century, retained too much salt for direct agriculture. In addition, wool production required very modest capital investment and resulted in large cash returns, thus maximizing the profits of producers. In addition to the wool needed for the cloth industry, animal husbandry produced a number of other commodities that could be used for the monastery's consumption or sold at local markets and fairs for profit, such as meat, leather, parchment, milk, cheese, and butter.

Since it required little manual labor, pastoralism allowed female foundations to participate as actively as their male counterparts in the expanding economy of the thirteenth century. The charters demonstrate the extent of such participation. In 1233, Jeanne granted the abbey of Marquette permission to pasture their herds on lands held from her without charge. The abbey of Marquette received an annual donation of 453 lambs from Jeanne in May 1236.[61] In another transaction, the nuns of Beaupré received permission from Marguerite in 1248 to pasture twenty cows free of charge on land called "La Gorgue."[62] The abbey of Ravensberg received an annual rent of eleven rams, to be valued at thirty *denari* each, by Jeanne and her husband Ferrand in November 1227, which would have contributed significantly to the abbey's herd.[63] In April 1244, the same month they received papal confirmation of their exemption from tithes on their flocks, Marguerite granted the nuns of Flines rights to pasture their flocks in the parishes of Flines, Raisce, Costices, Auchi, Orchies, and Bouvegnies. The nuns of Flines also owned pasture in the parish of Nomain, as revealed in a charter issued by Marguerite in 1271.[64] Participation in pastoral activities was not limited to Cistercian foundations, as revealed by a charter issued in 1241 by Jeanne to the Benedictine abbey of Oudenbourg, granting the nuns pasture rights in the dunes of Westende. The nuns were granted the right to prohibit all others from pasturing animals there.[65] By practicing animal husbandry, the nuns of Flanders avoided the economic difficulties experienced by many nunneries that have often been attributed to their reliance upon direct cultivation.[66] The profits generated by their participation in the wool trade would have not only proven lucrative for individual monastic foundations but would have stimulated the entire economy of the region, ultimately increasing comital revenue in the form of taxes and tolls exacted by the countesses.

Other economic privileges enjoyed by abbeys included the right to collect tolls on goods that traversed their domains en route to fairs or urban markets. Such rights, while proving lucrative privileges for individual abbeys, aided the countesses in regulating commercial activity and regularizing newly implemented systems of taxation that emerged as the direct result of the transformation of the Flemish economy. In May 1247, Marguerite arbitrated a dispute between the town of Audenarde and the Benedictine abbey of Eename regarding the right to collect a toll on wine being transported to the local market via the river Escaut, which traversed the abbey's domains. Marguerite settled the dispute in the abbey's favor, granting them sole rights to the toll.[67] In January 1256, Marguerite arbitrated a dispute between the nuns of Messines and several local "bateliers." The nuns demanded the right to tax boats using a canal that crossed the abbey's domains, which had recently been repaired at the nun's expense. Marguerite granted the nuns the right to exact a tax of 3 *deniers* per *marc* on all merchandise, not to exceed the sum of 342 *livres*, 14 *sols artois*, the approximate cost of the repairs.[68] In October 1270, Marguerite granted the nuns of Marquette the right to exact a toll on goods passing through the abbey's domains along the river Deule, from the "curtis" at Beaulieu to the bridge at Marquette.[69]

Abbeys were also frequent participants in the range of activities associated with the profit economy of urbanized Flanders in the thirteenth century, contributing to the economic well-being of the region in a variety of ways. Several Benedictine abbeys were integrally involved in the transportation of goods to the various urban centers of Flanders, a lucrative source of income during this period of burgeoning economic development. Charters issued to the abbeys of Messines and Marchiennes explicitly mention the presence of canals used to transport goods to local markets. The abbey of Saint-Bertin, near Lille, secured the right to hold a market at Poperinghe and to construct a canal that would facilitate the transportation of goods in the future.[70] The importance of canals to abbeys in Flanders is evident in an extended dispute between the abbey of Marchiennes and the neighboring Cistercian abbey of Flines. The canals, which traversed land owned by the nuns of Flines as well as that of the monks of Marchiennes, were carefully regulated by both abbeys and were frequently employed in the transport of goods to the markets in the nearby town of Lille.[71] The Cistercian monks of Loos also controlled a canal, as revealed in a charter issued by Marguerite in February 1271, which confirmed a donation made in 1243 by Jeanne.[72]

Direct control of such means of transportation facilitated the participation of abbeys in the profit economy that dominated Flanders, allowing them to transport surplus goods to local markets at minimal expense. The abbey of Mont Blandin benefited from participation in the commerce of wine, a privilege granted by Marguerite in 1258. Marguerite also granted the monks permission to hold a weekly Market at the nearby village of Tamise in 1264.[73] The abbey of Anchin was granted the right to use a road near Baise, controlled by Marguerite, and was exempted from the toll typically exacted from travelers.[74] The exemption suggests that the monks of Anchin routinely transported goods along the road to nearby markets. The Cistercian abbey of Ter Duinen, perhaps one of the wealthiest in the region, controlled sufficient resources to sustain a fleet of ships, as evidenced by a charter issued in 1233 in which Ferrand requested permission from the bailiffs of the coastal towns in England for the monks to build and repair ships in their ports.[75] The Cistercian monks of Ter Duinen were key participants in the wool trade which linked England and Flanders, providing the raw material on which the Flemish cloth industry depended.

Many abbeys also funded the construction of mills, or secured rights to those already in existence, further stimulating the economy of Flanders and Hainaut. Their participation in this sphere of activity is illustrated in several charters issued by the countesses to various foundations. In 1235, Jeanne ratified an agreement between the nuns of Notre-Dame-de-Près and Henri, the prévôt of Douai regarding a windmill built by the nuns without the consent of Henri. Despite the intervention of the countess, the dispute was not effectively resolved until 1242, when Henri, his wife Ida, and son William renounced all claims to the windmill "for the love of god and at the request of noble people and for our own peace."[76] The nuns of Marquette owned several mills in a variety of locations, including two at Houplines, donated by the abbey's founders, Ferrand and Jeanne, in 1231.[77] A charter issued in 1254 detailed an arrangement between Marguerite and the monks of Cambron regarding the construction of two mills at Hulst. The two parties agreed to divide the cost of construction, as well as any ensuing profits.[78] In June 1261, countess Marguerite purchased twenty-one *bonniers* of land and a windmill from Robert de Verlenghehem and his wife Maria, which she then donated to the abbey of Flines.[79] The monks of Anchin also controlled at least one mill, which they received in conjunction with the donation of an allod located at Montegni.[80] By encouraging monastic communities to engage in such activities, the countesses ultimately increased their own wealth and the resources at their disposal as rulers.

Commercial activity in Flanders would not have been possible without the ability to access large sums of money when necessary. The extant documents reveal numerous occasions in which abbeys functioned as institutions of credit, lending sizeable sums of money to the countesses. Perhaps the most obvious examples of this function occurred in conjunction with Jeanne's attempt to raise the ransom necessary to liberate her husband Ferrand. (In addition to the canons of Saint-Donatien, mentioned in chapter 1, the countess also received onetime loans from the abbeys of Saint-Vaast and Saint-Pierre of Lille.[81]) In a similar fashion, Jeanne and Ferrand guaranteed the sum of 700 *livres* borrowed from the community of Saint-Jean of Jerusalem on behalf of Gerard de Mons, who had been taken prisoner in the course of the Crusades.[82] The abbey of Saint-Bavon lent Jeanne and her husband Thomas 1,000 *pounds artois* for an indefinite amount of time.[83]

Perhaps the most visible contribution of religious communities to the region was their transformation of the topography of Flanders through their participation in comital reclamation programs. Examination of wider patterns of the countesses' patronage of monastic foundations in their domains indicates that a preponderance of donations to monasteries, regardless of spiritual affiliation, involved land subject to reclamation. Reclamation in Flanders during the thirteenth century targeted the northern periphery of the county near the city of Ghent and along the southern edge of the polders, where much of the land had been inundated by water for centuries.[84] Although this land had been drained decades earlier, the level of the land tended to fall following the removal of the water, requiring the construction of dikes to protect the recently drained land from the encroaching waters. Along with the diking of land that had already been drained, this second phase of reclamation involved drainage of the coastal marshes in the north, which until the eleventh century had been covered by the English Channel. It also involved clearance of land deemed "marginal" because its potential productivity seldom justified the expense and effort required to render it suitable for cultivation. Such land, located around Ghent and along the southern edge of the polders, was often covered by both water and small brush, or briar, and required several successive phases of drainage, diking, and clearance.

The majority of this reclamation was entrusted to the large abbeys of Flanders possessing the necessary resources to undertake such projects. Marshy land was distributed to monastic foundations by the countesses through sale or donation. The individual monasteries then implemented the measures required to convert the lands into suitable pasture, digging drainage ditches, building dikes, constructing additional polders to prevent future flooding, and clearing the land of any small brush.[85] The Cistercians were particularly prominent among the abbeys entrusted with reclamation activity during the thirteenth century, joining the countesses in their "fight against the sea."[86] In his study of the conversion of maritime Flanders, Adriaan Verhulst directly implicates the abbeys of Ter Duinen, Marquette, Spermalie, and Cambron in the reclamation activities that occurred under the auspices of the countesses. Such participation may have resulted from Cistercian emphasis on the importance of manual labor, even for choir, monks, and the presence of *conversi* (lay brothers).

Reclamation was particularly concentrated in the north of Flanders. The geography of this area made it particularly vulnerable to flooding, thus it was the last part of the county to be reclaimed from the sea.[87] Examination of the charters issued by the countesses on behalf of Cistercian foundations has revealed that very little of the land that constituted the initial endowment of many abbeys founded in the thirteenth century was suitable for immediate cultivation. Rather, the endowment of these foundations tended more frequently toward marsh, sandy coastal lands, and *wastine*. It was probably not a coincidence that Boudelo, the only abbey of the Order inhabited by monks founded during the reign of Jeanne and Marguerite, was located in the north of Flanders.[88] Donations made to men's houses in Flanders illustrate the preponderance of marsh and wasteland in grants or sales of land made by the countesses, land that would have been subject to reclamation. In a charter issued by Marguerite in 1276, over 842 *bonniers* of *wastine* are listed among the holdings of the abbey of Ter Doest, which was instrumental in the clearance of the less fertile areas of northern Flanders.[89] The monks of Ter Doest acquired 350 *bonniers wastine*, located near Maldegem, from Jeanne and Thomas in May 1243.[90] In June 1273, Marguerite donated twenty *bonniers* of land, located near Scipgragt and Wipen, to the abbey of Ter Doest.[91] The abbey of Ter Duinen alone was responsible for the conversion of at least 25,000 acres of land along the Flemish coast, on which it established 25 separate granges.[92] Though the majority of this reclamation occurred prior to the reign of Jeanne or Marguerite, Ter Duinen did receive a donation of 632 *verges* of land from Jeanne in 1235 to protect against the encroachment of the sea.[93]

One of the most interesting aspects of Flemish reclamation and clearance during this period is that Cistercian nuns participated in these activities nearly as often as Cistercian monks. The documents of several houses of Cistercian nuns in Flanders refer to activities associated with reclamation. In a charter issued in June 1228 by Jeanne and Ferrand, the nuns of Marquette were instructed to build a dike on the land at Calvekinscure.[94] A charter of 1265 refers to the diking of a polder on land near Lapscheure, conveyed in a separate donation to the nuns of Marquette by Marguerite.[95] Marquette and Flines are mentioned in conjunction with reclamation of land located in the north of Flanders, despite the fact that both abbeys were located in the southern half of the county near Lille. Donations made to Marquette included fifty *bonniers* of land located between Boudelo and Arteveld, made by Marguerite and approved by Jeanne and Thomas in December 1243.[96] Jeanne and Ferrand had already granted the abbey eleven *bonniers* of marsh in this same location in September 1233, and Jeanne added an additional 500 *bonniers* of marsh in December 1244, suggesting that the abbey's holdings in the region requiring reclamation were quite extensive.[97] In 1248, Marguerite confirmed a donation of fifty *bonniers wastine* located in Calve, and in January 1249, she approved another donation of fifteen *bonniers* of marsh.[98] In September 1269, Marguerite approved a donation of a polder near Bruges, made by Jeanne and Ferrand shortly after the abbey's foundation in 1226.[99] The abbey of Flines also possessed land along the northern coast in Flanders; in January 1265

Marguerite donated 40 *bonniers* located in Aardenburg, and in September 1276 she gave an additional 102 *bonniers* of land in the north of Flanders.[100] In addition to Marquette and Flines, the abbeys of Moorsele, Oosteeklo, Doornzele, Ravensberg, Bijloke, Notre Dame des Près, and Nieuwenbos were all recipients of marsh or wasteland in the north of Flanders. Marguerite granted the nuns of Oosteeklo a total of 183 *bonniers wastine* that was to be converted into arable, presumably through the construction and maintenance of several dikes.[101] A charter issued by Marguerite in 1265 addressed a dispute between Hugh, castellan of Ghent, and the abbey of Groeninghe concerning a tithe on land recently diked by the nuns of the abbey.[102] In 1250, Marguerite issued instructions to Willem of Boudelo concerning the extension of a canal constructed by the nuns of the abbey of Nieuwenbos, which traversed marshland owned by the monks of Boudelo.[103] The nuns of Nieuwenbos purchased 110 *bonniers wastine* from Jeanne in 1217. In 1227, Ferrand confirmed a sale made earlier by Jeanne of 310 *bonniers wastine*, all located in the parish of Lokeren. Jeanne also granted the abbey six *bonniers* of land located near "the marsh of the monks of Boudelo" at Coudenborne in October 1219. In October 1235, Jeanne sold the abbey of Bijloke near Ghent 126 *bonniers wastine* and 28 *bonniers* marsh near Sceldevelt, lying between Haghe and Langhe Triest.[104] The abbey of Doornzele also owned land in this area, including a prairie, wasteland, and marsh located near Haghe and Langhe Triest, purchased by Marguerite in July 1251 and donated to the nuns on behalf of her eldest son William.[105] In February 1250, Marguerite issued a charter extending comital protection to the nuns of Oosteeklo and all of their possessions, including 196 *bonniers* of *wastine* that the abbey had acquired.[106] In May 1266, the abbey of Oosteeklo received a donation of four *bonniers* of marsh in the parish of Kaprijke, made by Marguerite "for her souls and the souls of her ancestors and successors."[107] All of this land, whether *wastine* or *mori*, was located in the marshy, often briar-infested region of northern Flanders and would have required reclamation and clearance.

Although the Cistercians were the most prominent monastic order engaged in reclamation efforts, several Benedictine abbeys were involved as well.[108] The abbey of Saint-Bavon was perhaps the most active in reclamation. As early as 1215, Jeanne made a considerable contribution to the abbey's domain, including *wastine* located in the parish of Everghem, all of the woods located between Scaldem and Dormam, and twenty-four *bonniers* of uncultivated land located between the river Escaut and the river Dorme. Jeanne granted the monks permission to enclose the woods with a canal and a hedge. In November of the same year, she donated 500 *bonniers* of land located at Utdic, which included a dike. In September 1236, Jeanne donated land at Hodonc, including a chapel, and; granted the monks an additional five *bonniers* of land at Onlende.[109] Nearly all of the large tracts of land purchased from the countess by the monks of Saint-Bavon were located in the northern corner of the county, and involved land categorized as *wastine* or *bruyere*. In August 1221 Jeanne sold the abbey of Mont Blandin forty-five *bonniers* of *bruyere* located near Bulscamp. Three years later, in 1224, she granted the abbey an additional ninety *bonniers bruyere* located at Wachtebeke in return for an annual rent of twelve *deniers* per *bonnier*. The abbey also owned *wastine* near Scheldevelt, as revealed in a charter issued by Marguerite in 1249 regarding a dispute over jurisdiction in the area.[110] In May 1228, Jeanne and her first husband Ferrand donated twenty-eight *bonniers* of meadow located near the town of Clusa, and twenty-four *bonniers* of *wastine* located at Langhebeke to the abbey of Eename.[111] Eename also purchased land at Selzaete, in the parish of Assenede, from Marguerite, which was comprised of marsh and *wastine*.[112] Marguerite also granted the monks of Eename five *mensuras* of marsh in 1250, requesting an anniversary mass for her deceased sister Jeanne in return.[113]

The Benedictine abbey of Saint-Andre's participation in reclamation is not surprising in light of its location in the north of the county near Bruges. In two separate transactions in 1252, the abbey purchased ten *bonniers* of marsh from Johannes de Leffingha and 300 *bonniers* of *bruyere* from Marguerite.[114] In 1256, Marguerite approved the abbey's purchase of five *mesures* of *wastine*, sold for an annual rent of forty *sols flandrensis*.[115] The nuns of Bourbourg also received marsh and *wastine* subject to reclamation, further indication that the sex of an abbey's monastics had little or no bearing on the community's ability to succeed in the new economic climate of the thirteenth century. The nuns owned land that required drainage, as evidenced by a charter issued in 1244, in which Jeanne granted them permission to build a dike between the sea and their marsh at Fresdick.[116] In addition to a grant of four *bonniers* of marsh located near Rodembourg in 1269, the countess and her son Guy also donated twenty-nine *mesures* of *wastine* at Hemmekin in February 1272, which, according to the terms of the charter, required the construction of a dike.[117] In directing donations to abbeys that participated in such reclamation efforts, Jeanne and Marguerite successfully transformed the topography of Flanders, expanding the arable and ultimately stimulating future economic development.

Monastic and religious foundations were ideally positioned to contribute to the social well-being of the secular community, a function that clearly bridged any perceived divide between the practical and the pious. In the view of medieval society, providing care for the elderly and infirm was a manifestation of one's commitment to Christianity; such care simultaneously served a practical purpose in creating a safety net for the less fortunate. Both countesses exhibited a particular attraction to orders which embraced the ideals of the *vita apostolica*, an attraction illustrated by their actions as patrons. Although the countesses' interest in foundations that adhered to such ideals was undoubtedly prompted by pious concerns, their support for many of these communities may have also been informed by secular considerations. Foundations that embraced an active, rather than a contemplative, spirituality, were ideally suited to the highly urbanized and densely populated region.

The urban centers that dominated the Flemish landscape during the twelfth century proved to be especially receptive to the new religious movements of the thirteenth century. While the Flemish towns provided the new religious orders with the spiritual audience they required, the wealth generated by the booming textile industry produced the internal funds needed to support their religious ministrations to members of the urban communities. Such populous and prosperous communities were considered a necessity for the mendicants, who relied solely upon alms as their means of material support.[118] The towns served as a vital recruiting center for new adherents to orders such as the Franciscans and Dominicans. The preaching and poverty of the mendicants garnered support among popes and noble patrons alike, and they soon surpassed the traditional monks and canons in popularity, power, and prestige. The Dominicans and Franciscans were obviously valued by the countesses for the spiritual guidance they could provide to townspeople in Flanders and Hainaut. The Dominicans in particular, a prominent feature of most urban centers during the thirteenth century, would have emphasized the importance of preaching to the local community. The extent of the countesses' support for these communities, discussed earlier in this chapter, is an indication of the value placed upon their contribution to maintaining religious orthodoxy.

While the Franciscan and Dominican emphasis on preaching would have provided spiritual guidance for the inhabitants of Flemish towns, the beguinages functioned as a safety net for the many impoverished and infirm, caring for the sick and giving alms to the poor. Jeanne and Marguerite's intentions in supporting these women and the role they were expected to play within the wider secular community are often expressed in charters. For example, Jeanne revealed her understanding of the function of beguines in a charter issued in 1243 to the community at Valenciennes. The countess stated that her donation was intended "to aid them in their work on behalf of the poor and to support their infimary" [*omnino ad opus pauperum et infirmorum sustentationem habebat*].[119] Contrary to the assessment of some scholars, the women who became beguines were not poor themselves, but rather were women from the community who actively chose to serve the poor by providing care and shelter for those in need.[120]

Through their attempts to regulate these communities, the countesses demonstrate their dedication to ensuring that beguinages continued to perform the function for which they were originally established. Marguerite denounced the desire of the Dominican convent in Lille to alter the customs of the beguinage of that town, reprimanding them specifically for attempting to force the beguines to admit impoverished women into their community.[121] In May 1269, Marguerite issued orders that the statutes of the community, issued earlier by Jeanne, should be strictly observed.[122] In 1276, Marguerite ordered the grand mistress of the beguinage of Sainte-Élisabeth of Lille to banish any beguines whose conduct was deemed unbecoming to the community, as well as those individuals who refused to conform to the community's regulations.[123] Marguerite was involved in issuing the regulations for several beguine communities, determining the method by which the grand mistress of each was to be elected and dictating regulations for entrance. She also issued a code of conduct for beguines already residing in the community.[124] Clearly, the countesses did not view these foundations as merely a shelter for impoverished women, but rather as a community of pious, devout women dedicated to the service of the poor and infirm.

The form of life developed by these women under the direction of the countesses supports this view of the social function of beguines. Approximately twenty-one of the twenty-eight beguine communities in Flanders and Hainaut prior to 1280 were *curtis beguinages*. This organization seems to have been integral to comital policy. Eight of the foundations in their domains adopted this form, including Briel of Ypres, Sainte-Élisabeth of Ghent, Lille and Valenciennes, Champfleury of Douai, Cantimpré of Mons, Courtrai, and Wijngaard of Bruges. Clearly, the countesses preferred the communal form of beguine life, rather than that more common in the Rhineland, where beguines remained scattered throughout their urban communities, living independently or in small groups.[125] This preference may have resulted from Jeanne and Marguerite's understanding of the purpose of such communities. Unlike individual beguines living in private homes, the architectural complex of the *curtis beguinage* could include an infirmary. It also facilitated the distribution of alms for the poor. Although the endowment of such communities was often quite modest, the residents of the *curtis beguinage*, unlike their counterparts in the Rhineland, did have a source of communal wealth, which would sustain present as well as future generations. Such endowments provided stability and continuity, and they made the beguinage a stable element of many Flemish towns, where they cared for the poor and dispensed charity.

The countesses' concern for the poor is also reflected in their support of the numerous hospitals that, by the end of thirteenth century, had become a regular feature of the urban landscape in Flanders and Hainaut. Like the beguinages, these communities were expressly founded to tend to impoverished in the community. Count Ferrand's will, issued in 1230, provided

2,000 *livres* to be distributed in alms, along with an unspecified lump sum of money to be distributed to various charitable foundations by his executors. Jeanne administered the distribution of this money, directing sums to six hospitals in Flanders and Hainaut. The hospitals of Audenarde, Ghent, Lille, Gravelines, and Bruges were instructed to use the funds to provide beds for the poor.[126] The hospital of Saint-Sauveur in Lille, founded by Jeanne, was explicitly commanded by the countess to hear the confessions of the poor.[127] Jeanne was also actively involved in the administration of the leprosarium at Mons. In 1221, she ordered the aldermen of the city to consult with William, her chaplain, on all affairs concerning governance of the community, including the acceptance and dismissal of brothers and sisters,[128] and she directed several donations to the hospital at Ypres, founded by Marguerite, to pay for the services of a chaplain.[129] In 1265, Marguerite intervened in the administration of the hospital at Alost, ordering that the foundation should not support more than five sisters.[130]

Comital attempts to enlist monastic and religious communities in the maintenance of the social order of Flanders and Hainaut are also reflected in the responsibilities assigned to certain foundations regarding education. While such references to this type of function are elusive, charters do provide a glimpse of the role of pious foundations in regulating or supporting schools. The Victorine abbey of Sainte-Élisabeth of Quesnoy was granted the right to appoint individuals to vacated positions within the schools of Quesnoy by Jeanne, on the condition that these appointments were conferred free of charge and that the prior of the Dominican convent of Valenciennes was consulted.[131] The involvement of the canonesses in the local schools is characteristic of the congregation of Saint-Victor, which viewed education and the transmission of knowledge as one of the primary mandates of its members. In 1235, Jeanne issued a charter to the Arrouaisian abbbey of Sainte-Pharaïlde.[132] The countess agreed to cede to the dean of the chapter the right to appoint the directors of schools in Ghent. However, the terms of the agreement stipulated that the chapter was required to submit their choice in writing to the countess by Easter of each year. Their commitment to supporting education is generally reflected in a charter issued in 1247, in which the abbot of Clairvaux confirmed the donation made by Marguerite and her son Guy of an annual rent of thirty *livres parisis* to be used to support "the place called St. Bernard at Paris, where the brothers of the Order of Cîteaux go to live to pursue their studies."[133]

This discussion of the range of functions associated with monastic and religious foundations and the implications of such functions for potential patrons raises important questions about current attempts to characterize religious patronage. Such an approach also aids in assessing the impact of their actions. Past scholarship has often posited a particularly strong correlation between one's sex and one's predilection for religious patronage, identifying women as having a particular propensity to act as patrons. However, such attempts to understand patronage as a gendered activity have resulted in an underappreciation of the very political impact of such practices by categorizing it as a private rather than a public activity. The reasoning behind such categorization remains unclear. However, it has had important implications for the study of the position of women. This study does not challenge the characterization of women as more active patrons than men; that fact remains to be determined. However, it does question the various explanations provided for this discrepancy. In particular, scholars have often positioned patronage as one of the few realms of activity still available to women after their relegation to the domestic sphere after the year 1000.

According to such explanations, women were able to act privately as patrons, but their patronage often had very visible and political consequences, allowing them to circumvent the restrictions otherwise placed upon their activity in the public sphere.[134] Penelope Johnson has posited the theory that religious patronage, as evidenced in the actions of Agnes of Burgundy, provided noble women with an avenue by which to circumvent the traditional restrictions placed upon their exercise of "public power."[135] According to this view, reiterated in numerous studies, religious patronage provided women with access to secular authority without disrupting the medieval power structure, which relegated them to the margins of the political sphere. However, investigation of the experiences of Jeanne and Marguerite demonstrates their failure to conform to this expectation. Moreover, their activity on behalf of foundations challenges the view of religious patronage as a "private" activity. After considering the wider historical context in which these two women maneuvered, and the extent of their political activity, it becomes impossible to interpret their patronage as a response to restricted access to more public avenues of power.

Furthermore, attempts to categorize religious patronage as an activity located in the private sphere are complicated by the very public nature of these foundations. Any activity that has the power to publicly transform society politically, economically, and socially, defies the label of private. Perhaps religious patronage has been deemed a private activity because of its association with women and the tendency to view women's actions as restricted to the private sphere. However, this would prove to be circular reasoning, based upon assumptions about the division of society challenged in earlier chapters here, and by assuming that any activity available to women must fall into the category of private since women were supposedly unable to engage in actions deemed public. Religious patronage is categorized as a private activity due to its association with women, who were supposedly relegated to the private sphere. Women, who are relegated to the private sphere, can engage in religious patronage, hence it is categorized as a private activity (Women do it because it is private; it is private because women do it).

The tendency to view women as resorting to patronage as a result of their inability to act openly in the public sphere proves problematic. As the experience of Jeanne and Marguerite demonstrates, not all women were faced with such restrictions but were able to exercise power in the public sphere. Yet, Jeanne and Marguerite are just as inclined as many of their female counterparts to patronage. Rather than employing religious patronage as an alternative avenue to power, Jeanne and Marguerite both employed patronage as an additional avenue to power, along with the avenues typically employed by male rulers. Their actions in this respect challenge our current understanding of the relationship between women and patronage, and they suggest the need for a more complex view of women's patronage that is free from assumptions based upon modern perceptions of medieval gender distinctions.

Evidence of their ability to exercise power in both the public and the private sphere has significant implications for our understanding of the public/private dichotomy in thirteenth-century society, and it reinforces the need to reassess the use of this model as an interpretive device for medieval society. The various ways the countesses employed patronage challenge the very tendency to associate religious patronage with private, rather than public, power, and it suggests that a line demarcating public and private spheres of activity during this period was not nearly as rigid as previously assumed, if it existed at all.[136] Both women used their resources as countesses of Flanders and Hainaut in the course of patronage that often had political and economic ramifications. Once it is liberated from such an interpretive model, religious patronage can be more effectively used to understand the exercise of power in the Middle Ages. Clearly, both countesses employed patronage in a variety of ways to consolidate their authority, increase revenue, and regulate charity. Their actions in this respect reflect their understanding of the visibility of patrons and the public uses of patronage. It is clear that monastic communities in Flanders and Hainaut served as political agents, recruited by Jeanne and Marguerite to bolster their own position and more effectively exercise power.

CHAPTER 4

TRANSLATING SECULAR POWER INTO SPIRITUAL GAINS

In 1226, Jeanne established the Cistercian abbey of Marquette near Lille in the southern part of Flanders.[1] Ferrand, who was still in prison in Paris pending the successful outcome of negotiations concerning his release, participated from a distance. The foundation was expressly intended to represent their gratitude for Ferrand's imminent liberation and safe return home after twelve years, five months, and nine days in prison. From 1226 until her death in 1244, Jeanne issued over thirty-seven charters on behalf of Marquette, and secured its official incorporation into the Cistercian Order. The charters indicate that Jeanne was a frequent visitor at the abbey, making it one of the primary stops of her itinerant court. In 1233, she constructed a house within the abbey's walls, and petitioned Pope Gregory in 1239 for permission to be buried in its cemetery alongside her daughter, Marie, and her husband, Ferrand, both of whom had predeceased her.[2] After falling ill in December 1244, Jeanne retired to Marquette, taking vows just prior to her own death. She was then interred within the abbey's walls.

Marguerite, following her elder sister's lead, instigated a similar Cistercian foundation for women in southern Flanders in 1234, known as *Honor Beatae Marie*, or Flines.[3] Flines witnessed the burial of Marguerite's second husband, William of Dampierre, as well as the entry of her youngest daughter Marie as a member of the community. Marguerite built a personal residence within the abbey's enclosure, which she bequeathed to the nuns after her death.[4] Upon her abdication as countess of Flanders in 1278, Marguerite retired to Flines, where she spent the remaining two years of her life. She was buried in the abbey's church, positioned in the very middle of the transept. Such proximity to the altar, nuns, and relics ensconced within the church's walls were assuredly expected to increase her chance of a favorable destination in the afterlife.

Marquette and Flines are by no means the only examples of the countesses' patronage of monastic and religious foundations within their domains. Both sisters proved to be exceptionally generous, directing donations at a level unprecedented in Flanders and Hainaut, transforming the spiritual landscape of the region while they accrued reputations of extreme piety and devotion. While the previous chapter explored the various ways Jeanne and Marguerite employed religious patronage to consolidate their secular power, this chapter examines their patronage from a more spiritual perspective. It is based upon the premise that for individuals in the thirteenth century, secular power was valued in part for its ability to secure spiritual power, understood as the support and prayers of the monks and nuns that furthered one's chances of salvation. Examination of their actions reveals the various ways both countesses dispensed the material resources at their disposal and mined the political capital they had amassed over time to aid favored monastic and religious foundations. The recipients of their largesse were by no means determined by whim. In the increasingly diverse religious landscape of the thirteenth century, patrons were forced to make deliberate decisions about which communities to target with their generosity. Such decisions clearly involved careful calculation, taking into consideration the differences in practice that distinguished the monastic and religious orders that existed. Such discussion not only deepens our appreciation of the complexity of the spiritual landscape of the High Middle Ages, but it also facilitates our ability to determine which beliefs and practices held the most appeal for potential donors, providing a perspective of patronage from the view of the patron.

This study is premised upon the belief that the countesses of Flanders and Hainaut can be viewed as representative of members of society generally as well as members of their sex and social stratum more specifically in terms of religious patronage. Their motives in directing resources to monastic and religious communities, as conveyed in charters, express general concern for their salvation and, at times, an understanding of the spiritual obligation associated with people in positions of considerable authority. Not only were they expected to request spiritual aid from members of religious foundations for themselves and members of their families, but they were also expected to foster a positive spiritual climate within the territory they controlled. This task included using their secular power (the resources at their disposal and their political capital) to establish new foundations, hence transforming the spiritual aspirations of others into reality. In supporting monastic communities, patrons made religious life possible for those who, due to circumstance or conviction, desired entrance into a monastic community. Clearly, the presence of religious and monastic communities in a particular region can be directly correlated to demand among those interested in living such a life. The number of foundations in Flanders and Hainaut suggests that such a demand was particularly pronounced in this region, and the countesses were instrumental in responding to it.

Jeanne and Marguerite's awareness of the spiritual tasks and obligations they had inherited along with the counties of Flanders and Hainaut is articulated on occasion in the *arengae* [prefaces] of charters.[5] Although brief and often formulaic, such overt expressions of motive provide some insight into the concerns that prompted patronage. The disparity that existed between the ideals dictated by the church and the realities of medieval life were obvious to many individuals, who responded to their own inability to live in a truly Christian manner by seeking an alternative avenue to eternal life. According to Janet Burton, "Sermons and homilies constantly reminded medieval man and woman of the consequences of sin, and recalled for an aristocracy bred for war the need for intercessory supplication on its behalf. Their message was reinforced by monastic writers."[6] Clearly, society's awareness of the need for and purpose of patronage was translated by monastic scribes into *arengae*, which were inserted in charters and often prefaced the terms of a donation. These phrases clearly reflect individual attempts to secure salvations vicariously through the prayers of those who led lives of Christian perfection, namely the men and women who joined the monastic and religious orders that proliferated throughout Europe during the Middle Ages.

Furthermore, the rhetoric included in some charters suggests that Jeanne and Marguerite shared the concerns of their contemporaries regarding the responsibilities of a ruler in providing for the spiritual well-being of others. Such considerations are clearly expressed in the charters issued by Jeanne and Marguerite to the Cistercian abbey of Spermalie in 1239 and 1275 respectively quoted in the introduction. Both countesses were clearly cognizant of the origins of their own power, which had been "bestowed by God," as well as their obligation to exercise it on behalf of those who sought a religious life.[7] Although neither countess authored these charters, they undoubtedly shared the sentiment expressed concerning the role of a patron. Like many powerful rulers, Jeanne and Marguerite felt a particular obligation to use the resources at their disposal on behalf of monastic communities and the men and women who inhabited them.

The extent to which the countesses deliberately attempted to translate pious concerns into reality is revealed in a similar charter issued by Marguerite to the abbey of Val-des-Écoliers in Mons. It mentions the motives that prompted the initial foundation, as well as the considerations that influenced her decision regarding its affiliation:

> The sacred writers and the words of the saints make known to us clearly how it is pious, how it is necessary and profitable for the safety of our souls to give alms

o pious places and to the poor and to apply ourselves to works of mercy. Having carefully considered these obligations and wishing to anticipate the day of the supreme harvest by works of mercy, to sow in the earth in consideration of eternity in order to collect many fruits from God in heaven, to the religious, our esteemed brothers in Jesus Christ of the order of Val-des-Écoliers, out of generosity and of our own will, we honestly give and concede the inheritance which once belonged to Jean Noe and Sare, his wife, which we have purchased from them, located in our town of Mons.[8]

Although even more brief than these examples of *arengae*, the "donative phrases" present in charters also express the recognition by medieval men and women that attaining salvation was a collective responsibility.[9] In a charter issued by Jeanne in 1234 to the Dominican convent at Bruges, the countess stated that her actions on behalf of the abbey, including her participation in its foundation and a later donation of 300 *libras* from her husband Ferrand's will, were prompted by concern for her salvation, as well as the desire "to enhance the cult of the lord and contribute to the moral perfection of the people" ["ad ampliandum cultum domini et ad profectum populi"].[10] A charter issued by Jeanne to the Cistercian nuns of Bijloke in Ghent notes her intent to amplify the cult of the lord as well as "the glory of the virgin Mary" ["ad ampliandum cultum domini et gloriosae virginis matris dei"].[11]

According to André Vauchez, belief in the afterlife and the ability of individuals on earth to directly influence the outcome of the final judgment pervaded medieval society, and it encouraged religious patronage among the laity.[12] For medieval men and women, the foundation of a religious community was, with the exception of actual entrance into such communities, the most effective way to guarantee personal salvation. Religious patronage was a complex process, involving a series of deliberate, calculated decisions, intended to result in the foundation of a new community.[13] If the community itself was the product of careful consideration, than it stands to reason that examination of the various attributes of the community can provide insight into the concerns, interests, and ideals of the founder. When contemplating the foundation of a religious community, a patron was forced to consider a variety of factors, some personal, others practical. While decisions like size and geographic location would have been partially dictated by circumstance, other decisions, such as the affiliation of the community and the sex of its residents, would reflect the personal preferences of the founder. Thirteenth-century patrons in particular would have been presented with a wide array of options from which to chose, ranging from traditional monastic orders like the Benedictines and the Augustinian canons to the reform communities of the Cistercians, Arrouasians, and Victorines. They were also presented with more recent arrivals on the religious scene, such as the Franciscans, Dominicans, and beguines, who embraced a more active life, as dictated by the ideals associated with the *vita apostolica*.[14]

Quantitative examination of the countesses' patronage indicates that the two women issued charters to at least 98 of the 156 monastic and religious communities considered in this study.[15] While not all of the communities in question were the recipients of outright donations, nearly all of them benefited in some way from their interaction with Jeanne and Marguerite. By assessing the material support provided by the countesses to various foundations, it is possible to identify a range of concerns that informed their patronage, directing their actions toward certains orders or affiliated communities. The preferences that emerge during the course of the discussion here reveal how their personal concerns about their own salvation influenced their patronage and determined which communities they favored most. At the same time, it is possible to identify orders or individual communities presumed by the countesses to have the most potent or efficacious prayers. Jeanne and Marguerite, like most of their contemporaries, chose to direct donations to communities that, for various reasons, were deemed most capable of assisting them in their ultimate goal, securing salvation.

While both countesses would acquire a rather diverse portfolio in terms of religious patronage, several preferences emerge quite markedly in an examination of their role in the foundation of individual communities. Ultimately, this study argues that the countesses preferred communities that adhered to the *vita apostolica*. Within this broader category, Dominicans and beguines were singled out with the most frequency in terms of the establishment of new communities. However, Jeanne and Marguerite seem to have favored communities of women generally with similar intensity, exhibiting a particular propensity to orchestrate the foundation of Cistercian convents. The remainder of this chapter will discuss these preferences as they are illustrated by individual actions of the countesses, attempting to identify motives and isolate concerns that prompted their actions. It is quite possible that the two groups (Cistercian women and adherents of the *vita apostolica*) that benefited the most from the patronage of Jeanne and Marguerite were not distinguished by practices, but rather by chronology; the Cistercians received the bulk of the countesses' attention during the first few decades of the thirteenth century, prior to the arrival of the mendicants. As the discussion here indicates, by the time the countesses' turned their attention to supporting communities of friars and beguines, Cistercian foundation activity had slowed remarkably due perhaps to a glut of the spiritual market.

While their activity on behalf of Marquette (1226) and Flines (1234), as described earlier, was unusual in terms of the value and number of donations, their actions of behalf of several other Cistercian communities reflected the same spirit of piety combined with generosity.[16] Jeanne and Marguerite were responsible for a number of foundations including the abbeys of Nieuwenbos (1215), Bijloke (1228), Oosteeklo (1228), Zwijveke (1230), Ath (1216–34), and Ter Hagen (1230–34). Comital support for these abbeys was crucial for their formal admission into the Cistercian Order, and the extent of Jeanne and Marguerite's support illustrates the role played by the two sisters in the expansion of the female branch of the Order into northern Europe.

Marquette alone was the recipient of thirty-seven donations made by Jeanne or Marguerite during the course of the thirteenth century. Some of the more generous grants included an annual rent of 1,200 *modios* of oats, 463 lambs, and 15 *livres flandrensis* made by Jeanne in May 1236, and an annual rent of 5,000 eels to be taken from an eel pond located near Bruges in 1232.[17] In 1251, Marguerite added another lucrative rent of 14,000 herrings to be taken from the échevinage of Mardyck. In addition to annual rents, Marquette amassed a sizeable patrimony as a result of the countesses' generosity. Flines was equally fortunate, receiving a total of 429 *bonniers* of arable, woods, waste, and marsh from Marguerite alone during the course of her lifetime.[18]

In a number of transactions with the abbey of Nieuwenbos, founded near the city of Ghent in 1215, Jeanne provided a total of 332 *bonniers* of land for the nuns' use.[19] In 1228, the year of its foundation, the abbey of Bijloke possessed a patrimony sufficient to sustain twenty-five nuns and twenty lay sisters. In response to a direct petition by Jeanne and Ferrand, the abbey was accepted as an official member of the Cistercian Order, as a daughter house of Clairvaux. By 1243, due in no small part to the generosity of the countess, Bijloke received permission to increase the number of choir nuns to forty.[20] In November 1230, the year it was founded, the abbey of Zwijveke received a fief at Appels from Jeanne and her first husband Ferrand; the absence of other charters suggests that this fief most likely constituted the majority of Zwijveke's endowment.[21] In addition to Flines, Marguerite endowed the abbey of Ter Hagen, founded at Zuyddorp in the north of Flanders in 1230 but later moved because of the encroachments of the sea. By 1278, Marguerite had donated at least 242 *mesures* of land to the abbey of Ter Hagen, which she secured by authorizing the construction of a dike that surrounded the entire community.[22]

Although not typically recognized as the abbey's founder, Jeanne's contribution to the establishment of Épinlieu was not insignificant. While Beatrice de Lens provided the funds necessary for the construction of the monastic complex, Jeanne donated the six *bonniers* of land near Mons, that comprised the site of the convent.[23] While Jeanne is often cited as instrumental in the foundation of the abbey of Hemelsdale, established in 1237, it was Marguerite who orchestrated the community's transfer from its original location in Dixmude to a more conducive site at Zillebeke, near the city of Ypres. The charter that confirmed the relocation of the abbey, issued by Marguerite in 1270, also provided an annual rent of ten *livres* to compensate the canons of Saint-Martin for any loss of revenue incured as a result of the presence of the nuns.[24] Jeanne was also instrumental in the establishment of the abbey of Spermalie. Although its foundation was initiated by Egidius van Bredene, a canon of Saint-Donatien and clerk at the comital court, the abbey benefited considerably from the patronage of Jeanne. As countess, she petitioned the Cistercian General Chapter for incorporation in 1234 and confirmed the transfer of the original monastery to a more suitable location in 1239.[25]

In providing the initial endowment for these abbeys, the countesses played an instrumental role in ensuring their success, particularly in the thirteenth century, when changes in the economic climate and diminishing resources tended to limit the amount of land granted to monasteries in general. This was particularly true in regards to deliberate attempts by the Cistercians to prohibit the incorporation of additional female foundations that lacked the financial resources deemed necessary to sustain a community. The countesses appear in the statutes of the General Chapter of the Cistercian Order on seven separate occasions petitioning for the incorporation of the abbeys of Ath, Ter Hagen, Ter Roosen, Groeninghe, Soleilmont, Hemelsdale, and Flines.[26] By personally donating the necessary land and revenue and championing the attempt to secure official incorporation of individual abbeys, the countesses were able to secure the Order's acceptance of these new communities. Such appeals to the General Chapter reflect the willingness of the countesses to mobilize the political capital they had accrued on behalf of Cistercian women. In every instance, their request for official incorporation was eventually granted and the abbey in question was accepted into the Order.

As the wave of Cistercian foundation activity began to slow in the 1230s, the countesses turned their attention to other groups of religious women. As founders, Jeanne and Marguerite were extremely active on behalf of beguine communities. The sisters were instrumental in the establishment of at least nine of the twenty-eight beguinages in Flanders and Hainaut, working in tandem on several occasions. Examination of extant documents confirms the role of the countesses in the foundation of communities in Ghent (Sainte-Élisabeth and Saint-Aubert), Lille, Valenciennes, Mons (Cantimpret), Douai (Champfleury), Courtrai, and Bruges (La Vigne and Saint-Aubert).[27] Both Jeanne and Marguerite were active patrons of the beguinage of Sainte-Élisabeth of Ghent, as reflected in the numerous charters issued in conjunction with the community. In 1242, Jeanne arranged for the aldermen of the city of Ghent to cede land needed for the construction of the beguinage, and secured the consent of the nearby abbey of Saint-Bavon.[28] The countesses are also associated with the foundation of Ten Hoye, which was established in Ghent by 1234, as well as the beguinage of Sainte-Élisabeth in Douai.[29] In 1241, Jeanne confirmed the donation of land in Courtrai, and personally granted a house to provide a dwelling for the beguines of that city.[30] In a charter issued by Marguerite in 1245 to the beguines of Lille, she explicitly mentioned her earlier involvement in the community's foundation, as well as that of her "sister Jeanne of pious memory formerly countess of Flanders and Hainaut."[31]

The countesses also promoted mendicant communities in their domains. Along with the Franciscans of Valenciennes, whose foundation was initiated by Count Ferrand in 1225, Jeanne was instrumental in the establishment of the convent in Bruges in 1227. Overall, however, their patronage of Franciscan foundations was fairly modest, limited on most occasions to assisting existing communities in their attempts to relocate to more favorable sites. After the initial wave of foundation, Franciscans in Flanders and Hainaut were forced to re-evaluate the efficacy of their commitment to residences located along the outskirts of towns. Toward the middle of the thirteenth century, several communities were transferred to more spacious buildings in more accessible locations.[32] The community at Mons, established in 1228, was transferred in 1238 to a larger, central location, deemed more conducive to the pastoral activities of the friars. Jeanne, along with her second husband Thomas, funded the construction of new conventual buildings. They also granted the friars of Mons a large meadow and a chapel, located at Jonquoi. In order to secure an adequate water supply for the new community, the countess authorized the construction of a canal, which diverted water from the nearby Trouille river. Marguerite continued to support the community at Mons after Jeanne's death, funding the construction of a church and choir, and enlarging the surrounding buildings of the convent.[33]

The countesses were also instrumental in the transfer of the Franciscan community at Bruges, where friars were present as early as 1221. A permanent dwelling was constructed in 1227 on land owned by Jeanne. With the aid of Jeanne and Marguerite, the community moved to a new, more favorable site located in the city in 1246.[34] The Franciscan community at Ghent, initially located outside of the city walls in the hospice of Portaacker, acquired a new site within the city in 1226–27. The transfer is often attributed to the efforts of Jeanne and Ferrand.[35] The Franciscans at Lille, first established in 1226 by Walter de Marvis, bishop of Tournai, also changed locations when they were granted a site within the heart of the city in 1250. In conjunction with the transfer, they received a charter from Marguerite, feudal lord of the land which comprised their new location, exempting them from all taxes, tolls, and secular justice.[36]

Jeanne's esteem for Dominican ideals is clearly revealed in the support she extended to Dominican communities within Flanders and Hainaut over the course of her lifetime, support that contrasts starkly with her minimal involvement in Franciscan communities. From Paris, where a Dominican foundation was established as early as August 1218, Dominicans radiated northward, reaching Lille in 1224, Ghent in 1228, Valenciennes in 1233, and Bruges in 1234.[37] In 1228, Jeanne and Ferrand granted the Dominicans of Ghent a residence just outside the city, previously utilized as a hospital.[38] Their actions were in response to the petition of the friars, who had outgrown their current residence at Onderbergen, along the river Lys, and lacked sufficient space for expansion.[39]

Jeanne's involvement in the foundation and success of the convent of Bruges began as early as 1234, when she acted on the wishes of her recently deceased husband, Ferrand, who had expressed interest in establishing a community of Dominicans prior to his death. Jeanne assigned 300 *livres* from the testament of Ferrand for the purpose of erecting a convent for the Dominican friars in Bruges.[40] Jeanne used portions of this sum to purchase a house owned by Arnoul Voet, which she then donated to the Dominicans, exempt from all feudal rights and services. In May 1234, Jeanne ordered her bailiff of Bruges to officially transfer the house purchased from Voet to the Dominicans.[41] In July 1234, she entrusted a second residence, along with several dependencies, to Conrad, the provincial prior of Germany, on behalf of the Dominicans. This residence, also purchased from Arnoul Voet, was located "near the bridge called Oudemeulen," and it was freed from all debts, rents, services, and burdens.[42] In February 1241, Jeanne, in conjunction with her second husband Thomas of Savoy, granted the friars possession of a public path located in proximity to the convent, reportedly a source of noise and disturbances. The friars were granted permission to restrict its use to members of their community and, in 1242, Jeanne approved the decision of the Dominicans to incorporate the path into their enclosure.[43]

The Dominican convent in Valenciennes was first established in 1233, and officially affiliated to the Order in 1234. Godefroid de Fontaine, bishop of Cambrai, instigated the foundation by requesting that the General Chapter send a group of friars to the city. Four friars were dispatched from the convent in Lille in May 1233, including Jacques de Halle, confessor of the countess, Hellin de Templemart, Pierre du Quesnoy, and Nicolas l'Anglais. The friars were granted temporary residence in a house owned by Jacques de Champagne, as well as permission to erect a chapel on adjacent land, purchased by Jeanne on their behalf. Jeanne arranged for several prominent members of the clergy to arbitrate a dispute that resulted from the resistance of secular clergy to this Dominican intrusion into their community. The arbiters ordered the town of Valenciennes to cede four *bonniers* of public pasture to the chapter of Saint-Saulve, who in turn paid an annual rent of twenty *solidi* to the curé of Saint-Marie de la Chausée. In return for these concessions, the Dominicans were granted permission to build a chapel and a cemetery, to receive oblations, and to fulfill the pastoral mandate of their Order, which included the celebration of mass, preaching, administering the sacraments, and burying the dead.[44] The convent at Valenciennes was specifically mentioned in Jeanne's testament, receiving a donation of 100 *solidi* after her death.[45] Although not personally involved in the Dominican foundation at Lille, which occurred shortly before her death, Jeanne donated an ivory statue of the Virgin and several other relics to the priors, a clear gesture of her esteem. The Dominicans at Lille were also the recipients of Jeanne's sizeable library, which contained numerous hagiographies and other devotional texts.[46] After becoming countess in 1244, Marguerite became an equally avid patron of the Dominican Order, participating in the foundation of communities in Ypres and Douai and fulfillng her sister's wish to establish an abbey for women in Lille, the Abbiette.[47]

Both sisters were instrumental in the establishment of several canonical communities as well, further evidence of the diversity of their interests as patrons. Jeanne is often identified as the founder of the abbey of Zoetendale, a community affiliated to the order of Arrouaise. While the extent of her responsibility for the abbey's initial foundation remains unclear, the charter evidence reveals her role in determining the community's adherence to the rule of Saint Augustine and adoption of the customs of Arrouaise.[48] Marguerite orchestrated the establishment of an abbey at Mons affiliated with the order of Val-des-Écoliers in 1252.[49] The female branch of the order of Saint-Victor benefited considerably from the interest and attention of both countesses. The sisters acted in tandem when they founded a hospital in Quesnoy in 1233, which was later transformed into an abbey of Victorine canonesses under the guidance of Marguerite in 1261.[50] Marguerite was partially responsible for the re-foundation of the abbey of Saint-Trond. The canonesses, originally located adjacent to the Arrouasian community of Saint-Barthélemy of Eeckhout, founded near Bruges in 1149, accused the canons of that community of appropriating land and goods held jointly by both houses. Marguerite's involvement in the dispute resulted in the separation of the two communities and the relocation of the canonesses to Odegem. Under Marguerite's guidance, the canonesses formally withdrew from the order of Arrouaise and adopted the customs of the order of Saint-Victor in 1248.[51] The Victorine community of Bergues also received assistance from Marguerite, who orchestrated the transformation of the hospital of Sainte-Élisabeth into an abbey in 1248, and arranged for the transfer of the abbey, called Nieuclooster, to a more favorable location in the city.[52]

In addition to the foundation of new abbeys, acts on behalf of existing communities were also considered worthy of spiritual remuneration. In terms of donations, both countesses cast their net quite widely, directing material support to a number of different orders and a wide range of foundations. Charters that recorded such donations explicitly conveyed a sense of the donor's concern for his or her salvation. Brief and ubiquitous, scholars have in the past dismissed the *pro anima* clauses found in many charters as too conventional and formulaic in nature to reveal meaning. However, an alternative view does exist. Rather than detracting from their significance, their prevalence should reinforce the belief that all patrons, regardless of sex, status, or region, understood that the central purpose of patronage was securing prayers.[53] Furthermore, it is important to note that only charters conveying donations or transferring material wealth to a community included such phrases. In this manner, *pro anima* clauses functioned as part of an exchange, referring specifically to the prayers offered by the community in return for the patron's grant.[54]

Although not as elaborate as *arengae* or requests for prayers or anniversary masses, *pro anima* clauses nevertheless indicate that donors expected some type of compensation for their generosity. Jeanne and her husband Ferrand donated an annual rent of 5,000 eels to the abbey of Marquette in August 1228 after Ferrand's release from prison. The donation was made "...for the remedy of our souls and those of our ancestors, in pure alms."[55] Marquette also received a meadow between the abbey of Boudelo and Artevelde measuring eleven *bonniers* across "for the remedy" of the souls of Ferrand and Jeanne, and their ancestors and successors.[56] A donation made in 1228 by Jeanne and Ferrand to the canons of Zoetendale cited concern for "our souls and those of our ancestors."[57] In 1245, Marguerite donated six *bonniers* of land to the beguines of Sainte-Élisabeth in Ghent, "for the safety of our soul and the souls of our ancestors and successors."[58] The Dominicans of Ypres were granted a meadow and a portion of the garden behind the count's castle by Marguerite and her son Guy in 1268 "for the safety of their souls."[59] A donation made by Marguerite to the Abbiette in Lille was granted "for God and in alms, for the remedy of our soul and the souls of our ancestors and of our children."[60] These clauses did not appear in all documents issued on behalf of monastic and religious communities, but rather were restricted to those that conveyed something of value. Hence, their inclusion in a charter can be interpreted as a reflection of the donor's expectations that his or her generosity would elicit the goodwill of the community in question, a sentiment that would most likely be manifested in prayers on the donor's behalf.[61]

The spiritual benefits accrued from donations to monastic communities were by no means limited to the donor and his or her "ancestors and successors," but could be explicitly garnered for others as well, most often spouses, siblings, and parents, as evidenced in a number of the examples included above. According to Joel Rosenthal, the medieval patron generally ascribed to the view that the "fewer people one named, the greater the impact of the prayers," suggesting that such requests for others can be interpreted as an indication of a strong personal bond to the donor.[62] Their parents and husbands were among those most frequently mentioned by the countesses in charters. Jeanne specifically included prayer requests for her first husband Ferrand in donations on numerous occasions, both during his incarceration and after his death. In 1220, she granted possession of twenty *bonniers* to the canons of Zoetendale "for the salvation and prosperity of her lord and husband, Ferrand, count of Flanders and Hainaut, and herself and for the safety of the soul of her ancestors and successors."[63] Since Ferrand was still in prison when this donation was made, it was possible that Jeanne was particularly concerned for his spiritual well-being. In 1236, the abbey of Marquette received an annual rent of 1,200 *hodios* of oats, 463 lambs, and 108 *pensas* of cheese "for ourself and in good memory of F., once lord and our husband, count of Flanders and Hainaut."[64]

Marguerite was perhaps even more active than her sister in requesting prayers on behalf of family. In addition to requesting prayers for her second husband William of Dampierre, Marguerite frequently included Jeanne in requests that accompanied donations. In a charter issued to the Dominicans of Lille in 1245, Marguerite asked for the "secours" of their prayers for her sister, Countess Jeanne, in consideration of the goods that she had given them.[65] Marguerite requested prayers from the same community in 1249 in return for a donation of an annual rent of 50 *sous*.[66] A donation of 300 *libras*, made by the countess to the Dominicans of Bruges, was accompanied by requests for prayers from the friars for herself and for her sister.[67] In 1249, Marguerite confirmed the abbey of Ninove's possession of forty *bonniers* located at Calf, held in return for an annual rent of six *deniers*. Marguerite's confirmation was granted on the condition that the abbey celebrate the anniversary of her death and that of her mother, father, and sister.[68] Marguerite's mother figures prominently in prayer requests, including a charter issued in 1265, in which the countess ordered the bailiffs of Alost and Audenarde to defend and protect the hospital of Audenarde. Marguerite announced that her own protection had been extended to the residents of the hospital "in the memory of Marie, countess of Flanders and Hainaut, her mother."[69]

Marguerite also mentioned her sons with some frequency. In a charter issued by several leaders of the Trinitarian order in 1251, the grand master announced that, in response to letters sent by Marguerite informing them of the death of her eldest Dampierre son William the General Chapter planned to say prayers and celebrate an anniversary mass. They further agreed that every priest within the order would say two masses on William's behalf.[70] On a later occasion, Marguerite included her second eldest Dampierre son, Guy, who had become her primary heir after the death of William, in a prayer request made of the Premonstratensian abbey of Saint-Martin. In return for an annual rent of twenty *livres flandrensis*, Marguerite requested that the abbey "in full chapter" celebrate obits for her and Guy in vigil and mass "as for a canon."[71] As evidenced by the actions of the countesses, medieval patrons were aware that prayers from particularly saintly monks or nuns could not only ensure the donor a direct route to heaven, but they could also be requested on behalf of family members who had already departed, perhaps fated for an extended stay in purgatory.[72]

In order to ensure that their requests for prayers could be met by the foundation in question, willing donors like the countesses could facilitate the process by arranging for the construction of altars and ensuring the presence of chaplains to say prayers and anniversary masses by providing prebends. In 1223, Jeanne donated an annual rent of thirteen and one half *muids* of oats and two pigs to fund the construction of a chapel in the abbey of Cysoing. The countess stipulated the chapel was to be dedicated to the Virgin Mary, Saint John the Baptist, Saint John the Evangelist, Saint Nicholas, and Saint Mary Magdalene.[73] Jeanne also donated an annual rent of fifteen *livres*, fifteen *deniers* to the beguinage of Sainte-Élisabeth in Ghent, directing the chaplain of the community to say special prayers on her behalf and that of her husband.[74] In July 1232, as Lady of Dampierre, Marguerite donated a tithe at Orchies to the Cistercian abbey of Marquette, founded by her sister in 1226. The tithe was to be used to establish a chapel, in which daily prayers would be said on behalf of the Virgin Mary, Marguerite, and her husband William. Marguerite donated a second tithe to Marquette in 1245 to provide funds for a chapel, in which services were to be directed to the Virgin Mary on behalf of herself and William.[75] In 1263, Marguerite donated an annual rent of twenty-six *livres* ten *sols* to Marquette. Marguerite directed that the funds were to be used in part to support one of the abbey's chaplains to say daily masses on her behalf, as well as on the behalf of her husband William. The foundation to which Marguerite was the most attached, the abbey of Flines, was given a rent of ten *livres flandrensis* to provide a chapel in which divine services would be said daily for her soul and those of her ancestors.[76] Similarly, the abbey of Épinlieu received an annual rent of thirteen *livres* from Jeanne and Ferrand to provide for a chaplain, who was expected to perform divine services on their behalf.[77]

In addition to anniversary masses, the countesses also arranged for pittances to be distributed to monks or nuns of a particular community to commemorate their death or that of a loved one. In 1252, Marguerite dismissed a rent of four *livres* owed on four *bonniers* of meadow, land originally donated to the abbey of Salzinnes by her sister Jeanne. Instead of continuing to receive this payment herself, Marguerite assigned the sum to be used for a pittance to be distributed to the nuns on the anniversary of her death.[78] Of the seven rents Marguerite donated to the abbey of Marquette, three were intended to fund pittances for herself and her husband, William of Dampierre. In addition to those donations, Marguerite left the abbey 120 *livres* in her will to provide a pittance on the anniversary of her death.[79] Jeanne and her second husband Thomas also arranged for a pittance at the abbey of Marquette, granting 500 *bonniers* of marsh, and demanding that eight casks of wine be distributed to the nuns each year on their behalf.[80] In an especially detailed request, Marguerite remitted an annual rent of eight *livres* fourteen *solidi* nine *denaris flandrensis* owed to her by the nuns of the abbey of Bijloke. In return, she requested that the sum be used for a pittance of wine and fish worth 100 *solidi* to be distributed to the nuns and a second pittance of seventy-four *solidi* nine *denaris* to be given to the women of the hospital under the direction of the abbey.[81] Such actions would have served as a tangible reminder of the generosity of the countesses, drawing the attention of the entire community to their most avid patrons with some frequency for decades after the donation had been made.

Considering the range of options available to interested patrons in the thirteenth century, the decisions made by the countesses in determining which orders or individual foundations to support must be analyzed as the product of deliberate decision making. Examination indicates that while Jeanne and Marguerite's patronage was in many ways consistent with larger patterns discernible for thirteenth-century Europe generally, concerns unique to the countesses were also evident. The remainder of this chapter will attempt to illuminate such concerns, providing an opportunity to assess the spiritual considerations that informed patronage generally as well as the strategies employed by the countesses in particular to secure their own spiritual futures.

When the spiritual welfare of the countesses was in question, they looked to Cistercian foundations. Jeanne and Marguerite were much more likely to include requests for prayers, anniversary masses, and pittances in donations granted to Cistercian foundations than to those affiliated to any other order. This tendency is not surprising considering the prominence of the Cistercians in the religious landscape of Europe during this period.[82] By the thirteenth century, the Cistercians had clearly replaced the Cluniacs as the embodiment of the monastic ideal in medieval Europe, as evidenced by the stunning growth of the Order and the extensive fame of its most powerful member, Bernard of Clairvaux. Their emphasis upon reform, combined with their austerity and asceticism, earned the admiration of patrons, which fueled the unparalleled popularity of the Order. Cistercian dedication and devotion were interpreted by patrons as a manifestation of holiness, and who better to intercede with Jesus Christ than the monk or nun who most effectively emulated him?[83] As a result of Europe's esteem for their ideals and practices, Cistercian communities during this period were particularly recognized for the efficacy of their prayers and their ability to intercede with God.

That Jeanne and Marguerite shared Europe's faith in the efficacy of Cistercian prayers is evidenced by their actions on behalf of Cistercian communities generally. In addition to the extensive support directed toward individual communities, both sisters expressed a desire to secure prayers from these pious monks and nuns. Jeanne petitioned the abbey of Clairvaux directly, requesting that the monks celebrate annual masses for her and her husband Thomas of Savoy.[84] Jeanne also petitioned the General Chapter of the Cistercian Order for prayers to be said on her behalf by all Cistercian communities located in Flanders and Hainaut. In 1234, Jeanne wrote again, requesting prayers for her deceased husband Ferrand as well as for Marguerite's late husband, William of Dampierre. After Marguerite succeeded Jeanne, she herself requested prayers on behalf of her late sister, herself, and William of Dampierre.[85] One wonders if the they considered such prayers a privilege of their position as countess.

While Jeanne and Marguerite's preference for Cistercian abbeys is not surprising considering the preferences of patrons generally in this period, their propensity to direct more support to houses of Cistercian women than houses of Cistercian men is rather striking and unusual. Twenty-eight houses for female Cistercians were founded during the period generally associated with the expansion of the female branch of the order, which began around 1200, and accelerated between 1215 and 1217.[86] Extant documents indicate that Jeanne and Marguerite gave some type of support to at least nineteen of these communities during the course of their lives. Quantification of donations and the prayer requests that accompanied them reveals that Jeanne and Marguerite exhibited a particular preference for the prayers of Cistercian women not typical of patrons during this period, who normally favored male foundations in requests for prayers. Of the 241 donations made by the countesses to religious communities in their domains, 141 were directed toward Cistercian foundations. While Cistercian men received a total of twenty-seven donations from the countesses, Cistercian women's houses received 114. Of the charters issued to female foundations, eighty-four or 24.6 percent contained references to prayers, anniversary masses, pittances, or other special services, as compared to the sixteen or 13.3 percent for male foundations.[87] The countesses expressly arranged for pittances for Cistercian nuns on five occasions, requested anniversary masses from at least five different houses, and established chapels and provided funds for chaplains in the abbeys of Flines, Marquette, Épinlieu, and Ravensberg.[88] The countesses arranged for only one pittance for Cistercian monks, and they specifically requested masses from men's houses on only three occasions.[89] Marguerite's will, included in the cartulary of the abbey of Flines, perhaps best illustrates this preference. Donations were specifically made to a variety of Cistercian foundations "to buy a rent to provide a pittance for the convent on the day of my death." However, while leaving a total of 330 *livres* 100 *solidi* to Cistercian foundations for men, Marguerite left 740 *livres* to Cistercian foundations for women.[90]

Scholars have argued that the twelfth-century trend toward ordination for monks allowed men's houses to attract more patrons, since the presence of dozens of men capable of performing mass maximized the total number of masses that could be said by a community on behalf of patrons. Conversely, the prohibition against ordaining women by definition limited the number of masses women's houses could offer potential patrons, hence limiting their appeal to patrons.[91] However, such generalizations are challenged by the evidence available for Flanders and Hainaut. In fact, it is possible that the countesses, in personally funding the construction of altars in women's houses and supplying the stipends necessary for chaplains, were able to avoid the limitations in terms of number of masses said that other patrons may have experienced, allowing them to support the communities they personally preferred without forgoing the promise of prayers.[92]

Furthermore, Jeanne and Marguerite were not alone in looking to women's foundations for spiritual remuneration. In fact, during the thirteenth century, numerous women in similar positions of power shared their affinity for the Cistercians and can be identified as acting on behalf of the Order, initiating and endowing numerous foundations. Marguerite's own daughter-in-law, Beatrice of Courtrai, founded the abbey of Groeninghe in 1237, which benefited significantly from her extensive patronage.[93] Perhaps the most famous of these patrons was Blanche of Castile, who as queen regent of France, mobilized resources and revenues on behalf of Maubuisson and Notre-Dame-les-Lys. Isabelle, countess of Chartes, followed the tradition established by her cousin Blanche, founding two houses for Cistercian nuns in the 1220s, Lieu-Notre-Dame-lèz-Romorantin and Eau-lès-Chartres.[94] In England, Isabel, countess of Arundel, founded the abbey of Marham in Norfolk, and provided eleven individual grants that constituted the abbey's endowment.[95] Like Jeanne and Marguerite, Isabel also spent her last days in the convent that she had founded, requesting and receiving permission to be buried within the walls of the abbey. It is quite probable that further exploration of regions outside of England and northern France would multiply these examples, suggesting a need to reassess our understanding of the position of Cistercian nuns in both the secular and spiritual landscape of the thirteenth century. It seems quite possible that the prayers of these women were valued more than scholars have previously indicated and that such communities, in attracting wealthy patrons as a result of the perceived efficacy of such prayers, were more prosperous than prior studies have suggested.

The existence of such an affinity between powerful women and Cistercian nuns is testimony to the particular appeal exerted by the Order generally. Of all the monastic and religious orders that existed during this period, the Cistercians seemed to emphasize a spirituality that appealed particularly to powerful, secular women like Jeanne and Marguerite.[96] By this time, the teachings of the charismatic Bernard and other early, influential Cistercian writers had served as an inspiration for a group of female saints, all centered around the Low Countries. Such women as Ida of Nivelles, Juliana of Cornillion, Alice of Schaerbeek, and Beatrice of Nazareth lived and wrote in Cistercian communities during this second wave of Cistercian expansion of the early thirteenth century.[97] Their reputations for sanctity and holiness were noted by such figures as Jacques de Vitry, who brought them to the attention of some of the most powerful figures in western Europe, including the pope. In their daily lives, these women seemed to epitomize the Cistercian ideals of simplicity, charity, and union with the divine.

The countesses of Flanders and Hainaut were undoubtedly exposed to the existence and experiences of these female visionaries and their works.[98] It is more than plausible that they had access to the writings produced by these women, who attempted to reconcile the traditional monastic preoccupation with the contemplative life and chastity with a new emphasis on the active way.[99] The *vita* of Beatrice of Nazareth presents a way of life and mode of conduct based upon the belief that "perfection is attainment of the virtues, completed by charity."[100] Alice of Schaerbeek also emphasized the connection between salvation and the active way, expressing the conviction that her outward labors prepared her for eventual proximity to God. According to her biographer, it was precisely her charity, comportment, and concern with the needs of others that qualified her for God's favor and union with Christ.[101] Although chastity remained important for women, these writers emphasized the exterior manifestation of internal chastity in overt acts of charity and good works toward the less fortunate; this was behavior that individuals in secular positions like Jeanne and Marguerite not only could admire, but could emulate as well in directing patronage to Cistercian foundations.[102]

However, an added attraction of Cistercian nuns may have been the opportunities they offered female patrons in terms of forming personal connections to the communities they patronized. Jeanne and Marguerite would have occupied a particularly elevated position as founders of an abbey. The prerogatives they would have enjoyed would allow them to develop an intimate relationship with the members of the community, particularly if those members were also women.[103] The decision to retire to Cistercian nunneries toward the end of their lives reveals their attraction to the spiritual climate and connection that accompanied membership in a Cistercian community. Perhaps the countesses viewed the support of religious women as an opportunity to vicariously fulfill their own spiritual aspirations. Although they personally were unable to commit to a life dedicated to the contemplation of God or the service of the poor, they could create communities in which other women could realize similar ambitions. Their desire to participate in this type of religious life is demonstrated by the construction of personal residences in Cistercian communities, facilitating their ability to periodically seek refuge in the solace and security of the cloister.

A spiritual message that emphasized charity and obedience was ideally suited to powerful women who, because of the demands of family and politics, were unable to pursue a life of chastity, humility, and seclusion. As hereditary rulers of a wealthy principality such as Flanders and Hainaut, Jeanne and Marguerite were denied the avenues of spirituality available to other medieval women who could renounce the material world and seek peace and prayer in monastic communities. Their involvement in the material world of politics and economics was unavoidable. In addition, as women, the burden of procreation fell upon the shoulders of Jeanne and Marguerite, who would be expected to secure the future of the principality by providing heirs. Obviously, in light of these obligations, even such alternatives to the cloister as personal chastity and spiritual marriage would not have been considered viable options.

Perhaps the most telling example of the frustrations encountered by female rulers attempting to realize their spiritual ambitions is revealed in an anecdote related by Régine Pernoud regarding Blanche of Castile. When she expressed her desire to emulate the actions of John of Brienne, king of Jerusalem, who had recently journeyed to the grave of the Apostle James at Compostela, Blanche was chastised by Bishop William, her confessor. William offered Blanche a more suitable destination for her pilgrimage: "Take up your pilgrim's staff and bowl and go to Saint James-I mean to the Friars' convent here in Paris. Pay them their debt..."[104] While recent studies have suggested that women were more prominent among pilgrim bands than previously expected, such participation would have been difficult for the countesses since it mandated prolonged absence from the administration of the county.[105] Male rulers were able to take advantage of such opportunities as pilgrimage and crusade to further their spiritual aspirations and secure their salvations because they had capable wives who remained behind and assumed their secular responsibilities in their stead. Secular female rulers like Jeanne and Marguerite had no such luxury.

In contrast, the foundation and patronage of religious communities offered a viable spiritual alternative for women such as Jeanne and Marguerite, who could realize their religious ambitions vicariously through the actions of others. Although they themselves were unable to renounce the material world and devote themselves to the contemplation of God, they could use their power and wealth to help those who were in a position to enter monastic communities. Permanent withdrawal to the cloister was never an option for these women, whose political positions prevented them from seeking this ultimate path to salvation. Instead, they sought spiritual solace in supporting and protecting the women who could become nuns by creating and securing religious havens for them.

In part, Jeanne and Marguerite's affinity for Cistercian nuns can be explained as a part of a wider tendency to support communities of women more generally. As discussed earlier, the countesses were also extremely active on behalf of beguine and Victorine communities in their domains, providing donations of land and rents and administrative support in crucial moments. Their propensity in supporting beguines and Victorine canonesses was a result of interest in the *vita apostolica* generally, but also the manifestation of an affinity felt for members of their own sex. The evidence presented here certainly demonstrates that Jeanne and Marguerite personally influenced the individual experience of hundreds of women by providing them with the option of membership in a religious community. The marked tendency of Jeanne and Marguerite to direct donations to women certainly reflects the countesses' esteem for their prayers. However, it also suggests that the two sisters were sensitive to the religious ambitions of other women, and they made a concentrated attempt to facilitate the realization of these ambitions.

The interplay of these two preferences (women and the *vita apostolica*) is perhaps most effectively illustrated in their patronage of beguines, discussed above, and canonesses affiliated to the order of Saint-Victor. The ideals associated with the *vita apostolica* were clearly embraced by the Victorines, women who translated the ideal of service into the practice of providing for the poor. Nearly all the Victorine abbeys in Flanders and Hainaut were associated with charitable functions, particularly nursing and providing care and shelter for the impoverished and infirm. Similar to the beguines, these houses offered women the advantages of communal religious life without the confinement and restriction associated with the formal monastic cloister of the Benedictines and the Cistercians. Many of these communities originated as hospitals, and the canonesses continued to manage infirmaries after their elevation to abbatial status. Of the eight Victorine communities established in the counties of

Flanders and Hainaut during the thirteenth century, Jeanne and Marguerite were involved in the foundation of four, including Quesnoy, Beaulieu, Saint-Trond, and Bergues, and they promoted at least two others, making key donations to Bethleem and Waasmunster.

However, their support of communities associated with the ideals and practices of the *vita apostolica* was not limited to members of their own sex, as evidenced by the earlier discussion of their patronage of mendicant communities. Unlike the cloistered monks of the past, these new friars were visible members of society, adhering to the austerity and poverty of monastics while performing many of the functions of the local clergy. By adding a strong commitment to evangelical activity to the reform program of their twelfth-century predecessors, the friars intended to imitate the life of Christ and his apostles as completely as possible, aspiring to new levels of austerity and absolute freedom from the material trappings of the secular world.[106] By the end of the thirteenth century, the friars, like the Benedictines and Cistercians before them, had successfully parlayed their spiritual appeal into political and intellectual authority, becoming principle members of ecclesiastical administrations and key participants in the development of theology by their prominence in the universities of Europe. As a result of all these factors, the beliefs and practices advanced by the mendicant orders proved to be particularly suited to the highly urbanized, densely populated counties of Flanders and Hainaut, and it attracted the attention of their countess accordingly.

Examination of their patronage reveals the various ways their interest in the *vita apostolica* was translated materially into support for mendicant communities. Due in no small part to the efforts of its countesses, by the end of the thirteenth century, every major town in Flanders and Hainaut supported a Dominican convent. Jeanne and Marguerite were instrumental in the foundation of almost every one of these communities, providing the property and the political clout necessary for the establishment of new communities in an increasingly crowded and competitive spiritual market. Their preference for Dominicans was a function of their respect for the ideals and practices of these individuals, who immediately earned a reputation for extreme asceticism, austerity, and devotion to Christ. According to Lester Little, unlike the silent, stoic Benedictines, the gregarious mendicants appealed to a specific desire among the newly emerged urban elements of the laity that "fostered a need for a spirituality that would express itself in speech."[107] Their patronage indicated that the countesses were as susceptible as their contemporaries to Dominican emphasis on interaction with the community, preaching and pastoral services.

While the Cistercians attracted the attention of the countesses as a result of their reputation for piety and the perceived efficaciousness of their prayers, the mendicants' appeal, like that of the beguines and Victorines, was in part due to the countesses' understanding of the spiritual responsibilities that accompanied their office. The countesses, like many of their contemporaries, clearly responded to new currents in medieval spiritual life, preferring to direct patronage to communities that advocated an active, rather than isolated and contemplative, interpretation of the monastic ideal. Such orders must have impressed the countesses as particularly suited to their domains and especially conducive to fostering an ideal spiritual climate among the people of Flanders and Hainaut.

It seems clear that the ideals and practices of the Dominican friars appealed to the religious sensibilities of the countesses, who were attracted by their dual commitment to poverty and preaching. Unlike the Franciscans, whose regulations concerning ownership of property conflicted with the needs of their patrons, the Dominican constitution did not restrict possession of churches, priories, and the property on which these structures were built.[108] Although Dominicans were not able to accept donations of rents, tithes, or alms, they did offer patrons the opportunity of providing land and conventual buildings.[109] While all mendicants advocated an active interpretation of the *vita apostolica* that the countesses clearly found appealing and suited to their intensely urbanized domains, the Dominicans tended to privilege preaching over poverty, resulting in a religious order that was much more receptive to patronage as it was traditionally understood by medieval patrons.[110] Dominic clearly shared Francis's commitment to poverty and austerity, but he subordinated this ideal to that of preaching, which he deliberately placed at the forefront of his apostolate.[111] While he adopted many of the liturgical practices of the canons of Prémontré, he specifically granted his followers dispensations from any activity which interfered with their evangelism and the preparation necessary for it. By including such stipulations in his constitutions, Dominic clearly attempted to eliminate distractions before they became problematic, thus allowing the friars to dedicate their time to study and preaching.[112] Comital preference for Dominican communities reflects their tendency to privilege such concerns in directing patronage to new foundations. Clearly, in the view of the countesses of Flanders and Hainaut, the Dominicans, rather than the Franciscans, had more successfully translated the apostolic ideal into practice.

The countesses' promotion of communities like the Dominicans, beguines, and Victorines, communities that provided pastoral care for the laity, was a manifestation of the new spiritual trends that pervaded thirteenth-century society and transformed the approach to salvation. While the countesses still believed in the effectiveness of prayers and masses said on their behalf by monks and nuns, as evidenced by their support of the Cistercians, they also ascribed to a belief in the potential of individuals to secure their own salvation through meritorious acts, charity, and good deeds. For the countesses, the foundation of a community like the Victorines or beguines implied that their single act of charity, as represented by the foundation, was multiplied hundreds of times over in the charity dispensed by the women who inhabited the new community.

In light of their two obvious preferences in terms of directing their patronage (women's houses and foundations that adopted the practices associated with the *vita apostolica*), the relative indifference of the countesses to mendicant foundations for women is, at first glance, surprising. However, close examination of disparities between the way of life defined by the apostolic ideal generally and that dictated for these women by the male members of their orders provides a possible explanation for the relative indifference of the countesses to Franciscan or Dominican women. Their communities were subject to restrictions that seriously compromised their ability to minister to the poor and sick, challenging their ability to fulfill the mandate of the *vita apostolica*. The relative indifference of both countesses to mendicant women resulted in a dearth of foundations within their domains. The Poor Clares, or Clarisses, were significantly less prominent than their male counterparts in the spiritual landscape of Flanders and Hainaut.[113] In fact, during the thirteenth century, only two foundations associated with the Second Order of Franciscans were established in Flanders, Bruges in 1255–56, and Ypres, or Langemark, in 1256.[114] The countesses' interaction with both of these communities was limited to a donation of five *bonniers* of meadow made by Marguerite to the convent of Bruges in 1266[115] and two confirmations issued by Marguerite to Langemark in 1269 and 1273.[116] From 1204 to 1280, the Abbiette in Lille was the only foundation for Dominican women established in the counties of Flanders and Hainaut.[117]

The explanation for this relative neglect may lie in the position of mendicant women vis-à-vis the men in their respective orders. While mendicant men emphasized freedom from the constraints of the cloister, active involvement in the community, and poverty, most mendicant women were subjected to the same rigid rules regarding claustration that affected women in traditional, monastic communities. Activities such as preaching, interacting with the community, and begging, which earned the mendicants the respect and support of so many thirteenth-century patrons, were considered inappropriate for members of the female sex. In terms of actual practice, mendicant women hardly resembled their male counterparts and consequently would not have appealed to the same impulses in patrons.

Although few Dominican or Franciscan foundations for women were established in Flanders and Hainaut during the rule of Jeanne and Marguerite, the mendicant ideals of the *vita apostolica*, poverty, and ministrations to the poor clearly influenced the lifestyle developed by other religious orders that included women, particularly the beguines and Victorine canonesses. In many ways, the beguines served as the female counterpart to the mendicants in the counties of Flanders and Hainaut. These women were never subject to the strict laws regarding enclosure that applied to nuns, confining them to the monastery and prohibiting contact with the outside world. Rather, they were expected to interact with the secular community that surrounded their enclosures, engaging in manual labor, nursing, and various charitable activities. While the order of Saint-Victor lacked a strong central authority, thus allowing women's houses to affiliate without resistance, there was no male element in beguine life to curb the activities of these women. As discussed in chapter 3, Marguerite personally promulgated the statutes of many beguine communities in Flanders and Hainaut, allowing her considerable control over the regulation of their activities and formulating a daily regime that permitted extensive interaction with the laity. Clearly, the countesses' tendency to promote religious communities that embraced the ideals and practices associated with the *vita apostolica* was an element of their patronage that transcended gender boundaries. Their preference for communities that encouraged active involvement rather than contemplation was not sex-specific but applied to men and women alike.

Ultimately, this consideration of the religious patronage of Jeanne and Marguerite demonstrates the extent to which their position as countesses allowed them to translate secular power into spiritual power, that is, salvation. Although their personal preferences suggest that they were fairly typical as patrons in the thirteenth century, the extent of their patronage and the range of their activities on behalf of preferred communities are perhaps unusual. Clearly, both women were able to access their considerable material wealth without restriction, which they dispersed generously among various communities. Their repeated appeals to spiritual leaders as well as frequent interventions in local disputes on behalf of new communities demonstrate their recognition of the authority at their command and their ability to use their position to their advantage.

In part, Jeanne and Marguerite were willing to grant enormous sums of money and donate vast amounts of land to religious communities because, as countesses of an extremely wealthy principality, they could. The extensive financial resources of Flanders and Hainaut were at their disposal. It can hardly be considered a coincidence that these two particular women, whose lives were characterized by repeated personal loss, extended power struggles, and devastating interfamilial warfare expended so much time, energy, and financial resources on religious patronage. Perhaps their need to purchase so many prayers was prompted by remorse for actions on earth, actions that were guaranteed to cause eternal repercussions. Although a certain percentage of their interest was altruistic, their almost obsessive concern with their salvations was due to apprehension of the future. Like most medieval patrons, the countesses' generosity was prompted in part by genuine religious fervor, and in part by fear of what awaited them in death.

If donations to religious communities can be interpreted as investments in a spiritual future, examination of their patronage indicates that the countesses of Flanders and Hainaut were rather savvy investors. The comparative study of their actions employed here demonstrates that both Jeanne and Marguerite directed donations toward communities deemed most pious by their contemporaries and therefore considered capable of providing a maximum return on their investments. This examination of religious patronage and the motives that often precipitated it has provided a rare and fleeting glimpse into the minds of Jeanne and Marguerite of Constantinople, two particularly powerful, yet rather elusive, personalities in history. When one considers the range of motives most aptly characterized as spiritual, their understanding of the purpose of patronage emerges in clear relief.

CONCLUSION

In December 1244, Jeanne fell ill. She sought refuge at the abbey of Marquette, by far her favored foundation. Whether or not she was aware that her illness was to be fatal, the countess clearly viewed Marquette as a haven. Just prior to her death on December 5, Jeanne took vows. She was buried in the cemetery of this community to which she had clearly formed a very personal attachment, alongside her daughter Marie and husband Ferrand. In a similar fashion, Marguerite passed her final days at the abbey of Flines. Marguerite's attachment to Flines was at least as strong at Jeanne's to Marquette. Marguerite had previously arranged for the construction of a house within the abbey's walls, to which she retired in 1278 following her abdication as countess of Flanders in favor of her eldest son, Guy. Marguerite died in 1280 at the age of seventy-eight. She was buried in the center of the abbey's church, positioned at the very heart of the building for which she was primarily responsible, surrounded by the various altars and chapels she had previously commissioned.

While, in terms of religious patronage, the legacy of Jeanne and Marguerite cannot be disputed, enduring in the most visible way in the buildings they provided and the vocations they funded, their actions in some respects are open to interpretation. Clearly, like the vast majority of their contemporaries, Jeanne and Marguerite were concerned with the afterlife. They attempted to use the resources at their disposal to ensure a warm reception in heaven, for themselves as well as for members of their immediate family. Their actions reflect their conviction that such a reception could best be secured by prayers on their behalf and charity dispensed in their name. They chose orders and individual foundations as recipients of their patronage accordingly. However, as discussed in chapter 3, their actions had repercussions that cannot accurately be categorized solely as spiritual. Such practical outcomes were equally valuable to individuals, particularly those who occupied rather precarious positions, like the countesses of Flanders and Hainaut. For Jeanne and Marguerite, religious patronage was in many ways an obligation, a divine mandate stemming from the power entrusted to them by God. As rulers, they were expected to attend to the spiritual well-being of those who inhabited their domains. However, religious patronage was simultaneously a vehicle to further their own political agenda and bolster their ability to wield power.

The experience of Jeanne and Marguerite demonstrates that, in spite of assumptions about male dominance and the marginalization of women post-1000, female rulers were not only present in thirteenth-century society but continued to wield considerable power. However, without examining the social fabric from which these women emerged and the circumstances that precipitated their exercise of power, it is not possible to truly understand how the political functioned in the Middle Ages. Dismissing female rulers like Jeanne and Marguerite as isolated incidences of social dysfunction, anomalies produced by a rupture in the accepted political system, fails to further our understanding of the political and social conditions of power in the thirteenth century.[1] In spite of the emergence of aristocratic family strategies, which emphasized preserving the integrity of the patrimony and resulted in the entrenchment of primogeniture as the primary method of inheritance, women were not unilaterally excluded from access to authority. Although admittedly the outcome of such policies was to restrict the number of offspring eligible to inherit, including women, in the absence of men, the position of female heirs was actually strengthened. Rather than witness the devolution of the patrimony to a male from a lesser branch of the family, the eldest female was designated as the legitimate heir, becoming the repository of feudal authority. The presence of women inheriting fiefs accompanied by considerable authority in the twelfth and thirteenth centuries challenges assumptions about the increasing marginalization of women in the thirteenth century and their restriction to the periphery of politics. The number of women occupying positions similar to that of the countesses suggests the need to reconsider current notions about the position of noblewomen in medieval society and the mechanisms in that society that influenced their experience. In inheriting the counties of Flanders and Hainaut, the countesses inherited the right to act in a very public and political capacity, functioning as administrators, judges, and economic agents. They made laws, dictated foreign policy, regulated trade, defended religious institutions, and negotiated liberties for towns.

Evidence of their ability to exercise power in both the public and the private sphere have significant implications for our understanding of the public/private in the thirteenth century. The public/private model, as it was first conceptualized by scholars, relies upon the basic premise that public space is male space, and that public space is the primary locus of power in all societies. The association of women with private, or domestic, space resulted in a devaluation of their activities. However, employing the public/private model constructed in this fashion by definition divides space in the medieval world along a male/female axis without considering the influence of social stratification or examining the role of gender itself in this society. This approach assumes a uniform gender-based allocation of power at all levels of society, which is not necessarily reflected in the reality of the medieval world, particularly at the upper echelons of power. In other words, the imposition of the public/private model in this manner creates a rigid dichotomy that divides space without accounting for the peculiar nature of feudal, premodern society, where status often superceded gender in terms of opportunity and access to public power, and the boundary between the personal and the political remained extremely fluid in spite of recent changes to inheritance practices and modes of governing.²

However, in revising our understanding of the position of women in medieval society, this study is not suggesting a dramatic reversal of all current notions about women in the Middle Ages. Clearly they were most frequently positioned as subordinate to men in the political arena. This study does hope to demonstrate the complexities of the relationship between women and men, and between women and power, during this period. When combined with other recent, similarly focused studies, it emphasizes the need for a more complicated analysis of those relationships than currently available. The absence of a uniform experience for women during this period and the recognition of the diversity of opinions that influenced women's position encourage scholars to question continued attempts to impose the rigid, homogenizing model of public/private spheres upon medieval society. The norm of male dominance does not by any means preclude the presence of dissenting opinions or the possibility of female power. Appreciating the complexities of medieval society requires a recognition of the diversity of opinions that influenced individual experience.³ Such an appreciation is best achieved without reliance upon a model predicated upon a modern understanding of the division of space, labor, and sex in society.

Even if a public/private division of space may apply to most of medieval society, the example of women like the countesses demonstrates its inapplicability to the highest echelon, the nobility. In this stratum of society, the public and the private continued to overlap, creating a unique space that could be occupied simultaneously by members of both sexes. According to Kimberly LoPrete, "...modern scholars who take such pains to differentiate the fundamentally 'private' powers of the medieval lords from the truly 'public' powers of the authorized regents of modern states and then deny medieval women the exercise of acknowledged authoritative powers are blinded by their own dichotomies."⁴ This notion of separate spheres has implications for men as well as women by mitigating restrictions placed on members of each sex according to gender ideals and norms. Both men and women continued to derive authority from the family, since one's social status was the primary determinant of one's ability to access authority. Even in thirteenth-century France, after the emergence of a salaried bureaucracy and the augmentation of royal power, authority continued to remain in the hands of families, and land was associated with feudal offices. As long as offices were inherited, rather than appointed, public and private space remained synonymous at times.[5] The nature of public office may have been changing, and the royal curia dominated by salaried officials. However, the most powerful vassals in the realm still claimed their office as a result of familial ties, and they maintained it through a personal oath of homage sworn to the king.

However, while women's access to authority was seldom hindered by their sex, and they were often able to wield power, these women were not immune from prevailing notions of gender. In the Middle Ages, just like today, notions of gender were predicated upon a biological understanding of men and women and the perceptions of difference that resulted. However, as a cultural construct, notions of gender obviously vary over time, and across space. Any analysis of gender must incorporate the peculiar features of a society. As recent studies have very successfully demonstrated, it is impossible to impose a monolithic view of gender upon the Middle Ages.[6] Such studies demonstrate the need to account for the full range of factors that may have influenced a particular group's understanding of what it meant to be masculine or feminine, and how such an understanding would have translated into activities deemed appropriate for men and women. Not all women in medieval society shared similar experiences. In this particular study, the importance of status has proved to be a crucial determinant of the countesses' position, suggesting that their experience would have been radically different from women in other strata of society. When addressing the period in question here, any analysis must account for the extremely rigid social stratification of the Middle Ages when attempting to understand the influence of gender on one's relationship to power. Adopting a monolithic view of "woman" which does not take into account the importance of status in the medieval period will result in an inaccurate understanding of the position of many women. Just as the meaning and experience of "woman" differs among races and classes in the modern world, the meaning and experience of "woman" differed among social categories in the medieval world. This sentiment is conveyed by Carol Clover, who poses the question "was femaleness any more decisive in setting parameters on individual behavior than were wealth, prestige, marital status or just plain personality and ambition?"[7]

However, in spite of this divergence in experience among women in such a socially stratified society, it is important to acknowledge the presence of certain commonalities that would have transcended social status. There are some commonalities that seem to transcend social groups in influencing individual actions and experiences for men and women. For example, no matter what their social status, women were generally associated more directly than men with reproduction and child rearing. Even powerful women like the countesses would still be regarded as women, and consequently subject on occasion to polemical diatribes about the inherent weaknesses of their sex. Such views could manifest themselves as challenges to their ability to exercise power, or in obstacles encountered in their attempt to impose their will on others. In spite of the very overt demonstrations of their personal authority and the power they wielded in the office of countess discussed in previous chapters, the experience of Jeanne and Marguerite does suggest that their actions were on occasion circumscribed by notions of gender. On several occasions, their authority was challenged or obstacles were encountered that seemed to stem directly from perceptions about the limitations placed upon them because they were female.

It is quite possible that the two examples presented here of women who had access to considerable authority and were provided with the opportunity to wield power reflects a particular moment within the wider trajectory of the development of medieval political systems. In this moment, before the full impact of the shifts discussed earlier in family strategy, governing systems, and increasing bureaucratization were felt, a window may have existed which allowed female rule. Since the discussion here does not consider the period after the thirteenth century, and is almost exclusively concerned with northern France, larger questions about the experience of women more generally remain, and require additional examination. Ultimately, this study advocates the development of an interpretative model for medieval women which incorporates the unique features of feudal society in the Middle Ages and accounts for a range of factors that may have been constitutive of individual experience. The importance of family strategy and the centrality of status in determining one's ability to wield power, whether male or female, need to be incorporated into any analysis of medieval governance. Furthermore, any attempt to understand the experience of women in the Middle Ages must position them at the center of a matrix comprised of gender, social status, marital status, age and personality. In a society stratified sexually as well as socially, a myriad of combinations of gender and status existed to inform attitudes toward women, and influenced their relationship to power. Interpretive models that take such considerations into account avoid the difficulties which result from the identification of a woman who fails to conform to modern expectations about medieval norms, a difficulty that historians seem to be encountering with some frequency of late. Only additional investigation into the lives of women and their personal relationship to authority and power will provide the evidence needed to appreciate the diversity of experience that existed in the Middle Ages, and the range of opportunities open to individuals, hence broadening our appreciation of how power and political action were understood.

APPENDIX 1: MONASTIC AND RELIGIOUS FOUNDATIONS IN THIRTEENTH-CENTURY FLANDERS AND HAINAUT

Affiliation: Arrouaise

Name	Date of Foundation	Men/Women
Eeckhout	c. 1060/1146 Arrouaise	Men
Choques	1120/1138 Arrouaise	Men
Cysoing	855/1132 Arrouaise	Men
Phalempin	1039/1145 Arrouaise	Men
Saint-Jean Baptiste	c. 680/1142 Arrouaise	Men
Saint-Nicolas des Près	1125/1140 Arrouaise	Men
Warneton	1066/1142 Arrouaise	Men
Zoetendale	1162/1215 re-founded	Men
Zonnebeke	1072/1142 Arrouaise	Men

Affiliation: Augustinian Canons

Name	Date of Foundation	Men/Women
Saint-Aubert	963/1066 reformed	Men
Saint-Marie, Voormezele	1069/1110 reformed	Men
Saint-Martin, Ypres	1012/1102 reformed	Men
Saint-Pierre de Loo	c. 1050/1093 reformed	Men
Saint-Pierre et Saint-Vaast	c. 1091	Men

Affiliation: Beguines

Name	Date of Foundation	Men/Women
Aardenburg	1249	Women
Audenarde	1272	Women
Bardonck, Ypres	1271/1273	Women
Bergues	1259	Women

Binche	1248	Women
Briel, Ypres	1240	Women
Cambrai	1233	Women
Champfleury, Douai	1251	Women
Damme	1259	Women
Deinze	1273	Women
Diksmuide	1273	Women
Ijzendijke	1276	Women
Maubeuge	1273	Women
Cantimpré, Mons	1245	Women
Orchies	1267	Women
Portaaker (Ghent)	1273	Women
Quesnoy	1246	Women
Saint-Aubert (Bruges)	1270	Women
Sainte-Élisabeth (Courtrai)	1242	Women
Sainte-Élisabeth (Ghent)	1234	Women
Sainte-Élisabeth (Lille)	1244/1245	Women
Sainte-Élisabeth (Valenciennes)	1239	Women
Ter Hooie (Ghent)	1262	Women
Tournai	1241	Women
Wetz (Douai)	1245	Women
Wijngaard (Bruges)	1242	Women

Affiliation: Benedictine

Name	Date of Foundation	Men/Women
Anchin	1079	Men
Notre-Dame d'Avesnes	1028	Women
Bergues Saint-Winoc	1028	Men
Bourbourg	c. 1099	Women
Notre-Dame de Condé	c. 630	Women
Ghislenghien	1126	Women
Ghistelles	c. 1090	Women
Hasnon	c. 670	Double to 1065
Hautmont	649	Men
Liesses	751	Men
Marchiennes	c. 647	Double to 1028
Notre-Dame de Merkem	1090	Women
Notre-Dame de Messines	1060	Women
Nonnenbossche	1101	Women
Oudenbourg	c. 1083	Men
Saint-Adrian Grammont	733	Men

Saint-Amand les Eaux	c. 639	Men
Saint-André-les-Bruges	1098	Men
Saint-André-du-Cateau	c. 1030	Men
Saint-Bavon	c. 639	Men
Saint-Bertin	c. 847	Men
Saint-Denis-en-Broqueroye	1081	Men
Saint-Ghislain	c. 681	Men
Saint-Jean-au-Mont	1080	Men
Saint-Martin	c. 652	Men
Saint-Pierre à Dickelvenne	734	Men
Saint-Pierre de Lobbes	654/691	Men
Saint-Pierre au Mont Blandin	c. 650	Men
Saint-Sauveur à Eename	1064	Men
Saint-Saulve	c. 850	Men
Saint-Sepulcre	1064	Men
Saint-Waudru	c. 686	Women

Affiliation: Cistercian

Name	Date of Foundation	Men/Women
Aulne	868/1147 incorporation	Men
Boudelo	1225/1245	Men
Beaupré, Grimminge	1228	Women
Beaupré-sur-la-Lys	1220/1224 incorporation	Women
Bijloke	1228	Women
Blendecques	1186/1201 incorporation	Women
Bonham	c. 1233	Women
Brayelle	1196/1212 incorporation	Women
Cambron	1148	Men
Clairmarais	1128/1140 incorporation	Men
Doornzele	1234	Women
Ter Doest	1106/1174 incorporation	Men
Ter Duinen	1107/1139 incorporation	Men
Épinlieu	1216	Women
Flines	1234	Women
Fontenelle	1212	Women
Groeninghe	1236	Women
Ter Hagen	1230/1236 incorporation	Women
Hemelsdale	1238/1241 incorporation	Women
Loos	1149	Men
Marquette	1224	Women
Mont d'Or, Guldenberg	1214	Women

Nieuwenbos	1215	Women
Olive	c. 1233	Women
Oosteeklo	c. 1228	Women
Notre-Dame des Près	1218	Women
Ravensberg	1194	Women
Refuge-Notre-Dame, Ath	1234	Women
Ter Roosen	1228/1235 incorporated	Women
Saulchoir	1233/1234	Women
Soleilmont	1088/1237 incorporated	Women
Spermalie	1200/1234 incorporated	Women
Verger	1227	Women
Vivier	1219	Women
Woestine	c. 1244	Women
Zwijveke	1221/1228 incorporated	Women

Affiliation: Order des Écoliers

Name	Date of Foundation	Men/Women
Notre-Dame des Écoliers	1252	Men

Affiliation: Franciscan

Name	Date of Foundation	Men/Women
Audenarde	1273	Women
Audenarde	1252	Men
Bourbourg	1251	Men
Bruges	1227/1233	Men
Bruges	1255/1256	Women
Cambrai	1251	Men
Douai	1246	Men
Ghent	1223/1226	Men
Langemark (Ypres)	1255	Women
Lille	1226/1227	Men
Mons	1228	Men
Tournai	1235	Men
Valenciennes	1225	Men
Ypres	1249	Men

Affiliation: Dominican

Name	Date of Foundation	Men/Women
Abbiette	1275	Women
Bergues	1244/1245	Men

Bruges	1234	Men
Douai	1268	Men
Ghent	1228	Men
Lille	1225	Men
Valenciennes	1233	Men
Ypres	1268/1269	Men

Affiliation: Prémonstratensian

Name	Date of Foundation	Men/Women
Bonne Espérance	1125/1126	Men
Chateau l'Abbaye	c. 870/1155 Prémontré	Men
Cherscamp	1147	Women
Herlaimont	1135	Women
Heylissem	1129	Women
Hof ten Vrouw	1167/1179	Women
Ninove	1137	Men
Petegem	1135	Women
Rivreulle	1140	Women
Seneffe	1181	Men
Saint-Feuillan	1126	Men
Saint-Nicolas, Furnes	1120/1135 Prémontré	Men
Tronchiennes	1136	Men
Tusschenbeek	1256	Women
Vicoigne	1125	Men

Affiliation: Order of Saint-Victor

Name	Date of Foundation	Men/Women
Beaulieu-sin-le-noble	1224	Women
Bethleem	1244	Women
Notre-Dame de Cantimpré	1180	Men
Notre-Dame de la Nouvelle Plante	1236	Women
Roosenberg	1235/1238 incorporated	Women
Sainte-Élisabeth, Bergues	1227/1248 incorporated	Women
Sainte-Élisabeth, Quesnoy	1233/1261 incorporated	Women
Saint-Trond	1149/1248 incorporated	Women
Près-Porcins	1231	Women
La Thure	1244	Women

APPENDIX 2: GENEALOGY OF THE COUNTS OF FLANDERS AND HAINAUT

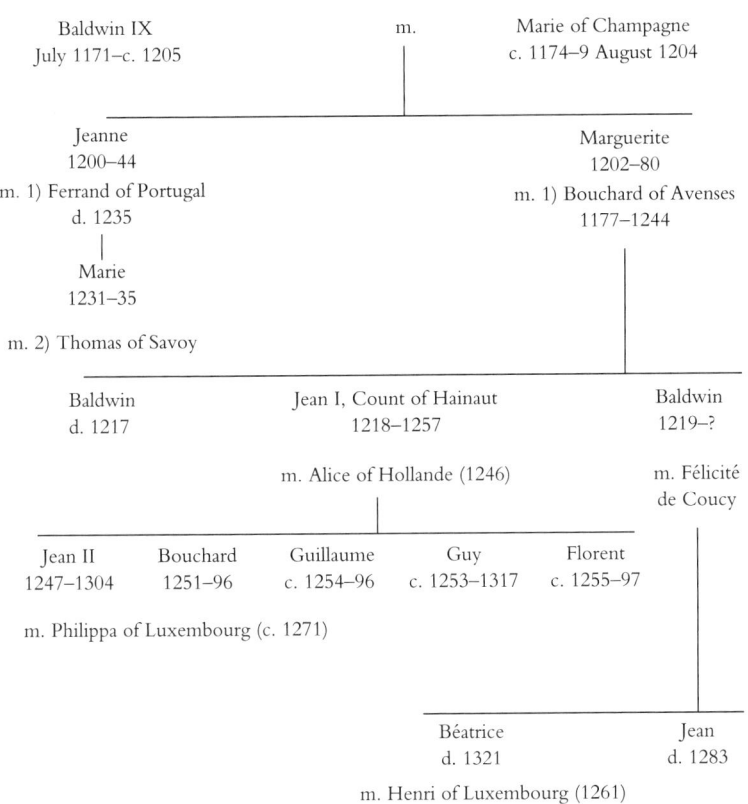

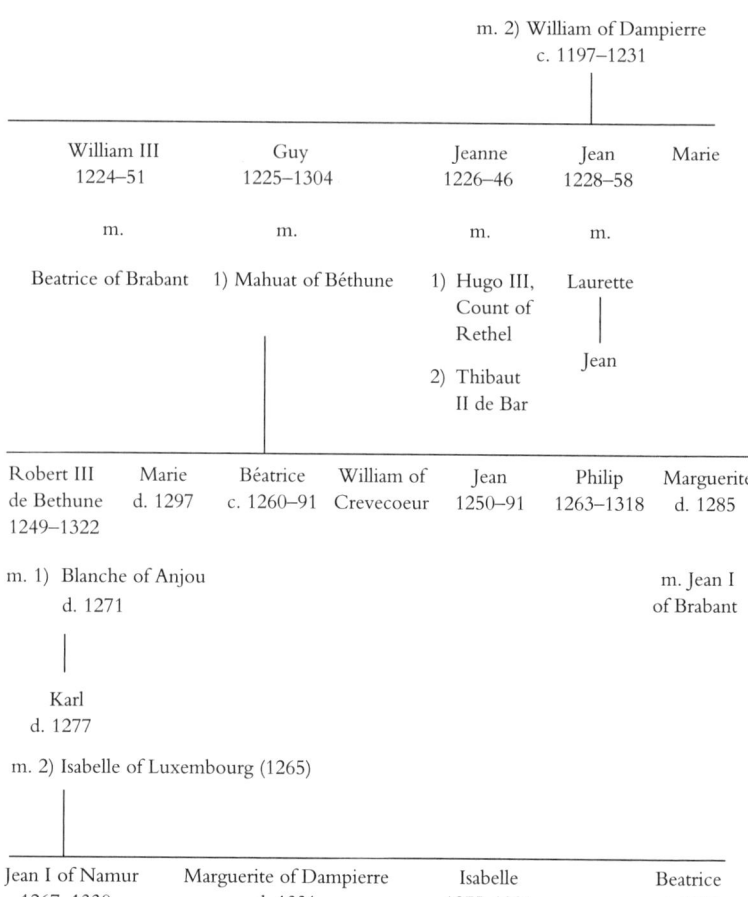

NOTES

Introduction   Powerful Women and Religious Patronage

Epigraph. Jean Francois Foppens, *Diplomatum Belgicorum Nova Collection sive Supplementum ad Opera Diplomatica Auberti Miraei*, vol. 1 (Brussels, 1734), no. 33 (July 1239), pp. 586–87.

1. Such views were presented by Joanne McNamara and Suzanne Wemple in "The Power of Women through the Family," in *Women and Power in the Middle Ages*, ed. Mary Erler and Maryanne Kowaleski (Athens, 1988), pp. 83–101. They conclude that "[t]he public power of artistocratic women...decreased significantly after the twelfth century when the growing power of the state and the rise of formal education restricted women from following previous avenues of power. At the same time, changes in inheritance practices, dowry, and dower reduced the economic power women enjoyed within families," p. 5. See also Susan Mosher Stuard, "The Dominion of Gender or How Women Fared in the High Middle Ages," in *Becoming Visible. Women in European History*, ed. Renate Bridenthal, Claudia Koonz, and Susan Stuard, 2nd ed. (Boston, 1987), pp. 129–50. Recent research has continued the discussion initiated by McNamara and Wemple, debating the extent to which the year 1000 witnessed dramatic changes regarding female inheritance. See Pauline Stafford, *Queens, Concubines and Dowagers. The Kings Wife in the Early Middle Ages*, 2nd rev. ed. (London, 1998), p. xvii; Theodore Evergates, ed., *Aristocratic Women in Medieval France* (Philadelphia, 1999) and Erler and Kowaleski's own reassessment in *Gendering the Master Narrative. Women and Power in the Middle Ages* (Ithaca, 2003), most notably Mary Erler and Maryanne Kowaleski, "A New Economy of Power Relations: Female Agency in the Middle Ages," pp. 1–16 and JoAnn McNamara, "Women and Power through the Family Revisited," pp. 17–30. McNamara affirms her earlier conclusion that after 1000 "...women were disadvantaged by the development of more centralized states, a more hierarchical church and an urban society based on the money economy" p. 22.

2. For a brief of summary of medieval views as they related to powerful women see Georges Duby, "Women and Power," in *Cultures of Power: Lordship, Status, and Process in Twelfth-Century Europe*, ed. Thomas N. Bisson (Philadelphia, 1995), pp. 69–85. For a slightly later period see Joel T.

Rosenthal, *Patriarchy and Families of Privilege in Fifteenth-Century England* (Philadelphia, 1991), pp. 15–17.
3. Baldwin's successes on the Fourth Crusade are presented in detail by R.L. Wolff, "Baldwin of Flanders and Hainaut, First Latin Emperor of Constantinople: His Life, Death and Resurrection, 1172–1225," *Speculum* 27 (1952): 281–322.
4. R.L. Wolff provides the most detailed discussion of the thirteenth-century sources that addressed Baldwin's fate, attempting to sort between fact and the fanciful. See Wolff, "Baldwin of Flanders and Hainaut," pp. 298–300.
5. Charles Duvivier, *Les Influences Française et Germanique en Belgique au XIII siècle. La Querelle des d'Avesnes et des Dampierres jusqu'a la mort de Jean d'Avesnes (1257)*, 2 vols. (Bruxelles, 1894), p. 94.
6. There are several recent articles that contribute to the reassessment of the public/private dichotomy as it functioned in the Middle Ages. Of particular note are Janet Nelson's response to the adoption of this dichotomy as a primary organizing principle of medieval society by Georges Duby in *A History of Private Life*, ed. Philippe Aries and Duby (Cambridge, 1988). Nelson questions the applicability of the public/private dichotomy, suggesting that modern authors often equate a conceptual divide with a nonexistent physical divide in what amounts to an anachronistic approach to understanding medieval society. Janet L. Nelson, "The Problematic in the Private," *Social History* 15 (1990): 355–64, especially p. 363. See also Pauline Stafford, *Queens, Concubines and Dowagers*, p. xviii. Stafford revisits her argument as it was presented in the first edition, questioning earlier conclusions about the position of women in post-1000 in light of more recent scholarship. Amy Livingstone provides a succinct and extremely useful summary of the debate in "Noblewomen's Control of Property in Early Twelfth-Century Blois-Chartres," *Medieval Prosopography* 18 (1995): 55–72.
7. See most notably Evergates, *Aristocratic Women in Medieval France* and Susan M. Johns, *Noblewomen, Aristocracy and Power in the Twelfth-Century Anglo-Norman Realm* (Manchester, 2003). Jane Martindale argues that shifts in inheritance practice and dynastic alignment resulted in female heiresses with some frequency by the early twelfth century. Jane Martindale, "Succession and Politics in the Romance-speaking World, c. 1000–1140," in *Status, Authority and Regional Power. Aquitaine and France, 9th to 12th Centuries*, ed. Martindale (Aldershot, Great Britain, 1997), pp. 19–41.
8. See Fredric Cheyette, *Ermengard of Narbonne and the World of the Troubadours* (Ithaca, 2001); Miriam Shadis, "Piety, Politics, and Power: The Patronage of Leonor of England and her Daughters Berenguela of Leon and Blanche of Castile," in *The Cultural Patronage of Medieval Women*, ed. June Hall McCash (Athens, 1996), pp. 202–216; Kimberely A. LoPrete, "The Gender of Lordly Women: The Case of Adela of Blois," in *Pawns or Players? Studies on Medieval and Early Modern Women*, ed. Christine Meek and Catherine Lawless (Dublin, 2003), pp. 90–110; Amy Livingstone, "Noblewomen's Control of Property in Early Twelfth-Century Blois-Chartres," pp. 55–72;

Penelope Adair, "Countess Clemence: Her Power and Its Foundation," pp. 63–72; Patricia Humphrey, "Ermessenda of Barcelona: The Status of her Authority" and Douglas C. Jensen, "Women and Public Authority," all in *Queens, Regents and Potentates*, ed. Theresa M. Vann (Dallas, 1993).
9. Few such studies have been attempted, as discussed by Julia M.H. Smith, "Gender and Ideology in the Early Middle Ages," *Studies in Church History* 34 (1998): 51–74.
10. For example, studies such as that of Penelope Johnson are based upon the premise that religious patronage was considered an activity that occurred within the private sphere and hence was available to women. See Penelope Johnson, "Agnes of Burgundy: An Eleventh-Century Woman as Monastic Patron," *Journal of Medieval History* 15 (1989): 93–104. This sentiment is echoed in studies of patronage generally such as that by June Hall McCash, "The Cultural Patronage of Medieval Women. An Overview," in *The Cultural Patronage of Medieval Women*, pp. 1–49.
11. Théo Luykx, *Atlas Historique et Culturel de la Belgique* (Brussels, 1959), p. 39. See also Émile Varenbergh, *Histoire des Relations Diplomatiques entre la Comté de Flandre et l'Angleterre au Moyen Age* (Brussels, 1874) and Charles Petit-Dutaillis, *The Feudal Monarchy in France and England from the Tenth to the Thirteenth Century*, trans. E.D. Hunt (New York, 1966).
12. John Baldwin discusses the subjectivity of many medieval chroniclers whose "points of view were almost always shaped by the vocations of their authors and by their patrons." See John Baldwin, *The Government of Philip Augustus. Foundations of French Royal Power in the Middle Ages* (Berkeley, 1986), p. 381. For a discussion of specific sources and their patrons, see Diana B. Tyson, "Patronage of French Vernacular History Writers in the Twelfth and Thirteenth Centuries," *Romania* 100 (1979): 180–222. Linda Mitchell addresses the problems associated with the use of chronicles as they apply specifically to women who appear in such sources. Mitchell suggests that historians are generally less critical of depictions of women than they are of depictions of men, resulting in a skewed understanding of medieval attitudes toward women. She encourages scholars to subject chronicles and their authors to questions about perspective, and warns against unequivocal acceptance of the authenticity of the author's view. See Linda E. Mitchell, *Portraits of Medieval Women. Family, Marriage and Politics in England, 1225–1350* (New York, 2003), pp. 2–3.
13. Philippe Mouskes, *Chronique Rimée*, ed. Baron de Reiffenberg, vol. 1 (Bruxelles, 1836), pp. cl–cli. Philippe Mouskes was a canon of Tournai who garnered the favor of the French king. His history of France begins with King Priam and traces events to the mid-thirteenth century. Although he includes information not found in any other contemporary source, the nature of his work as well as his anti-Flemish perspective forces one to question its reliability. Consequently, he is incorporated in this study only when the information can be corroborated by other narrative sources or by documents of practice.

14. Guillaume le Breton, "Gesta Philippi August," in *Oeuvres de Rigord et de Guillaume le Breton*, ed. Henri-Francois Delaborde, vol. 1 (Paris, 1882). Also his "Philippide," in *Oeuvres de Rigord et de Guillaume le Breton*, vol. 2 (Paris, 1885).
15. For example, the *Chronique latine de Baudouin d'Avesnes*, written near 1289, presents an anti-Flemish perspective, and condemns both countesses for their complicity with the French. This text, most likely commissioned by Marguerite's son Baldwin, originated in Hainaut, and it embodies the feelings of many members of the county's nobility, who thought they were increasing marginalized in the court of the countesses. According to Diana Tyson, the first version was most likely completed during the last two decades of the thirteenth century, and it was subject to several revisions in the fourteenth. Tyson, "Patronage of French Vernacular History Writers," pp. 180–222, especially p. 209.
16. The veracity of de Guyse's account is challenged by a variety of authors, including L.A. Warnkoenig, *Histoire de la Flandre et de ses Institutions Civile et Politique jusqu'a l'Annee 1309*, vol. 1 (Bruxelles, 1835), p. 69 and Theo Luykx, *Johanna van Constantinopel, Gravin van Vlaanderen en Henegouwen, haar Leven (1199/1200–1244), haar Revgeering (1205–1244), vooral in Vlaanderen* (Antwerp, 1946), p. 56.
17. Duvivier suggests that Paris's stance is due in part to his support for Jean of Avesnes, Marguerite's son from her first marriage who contested the inheritance settlement that divided up the two counties, leaving him with Hainaut and granting control of Flanders to his Dampierre brothers. Charles Duvivier, *Les Influences Française et Germanique en Belgique au XIII siècle. La Querelle des d'Avesnes et des Dampierres jusqu'a la mort de Jean d'Avesnes (1257)*, vol. 1 (Bruxelles, 1894).
18. In his report of the battle of Westkappelle in 1253, Matthew Paris attributes all blame to Marguerite, placing her in a long line of women responsible for the destruction of men: "There perished in divers ways more than twenty thousand fighting men, who had congregated from the various provinces of the kingdom of France, as well as of the empire...of Germany...; and all these men died on account of one immodest woman. And as the whole of Troy, or Pergamus...was reduced to ashes through a woman, and as Greece was deprived of its inhabitants at the instigation of Venus, so by this catastrophe...the whole of France, Germany, and Flanders were covered with confusion and grief." See Matthew Paris, *Chronica Majora*, ed. Richard Vaughn (Cambridge, 1958), p. 74.
19. See Varenbergh, *Histoire des Relations Diplomatiques*.
20. See Edward Le Glay, *Histoire de Jeanne de Constantinople, Comtesse de Flandre et de Hainaut* (Lille, 1841) and J. de Mersseman, "Étude Historique sur Jeanne de Constantinople, Comtesse de Flandre," in *Annales de la Société d'Émulation pour l'Histoire et les Anitquités de la Flandre Occidentale*, vol. 2 (Bruges, 1840), vol. 1, pp. 73–87, 109–132; (1841), vol. 3, pp. 15–52, 281–330, 359–422.
21. Baron Kervyn de Lettenhove, *Histoire de Flandre*, vol. 1 (Bruxelles, 1847).
22. Warnkoenig, *Histoire de la Flandre*. More reliable studies of Flemish affairs during this period include Gaston G. Dept, *Les Influences Anglaise et Française*

NOTES 129

dans le comté de Flandre au Debut du XIIIe Siècle (Paris, 1928) and Duvivier, *Les Influences Française*. Duvivier in particular includes a number of charters in the appendix to the second volume.

23. Theo Luykx, "Gravin Johanna van Constantinople en de godsdienstige vrouwen-begegingen in Vlaanderen gedurende de eerste helft der XIII de eeuw," *Ons Geestelyk Erf* 17 (1943): 5–30. In addition to his two studies of Jeanne, Luykx provides an exhaustive account of the finances of Flanders during the reign of Marguerite, *De grafelije financiele Bestuursinstellingen en het grafelijke patrimonium in Vlaanderen tijdens de regering van Margareta van Constantinople (1244–1278)* (Brussels, 1961). Also available are Thérèse de Hemptinne, "Vlaanderen en Henegouwen onder de ergenamen van de Boudewyns, 1070–1244," *Algemene geschiedenis der Nederlanden* 1 (1977): 372–98 and Maurice Vandermaesen, "Vlaanderen en Henegouwen onder het Huis van Dampierre, 1244–1384," *Algemene Geschiedenis der Nederlanden* 2 (1982): 400–414.
24. Geneviève de Cant, *Jeanne et Marguerite de Constantinople, Comtesses de Flandre et de Hainaut au XIIIe siècle* (Brussels, 1995).
25. See Henri Pirenne, *Histoire de Belgique*, vol. 1 (Brussels, 1929); David Nicholas, *Medieval Flanders* (New York, 1992); Gabrielle M. Spiegel, *Romancing the Past. The Rise of Vernacular Prose Historiography in Thirteenth-Century France* (Berkeley, 1993). Unfortunately, the countesses themselves are only briefly mentioned by Spiegel since they fall outside the parameters of her discussion.
26. Karen Nicholas, "Countesses as Rulers in Flanders," in *Aristocratic Women in Medieval France*, ed. Theodore Evergates (Philadelphia, 1999), pp. 111–37. Also Karen Nicholas, "Women as Rulers: Countesses Jeanne and Marguerite of Flanders," in *Queens, Regents and Potentates*, pp. 73–90.
27. Linda Mitchell's discussion of the treatment of women in medieval narrative sources has informed this discussion considerably. She suggests a new approach to assessing the position of women in medieval society which accounts for the bias unavoidable in medieval sources which is extremely productive. Mitchell, *Portraits of Medieval Women*, p. 3.
28. Advantages and disadvantages of charters as sources are addressed in a wide array of studies, most notably Stephen D. White, *Custom, Kinship and Gifts to Saints: The Laudatio Parentum in Western France 1050–1150* (Chapel Hill, 1988), p. 11 and Emily Zack Tabuteau, *Transfers of Property in Eleventh-Century Norman Law* (Chapel Hill, 1988), p. 11. Janet Burton discusses the relative merits of charter evidence concerning motives in *The Monastic Order in Yorkshire, 1069–1215* (Cambridge, 1999), p. 139.
29. For a list of communities included in this study, see appendix 1. This list, however, is not exhaustive as it does not include hospitals or communities outside of their domains, which are included in qualitative, but not quantitative, discussion. The primary collections of secular charters consulted here are the Chartes des Comtes de Flanders, located in the Rijksarchief te Gent and the Archives Départementales du Nord (ADN), Lille. Other collections include those charters recorded by the court of France, most notably the Trèsor des Chartes and the Registres de Philippe Augustus. The latter two

are available in published collections. Alexandre Teulet, Joseph de Laborde, Elie Berger, and Henri Francois Delaborde, eds., *Layettes du Trésor des Chartes*, 4 vols. (Paris, 1863–75) and M. Charles Samaran, ed., *Recueil des Actes de Philippe Auguste*, 4 vols. (Paris, 1966).
30. An example of a discussion about the limitations placed on women is Duby, "Women and Power," p. 71.
31. Studies such as Penelope Johnson's *Prayer, Patronage and Power: The Abbey of La Trinité, Vendôme, 1032–1187* (New York, 1981) and J. Wardrop, *Fountains Abbey and its Benefactors, 1132–1300* (Suffolk, 1987) have investigated the relationship between individual religious communities and local patrons. For discussions of the meaning of patronage more generally over a substantial chronological period see Emma Cownie, *Religious Patronage in Anglo-Norman England, 1066–1135* (Suffolk, 1998); Bennett Hill, *English Cistercian Monasteries and their Patrons in the Twelfth Century* (Urbana, IL, 1968). More regionally focused studies include Constance Brittain Bouchard, *Holy Entrepreneurs: Cistercians, Knights and Economic Exchange in Twelfth-Century Burgundy* (Ithaca, 1991) and Barbara Rosenwein, *To Be the Neighbor of St. Peter: The Social Meaning of Cluny's Property, 909–1049* (Ithaca, 1989). A very succinct discussion of the motives of benefactors can be found in White, *Custom, Kinship and Gifts to Saints*, pp. 28–29.
32. The advantages of comparative study in revealing motives prompting patronage are addressed by Jane Martindale, "Monasteries and Castles: the Priories of St.-Florent de Saumur in England after 1066," in *England in the Eleventh Century*, ed. Carola Hicks (Stamford, 1992), pp. 135–57. This type of comparative study is effectively employed by J.C. Ward in "Fashions in Monastic Endowment: The Foundations of the Clare Family, 1066–1314," *Journal of Ecclesiastical History* 32 (1981): 427–51.
33. See Emma Cownie, "Religious Patronage at Post-Conquest Bury St. Edmunds," *Haskins Society Journal* 7 (1997): 1–9 and *Religious Patronage*, pp. 7–8.
34. Wendy Davies and Paul Fouracre, eds., *Property and Power in the Early Middle Ages* (Cambridge, 1995), pp. 2–3 and Chris Wickham, "Property Ownership and Signorial Power in Twelfth-Century Tuscany," pp. 221–44, especially p. 243.
35. See most recently Burton, *The Monastic Order*, pp. 193–94; Ludo Milis, *Angelic Monks and Earthly Men: Monasticism and Its Meaning to Medieval Society* (Woodbridge, 1992), pp. 87–91 and Megan McLaughlin, *Consorting with Saints. The Ideology of Prayer for the Dead in Early Medieval France* (Ithaca, 1994), pp. 179–80.

1 Accessing Authority: 1206–14

1. Gaston Dept, *Les Influences Anglaise et Française dans le comté de Flandre au Début du XIIIe siècle* (Paris, 1928), p. 47.
2. The treaty was witnessed by Jean of Nesle, siger of Ghent and Guillaume, Baldwin's uncle. The remainder of the leading nobles of Flanders attempted

to render the treaty invalid by refusing to act as witnesses. Geneviève de Cant, *Jeanne et Marguerite de Constantinople, Comtesses de Flandres et de Hainaut au XIIIe siècle* (Brussels, 1995), p. 32. For the terms of the treaty see M. Charles Samaran, ed., *Recueil des Actes de Philippe Auguste*, vol. 3 (Paris, 1966), no. 1043, pp. 110–111.

3. Although the contract was signed in August 1206, Marie was still a minor at that time, and the actual marriage did not occur until January 15, 1211. Theo Luykx, *Johanna van Constantinopel, Gravin van Vlaanderen en Henegouwen, haar Leven (1199/1200–1244), haar Revgeering (1205–1244), vooral in Vlaanderen* (Antwerp, 1946), p. 81. The marriage lasted less than a year, since Philip died in October 8, 1212. Dept, *Les Influences Anglaise*, p. 75.

4. In order to secure physical control of the two girls, Philip had to buy the "droits de tutelle" over them from the bishop of Liège, into whose care they had been placed by their mother Marie prior to her departure to the Holy Land in 1203. See William Mendel Newman, *Les Seigneurs de Nesle en Picardie (XIIe–XIIIe siécle). Leurs Chartes et Leur Histoire. Étude sur la Noblese Régionale Ecclésiastique et Laïque*, vol. 1 (Philadelphia, 1971), p. 38.

5. Although harshly criticized by nobles of Flanders and Hainaut, Philip Augustus was acting within his rights as feudal lord when he asserted authority over the marriages of Jeanne and Marguerite. During this same period, he assumed similar control over minor heirs of the counties of Champagne and Navarre and placed restrictions on the actions of the countesses. See John Baldwin, *The Government of Philip Augustus. Foundations of French Royal Power in the Middle Ages* (Berkeley, 1986), p. 271. See also Michel Bur, "Rôle et Place de la Champagne dans le Royaume au Temps de Philippe Auguste," in *La France de Philippe Auguste. Le Temps des Mutations*, ed. R.H. Bautier (Paris, 1982), pp. 237–54. Much of the outcry in the case of Jeanne and Marguerite was due to the dual infeudation of Flanders, since portions of the county were held in fief of the Holy Roman emperor, and the county of Hainaut was held in fief of the bishop of Liège. See David Nicholas, *Medieval Flanders* (New York, 1992), p. 152.

6. Philippe Godding, "Le droit au service du patrimoine familial: Les Pays-Bas Méridinaux (12e–18e siécles)," in *Marriage, Property and Succession*, ed. Lloyd Banfield (Berlin, 1992), pp. 15–35, especially p. 15. The discussion of feudal law as it pertains to female inheritance is considerably more developed for thirteenth-century England than for France during the same period. See, e.g., Scott L. Waugh, *The Lordship of England. Royal Wardships and Marriages in English Society and Politics, 1217–1327* (Princeton, 1988); J.C. Holt, "Feudal Society and the Family in Early Medieval England: The Heiress and the Alien," *Transactions of the Royal Historical Society* 35 (1985): 1–28.

7. Georges Duby, *The Chivalrous Society*, trans. Cynthia Poston (Berkeley, 1980), p. 74.

8. Philippe Godding, *Le droit privé dans les Pays-Bas méridinaux du 12e au 18e siècle* (Brussels, 1987), p. 336. Godding dates primogeniture as the established inheritance practice in the Pays-Bas and northern France to the beginning of the eleventh century.

9. Jane Martindale, "Succession and Politics in the Romance-speaking World, c. 1000–1140," in *Status, Authority and Regional Power. Aquitaine and France, 9th to 12th centuries*, ed. Martindale (Aldershot, Great Britain, 1997), pp. 19–41. Martindale acknowledges that, while widely accepted among scholars, the model described requires further investigation regarding its applicability to political systems as they functioned in the thirteenth century.
10. Godding, "Le droit au service patrimoine," p. 16. See also the discussion by Theodore Evergates concerning feudal tenure, *Feudal Society in Medieval France. Documents from the County of Champagne*, trans. and ed. Evergates (Philadelphia, 1993), pp. 49–53.
11. Godding, *Le droit privé*, p. 371. See also John Glissen, "Le Privilège de Masculinité dans le droit coutumier de la Belgique et du nord de la France," *Revue du Nord* 43 (1961): 201–16.
12. This summary of the views of Duby and others is provided by Amy Livingstone, who challenges conclusions about the monolithic view of noble family dynamics they advance. Her study of family strategy in the Chartrain questions notions about the uniformity of such shifts and the assumption that primogeniture and patrilineage were always practiced in tandem. See Amy Livingstone, "Kith and Kin: Kinship and Family Structure of the Nobility of Eleventh- and Twelfth-Century Blois-Chartres," *French Historical Studies* 20 (1997): 419–58, p. 420. Livingstone is joined by Kimberly A. LoPrete, who has also posited the existence of more continuity in family dynamics between the eleventh and twelfth centuries than Duby's model demonstrates. The discrepancy between her findings and those of Duby has led her to suggest that "the current evaluation of the status of noblewomen in particular, and the fabric of the noble family in general, are in need of revision." See Kimberly A. LoPrete, "Adela of Blois and Ivo of Chartres: Piety, Politics and the Peace in the Diocese of Chartes," in *Anglo-Norman Studies XIV: Proceedings of the Battle Conference*, ed. Marjorie Chibnall (Woodbridge, 1992), p. 23.
13. Pauline Stafford, *Queens, Concubines and Dowagers. The King's Wife in the Early Middle Ages*, 2nd. rev. ed. (London, 1998), p. 195. In the second edition of the text, Stafford herself questions her earlier conclusions, suggesting that notions of the position of women post 1100 are in need of further examination. Arguments that outline the supposed negative impact of primogeniture and patrilineage on women during this period are summarized in Theodore Evergates, ed., *Aristocratic Women in Medieval France* (Philadelphia, 1999), p. 1. Jane Martindale dates the shift from "loosely organized medieval groupings" to "lineages which traced descent and affiliation in the masculine alone" to the late twelfth century. Martindale, *Status, Authority and Regional Power*, p. 23.
14. Waugh, *The Lordship of England*, p. 16. One key difference between the system in England and that on the continent was the English custom of dividing inheritance equally among all daughters in the absence of a male heir. Such division would have diminished the potential authority of each heiress.

15. According to Duby, this particular outcome provided added proof that by the eleventh century, seniority had became one of the primary considerations in determining inheritance. Duby, *The Chivalrous Society*, p. 75. Glisson concludes that "la fille est écartée par les fils, mais elle est préférée au frère et au neveu." Glissen, "Le Privilège de Masculinité," p. 202.
16. Miriam Shadis and Constance Hoffman Berman, "A Taste of the Feast: Reconsidering Eleanor of Aquitaine's Female Descendants," in *Eleanor of Aquitaine. Lord and Lady*, ed. Bonnie Wheeler and John Carmi Parsons (New York, 2003), pp. 177–211. Many of these women are discussed by John Baldwin due to the role they played in Philip's attempt to consolidate power through the manipulation of marriage. Baldwin, *The Government of Philip Augustus*, p. 270. For Brittany during the rule of Constance, see Yannick Hillion, "La Bretagne et la Rivalité Capétians-Plantagenets. Un Exemple: La duchesse Constance (1186–1202)," *Annales de Bretagne et du pays de l'Ouest* 92 (1985): 111–44. Isabelle, countess of Ambois and Alix, countess of Eu can also be added to this list, although little information is known of their activities. To date, I have identified twenty-nine women at the seigneurial level acting in their own name in charters as countesses or duchesses during the four decades spanning the reign of Philip Augustus. While a number of these women have been the subjects of study, many remain quite elusive in the historical record, and further research is needed before conclusions about their individual experiences can be formed.
17. The marriage between Ida and Renaud occurred without the king's consent, and caused much consternation in the royal court at Paris. Baldwin, *The Government of Philip Augustus*, pp. 200–201. While scholars often suggest that the marriage to Renaud occurred without Ida's consent as well, this interpretation seems open to consideration. See Henri Malo, *Un Grand Feudataire. Renaud de Dammartin et la Coalition de Bouvines* (Paris, 1898) and Erin Jordan, "The Abduction of Ida of Boulogne," *French Historical Studies*, Winter 2007.
18. Susan Mosher Stuard, *Women in Medieval Society* (Philadelphia, 1976); Penny Schine Gold, *The Lady and the Virgin. Image Attitude and Experience in Twelfth Century France* (Chicago, 1985).
19. Linda E. Mitchell, *Portraits of Medieval Women. Family, Marriage and Politics in England, 1225–1350* (New York, 2003): "Theoretically, the inheritance of property by women should not have disrupted the feudal structure, since unmarried heiresses were governed by male guardians and married heiresses relinquished virtually all control over their property to their husbands" p. 12. See also Waugh, *The Lordship of England*, p. 67.
20. Georges Duby, "Women and Power," in *Cultures of Power: Lordship, Status and Process in 12th-Century Europe*, ed. Thomas N. Bisson (Philadelphia, 1995), pp. 69–85, p. 74: "This said, the fact remains that it was he who wielded his wife's power, not she. She was merely at his side when he exercised it. She had to be there, in token of adhesion, of assent, of association."
21. Michelle Zimbalist Rosaldo, "Women, Culture and Society: A Theoretical Overview," in *Women, Culture and Society*, ed. Rosaldo and Louise

Lamphere (Stanford, 1974). Rosaldo makes the distinction between authority, legitimate action associated with men, and power, a more subversive way to exert influence, often associated with women, p. 22.
22. Douglas C. Jansen, "Women and Public Authority in the Thirteenth Century," in *Queens, Regents and Potentates*, ed. Theresa M. Vann (Dallas, 1993), pp. 91–103. While I concur with Jansen's definition of authority as it functioned during this period, I disagree with his characterization of Isabella de Clifford, who he describes as "extraordinary" in the extent of the authority she wielded. The numerous examples of similar women cited throughout this study suggest that such women were more commonplace than the term "extraordinary" would convey.
23. This discussion is informed primarily by the theories of authority developed by Weber. Feudal society at this juncture exhibits traits of authority based on rational and traditional grounds; while Jeanne's ability to exercise authority was based upon tradition, it was combined with recognition of the authority of her office. See Max Weber, *The Theory of Social and Economic Organization*, trans. A.M. Henderson and Talcott Parsons (New York, 1947), p. 328. A similar distinction is used quite effectively by Helen Maurer in her examination of Margaret of Anjou: "Following M.Z. Rosaldo and L. Lamphere, I understand 'authority' to be the socially recognized right to make certain decisions and to require obedience. 'Power'is the more informal 'ability to gain compliance.' " Helen E. Maurer, *Margaret of Anjou. Queenship and Power in Late Medieval England* (Suffolk, 2003), p. 5. I would like to thank Helen Maurer for bringing this similarity in our respective approaches to my attention.
24. The reversal of his position vis-à-vis Flanders is discussed in detail in John Baldwin, *The Government of Philip Augustus*. See also Elizabeth M. Hallam and Judith Everard, eds., *Capetian France, 987–1328*, 2nd ed. (New York, 2001).
25. Rosaldo, "Women, Culture and Society."
26. This approach is perhaps best represented by the articles in *Women and Power in the Middle Ages*, ed. Mary Erler and Maryanne Kowaleski (Athens, 1988). A number of women clearly existed in this period who exercised what this model would consider authority. Such action, which seems to contradict the basic understanding of society upon which this model is predicated, is explained as the result of the overlap that existed between the public and the private spheres during this period. In other words, as long as the lines between these two spheres of action remained blurred, women were able to access authority with some frequency. For the most part, such studies suggest that these spheres of activity became more distinct after the year 1000, with dramatic implications for women, henceforth consigned to wielding power, but rarely given access to authority.
27. A variety of studies address the effectiveness of the public/private model as an organizing principle for medieval society. Of most use here are *The Texture of Society. Medieval Women in the Southern Low Countries*, ed. Ellen Kittell and Mary A. Suydam (New York, 2004), pp. xix–xx and Kimberly A. LoPrete, "Historical Ironies in the Study of Capetian Women," in *Capetian Women*, ed. Kathleen Nolan (New York, 2003), pp. 271–86.

28. A similar attempt to integrate women into our understanding of power as it operated in the Middle Ages can be found in Carol J. Clover, "Regardless of Sex: Men, Women and Power in Early Northern Europe," *Speculum* 68 (1993): 363–87. For a discussion of the problems that arise when such women are dismissed as anomalous, see Kimberly A. LoPrete, "The Gender of Lordly Women: The Case of Adela of Blois," in *Pawns or Players? Studies on Medieval and Early Modern Women*, ed. Christine Meek and Catherine Lawless (Dublin, 2003), pp. 90–110.

29. Georges Duby, "Women and Power," p. 7. According to Duby, by the twelfth century, *potestas* was incorporated into the patrimony, and subsequently transmitted by inheritance. "Normally, sons prevailed over their sisters and inherited the *potestas*. But if it happened that there were no sons, it was a woman, the eldest of the girls, who inherited" p. 70. This study equates Duby's notion of *potestas* with authority, rather than with power, as it would be most closely translated.

30. This distinction is consistent with Rosaldo's discussion of these two terms. Authority, or the legal right to act, is most often associated with men, and power, extra-legal but equally important in terms of exerting influence, is associated with women acting "behind the scenes." While this study accepts Rosaldo's distinction between the two concepts, it argues for a less clear connection to gender. Obviously, in the case of feudal society, the positions were somewhat more fluid due to the role played by inheritance. See Rosaldo, "Women, Culture and Society," p. 23.

31. In her discussion of this period in Flemish history, Gabrielle Spiegel identifies the dispute over the Vermandois succession as the event that triggered the conflict between the Flemish counts and Philip Augustus during the twelfth century, which eventually culminated in Flemish subservience to French control. See Gabrielle Spiegel, *Romancing the Past. The Rise of Vernacular Prose Historiography in Thirteenth-Century France* (Berkeley, 1993), p. 43. However, the loss of the Vermandois, which passed from Flemish to French control in the form of the dowry of Isabelle of Hainaut, the first wife of Philip Augustus, was merely the first stage in the gradual decline of Flanders. It did not hinder Baldwin IX, who established Flanders as one of the main political and military powers of Europe. The ultimate decline of Flanders was precipitated by the interregnum of 1206 to 1212, when the absence of comital authority allowed Philip Augustus to consolidate control of his vassals. This decline was later exacerbated by losses, both political and economic, incurred as a result of the defeat at Bouvines, which will be discussed later. Spiegel provides a concise discussion of the history of Flanders during the century prior to the reign of Jeanne and Marguerite in *Romancing the Past*. Duvivier claims that the political decline of Flanders was precipitated by Jeanne and Marguerite. He blames Marguerite in particular for the devastation and disruption that resulted from her children's quarrel regarding the succession. Many modern scholars have relied upon Duvivier's work, thus incorporating his views into their own accounts. Although the disputes between Marguerite's heirs were certainly disruptive, the political decline of Flanders and its submission to France began much

earlier, when Baldwin IX was murdered and Philip of Namur confirmed as regent. This decline was then exacerbated by Ferrand's political stance, and his overt opposition to Philip Augustus. The thirteenth century in Flanders would have been dramatically different if Ferrand's coalition had been victorious at Bouvines. For Duvivier's presentation of events see *Les Influences Française et Germanique en Belgique au XIIIe siècle, La Querelle des Avesnes et des Dampierres jusqu'a la mort de Jean d'Avesnes (1857)* (Bruxelles, 1894).
32. The situation in Flanders as it existed prior to the reign of Philip Augustus is discussed by Jean Dunbabin, *France in the Making, 843–1180*, 2nd. ed. (Cambridge, 2000), pp. 318–20.
33. This discussion is only concerned with the county of Flanders since the other half of the countesses' domains, the county of Hainaut, was held in fief of the Holy Roman emperor, and was only indirectly affected by French royal policy. Baldwin, *The Government of Philip Augustus*, p. 8. The boundary between the two entities was the river Scheldt.
34. Dept, *Les Influences Anglaise*, p. 21.
35. Although Flanders was traditionally connected by feudal ties to France, an even more compelling connection was created by Flemish dependence on English wool. Gaston Dept's study of French and English competition for Flemish support remains the most accurate and informative study of the relationship between these three countries and its gradual change over time. Dept, *Les Influences Anglaise*, p. 21. See also Émile Varenbergh, *Histoire des Relations Diplomatiques entre le Comté de Flandre et l'Angleterre au Moyen Age* (Brussels, 1874).
36. For Philip's designs on Flanders and the events that culminated in the battle of Bouvines, see Jim Bradbury, *Philip Augustus. King of France. 1180–1223* (New York, 1998).
37. Apparently, Elizabeth's concession of her lands was forced upon her by Philip as punishment for an adulterous affair. Although most historians have tended to accept this explanation without hesitation, it only appears in one medieval account, authored by Ralph de Diceto of London, and remains uncorroborated by any other contemporary source. The tale appears in *The Historical Works of Master Ralph de Diceto, Dean of London*, ed. William Stubbs, vol. 1 (London, 1876), p. 402. It is cited by Nicholas, *Medieval Flanders*, p. 72 and Baldwin, *The Government of Philip Augustus*, pp. 24–25.
38. Although not technically appointed regent for the young king, the count of Flanders, as the most powerful magnet of the realm, assumed control of French policy after the death of Louis VII in 1179. He retained this control until the 1180s, when the increasingly resentful Philip Augustus began to assert his own authority at the count's expense. Baldwin, *The Government of Philip Augustus*, p. 17.
39. According to Baldwin, Philip Augustus's immediate response to Philip of Alsace's retraction of the Artois was to declare his intention to divorce Isabelle. She was only able to prevent this from happening by walking barefoot through the streets of Paris, clothed in a white gown, carrying a candle, and pleading for her husband to reverse his decision. Baldwin, *The Government of Philip Augustus*, p. 18.

40. After the peace of Amiens, Philip of Alsace apparently reconciled himself to his losses, accompanying the pious king on crusade and dying at the siege of Acre in June, 1191. Spiegel, *Romancing the Past*, p. 33.
41. Nicholas, *Medieval Flanders*, p. 73.
42. This explanation appears in the chronicle of Rigord, written in 1204. Baldwin notes that the chronicle was written prior to the acquisition of the Artois, which further solidified Philip's prominence in French history. J.W. Baldwin, "La décennie décisive: les années 1190–1203 dans le règne de Philippe Auguste," *Revue Historique* 266 (1981): 311–37, p. 325.
43. Baldwin, "La décennie décisive," p. 315.
44. Spiegel, *Romancing the Past*, p. 39.
45. JoAnn McNamara and Suzanne Wemple, "The Power of Women Through the Family," p. 95.
46. See Baldwin, *The Government of Philip Augustus*. See also Achille Luchaire, *Histoire des Institutions monarchiques de la France sous les premier Capetians* (987–1180), 2 vols. (Bruxelles, 1891); *Capetian France, 987–1328*, ed. Everard and Hallam; Andrew W. Lewis, *Royal Succession in Capetian France: Studies on Familial Order and the State* (Cambridge, 1981).
47. Philip's success in enticing the Flemish nobility away from their allegiance to England was due primarily to the number of money fiefs he distributed. By 1212, at the end of the regency of Philip of Namur, at least fifteen Flemish nobles were receiving money fiefs from Philip. His successful campaign in Normandy made it possible for Philip to concentrate his energies and his resources on Flanders. In 1212, 49 percent of French money fiefs were paid to nobles in Flanders and Hainaut. Baldwin, *The Government of Philip Augustus*, p. 274. See also Spiegel, *Romancing the Past*, p. 42. Philip was successful in part because of the turmoil in England, and the abrupt cancellation of many of the English money fiefs formerly enjoyed by Flemish nobles.
48. *Alberic de Troisfontaines, MGH, Scriptores*, vol. 23, p. 896.
49. Among these nobles was Jean of Nesle, the king's staunchest supporter among the nobles of Flanders and Hainaut. See Newman, *Les Seigneurs de Nesle*, p. 38.
50. While Philip was attempting to solidify his control of Flanders through securing the support of leading Flemish nobles, John was experiencing numerous reversals on French soil, culminating in the loss of Normandy in 1204. John's position was seriously weakened by his nephew Arthur, count of Brittany. Sparked in part by rumors of Arthur's death at the hands of his uncle, John faced growing opposition at home. John attempted to counter his rival's generosity, promising fief rents to at least twenty-four Flemish nobles, including eight who were already on the French payroll, in return for their support. In spite of his best efforts, John's waning position on the continent, combined with the absence of count in Flanders, failed to produce the desired results. For waning English influence on the continent see Maurice Powicke, *The Loss of Normandy, 1189–1204* (Manchester, 1960).
51. The terms of the agreement were revealed in a charter issued in 1208, when the girls were officially transferred to the French royal court. The agreement

stipulated that if the girls had not been married by the time they reached the "*etatem legitimam*" [state of legitimacy] control of their marriages would revert to Philip of Namur. Samaran, *Recueil des Actes de Philippe Auguste*, no. 1043, pp. 110–11.

52. By 1212, Philip had already rejected a proposal made by Enguerrand de Coucy. Enguerrand's bid for the countess initially amounted to 30,000 *livres parisis*, and stipulated that Marguerite would marry his younger brother Thomas. Despite his willingness to raise the amount to 50,000 *livres parisis*, Enguerrand's suit was denied by Philip Augustus. Samaran, *Recueil des actes de Philippe Auguste*, no. 1227, pp. 340–41. Enguerrand eventually found an heiress in Matilda of Saxony, the dowager countess of the county of the Perche. Kathleen Thompson, *Power and Border Lordship in Medieval France. The County of the Perche, 1000–1226* (Woodbridge, 2002), p. 147.

53. This suggestion is proffered by several authors, including Henri Pirenne, *Histoire de Belgique*, vol. 1 (Brussels, 1929), p. 229. Ferrand was the nephew of Matilda, widow of Philip of Alsace and dowager countess of Flanders, who remained a player in Flemish politics until after Bouvines.

54. Archives Départementales du Nord, Lille, Inventaire Chronologique et detaille des chartes de la Chambre des comptes à Lille, par Denis Joseph Godefroy, 2187, H 51, no. 276 (1212).

55. Dept, *Les Influences Anglaise*, p. 94. Ferrand was accompanied by Philip of Namur, Jean of Nesle, and Siger of Gand. While he was cordially received and acknowledged by Ypres and Bruges, he encountered extreme hostility upon his arrival in Ghent, led by Arnoul of Audenarde and Rasse of Gavre.

56. Duby, "Women and Power," p. 70: "If the males who blocked them from possession of this dominium happened to disappear, or if such a condition were already fulfilled, and if she chanced to be an orphan without a brother, then the husband gathered up with her the power of which she was the legitimate holder."

57. Three of the six charters reiterated donations made to monastic communities by Jeanne's predecessor, Count Baldwin, suggesting they were pro forma confirmations of grants made by their predecessor rather than new donations. Two others, both issued in 1213, confirmed sales to monastic foundations made by a third party. The remaining charter, issued in 1212 to the abbey of Saint-Waudru, concerned the administration of the community.

58. The first charter was issued from Mons in May 1212. See Alphonse Wauters, ed., *Table Chronologique des Chartes et Diplômes Imprimés Concernant l'Histoire de la Belgique*, vol. 3 (Brussels, 1903), p. 359. The second was issued from Valenciennes, May 31, 1214. See Wauters, *Table Chronologique*, vol. 3, p. 385. During this same period, Ferrand issued four charters in conjunction with patronage. All of these charters involved confirmation made by previous counts or consent to transactions made by a third party.

59. In charter issued in January 1212 Ferrand swore to be the "liege man of his illustrious lord Philip king of France." Samaran, *Recueil des Actes de Philippe Auguste*, no. 978, pp. 373–74. Pledges followed from Siger, castellan of Ghent (no. 979, pp. 371–72), Jean, castellan of Lens (no. 980, p. 374), and

Jean of Nesle (no. 981, p. 74). The charter recording Ferrand's pledge is also included in *Layettes du Trésor des Chartes*, ed. M. Alexandre Teulet, vol. 1 (Paris, 1863), no. 978, p. 373. For Matilda's pledge see *Table Chronologique*, vol. 3, p. 352.

60. ADN, Lille, Inv. Chron., 2187 H 51, no. 276 (1212). According to the text of the charter, Louis claimed the cities, previously forfeited by the French in the treaty of Peronne, by right of his mother Isabelle of Hainaut. Witnesses included most members of the pro-French nobility of Flanders, including Jean of Nesle, Siger of Ghent, and Michel of Harnes.
61. ADN, Lille, Inv. Chron., 2187 H51, no. 293. The charter alludes to a dispute between Ferrand and Jeanne and Bouchard regarding the marriage settlement to be conferred on Marguerite, citing Gérard of Jauce, Guillaume, his uncle, the castellan of Beaumont, Arnould of Audenarde, Bauduin of Comines, and Gilbert of Berghelles as arbiters. The marriage of Marguerite will be discussed at length in chapter 2.
62. This charter confirmed the laws and customs previously established for the city by Philip of Alsace, and it expressly prohibited them from forming peace with either Ferrand or Matilda. Samaran, *Receuil des Actes de Philippe Auguste*, no. 1304, pp. 442–43.
63. Gender as it is understood in this study is based on the definition and discussion provided by Joan Scott and Elaine Showalter. Scott defined gender as "A constitutive element of social relationships based on perceived differences between the sexes." Joan Wallach Scott, "Gender: A Useful Category of Historical Analysis," in *Feminism and History*, ed. Scott (Cambridge, 1986), pp. 152–86, especially p. 54. Elaine Showalter, "Introduction: The Rise of Gender," in *Speaking of Gender*, ed. Showalter (New York, 1989), pp. 1–4. Both Scott and Showalter qualify the use of a theoretical model based on gender in the endeavor to understand the experience of women, warning against the tendency to view individuals in a vacuum. Both suggest that women should not be viewed as discrete subjects, removed from the historical context in which they operated. In addition, they expressed concerns that while gender could be useful in attempts to determine the relationship between women and power, it should not be analyzed as the only signifier of power but merely one among many. However, in spite of this caution, the tendency of some historians to position gender as the central, and primary, determinant of women's experience has been called to question in recent studies of the Middle Ages. An example of this tendency to position gender as the key determinant of experience can be found in the recent article of JoAnn McNamara, "Women and Power through the Family Revisited," in *Gendering the Master Narrative. Women and Power in the Middle Ages*, ed. Mary Erler and Maryanne Kowaleski (Ithaca, 2003). In her study of shifts in the position of women during this period, McNamara concludes that by the year 1000, gender replaced class as "the basic organizing principle in the new society," and consequently contributed to the further marginalization of women, p. 22. In discounting a range of other, equally important factors, such as age, social status, and marital status, conclusions are predicated upon monolithic

assessment of female experience. The result is described by Kimberly A. LoPrete as an "idealising essentialism," where "individual women are ahistorically reduced to what men thought all females were (or ought to have been)." Kimberly A. LoPrete, "The Gender of Lordly Women," pp. 90–110. These scholars are not suggesting that gender be discarded as a normative category, but rather that historians should resist the tendency to view it as binding, recognizing the frequency with which people tend to diverge from the norm in any society. See, e.g., the discussion by Carol J. Clover, "Regardless of Sex: Men, Women and Power in Early Northern Europe," *Speculum* 68 (1993): 363–87.
64. Duby, "Women and Power," p. 71.
65. Mitchell discusses the potential that divergent views existed in society concerning the position of women, suggesting that the uniformity that pervades modern notions may in fact be a product of modern, rather than medieval, prejudices concerning women. See Mitchell, *Portraits of Medieval Women*, p. 134: "The conflict might arise between competing cultural norms within a given society and historical analysis exterior to it. In other words, civilizations might have conflicting conceptions of gender embodied in their cultures; the historian might privilege one conception over another and thereby fail to acknowledge both the validity of the other conception and the prevalence of interior conflict."
66. As quoted in Duby, "Women and Power," p. 78.
67. This is a much different interpretation of Bernard's statement than that found in Duby's discussion of women and power. Duby cites this passage as evidence for his understanding of the medieval view of women as unilaterally denied access to power due to notions of gender. Duby, "Women and Power," p. 84: "By reason of their physical constitution, of the nature of their body, and the sex which defines them, women were deemed incapable of exercising the power of command, *potestas*." The possibility of two such dramatically different modern interpretations of this text illustrates the problems encountered by historians in their attempt to ascertain medieval views of gender. This example supports the views presented by Kimberly LoPrete, who argued that the medieval perception of powerful women has been frequently misconstrued by modern scholars, resulting in confusion and inaccurate conclusions. LoPrete, "The Gender of Lordly Women," p. 91.
68. See most recently Sharon Farmer, *Surviving Poverty in Medieval Paris. Gender, Ideology and the Daily Lives of the Poor* (Ithaca, 2002) and Ruth Mazo Karras, *From Boys to Men. Formations of Masculinity in Late Medieval Europe* (Philadelphia, 2003).
69. Clover, "Regardless of Sex," p. 371.
70. It seems that King John made overtures to Ferrand concerning an alliance between England and Flanders. Philip Augustus issued a charter at the end of May 1213, announcing Ferrand's defection and his refusal to participate in his proposed invasion of England, published in *Receuil des Actes de Philippe Auguste*, no. 1302, pp. 439–40.

71. Philip Augustus was forced to abort his invasion of England in May 1213. Teulet, *Trésor des Chartes*, no. 1304, pp. 442–43. From Lille they proceeded to Ypres, Bruges, and Ghent. See Nicholas, *Medieval Flanders*, p. 152 and Baldwin, *The Government of Philip Augustus*, p. 209.
72. Baldwin, *The Government of Philip Augustus*, p. 209 and Speigel, *Romancing the Past*, p. 47.
73. The alliance between England and Flanders was formalized in January, 1214 during Ferrand's visit to England. Baldwin, *The Government of Philip Augustus*, p. 209. According to the figures quoted by Baldwin, the French army at Bouvines consisted of 1,300 knights and 4,000–6,000 foot soldiers. The allies were able to field a slighter larger number of troops, with 1,300–1,500 knights and 7,500 foot soldiers. Despite the church's restrictions, the battle actually occurred on a Sunday, as the allies attempted to catch the French troops by surprise. As evidenced by the outcome of the battle, their attempt failed. Baldwin, *The Government of Philip Augustus*, p. 209. For a careful reconstruction of the actual battle, see Georges Duby, *The Legend of Bouvines. War, Religion and Culture in the Middle Ages* (Berkeley, 1990).
74. In the months following Bouvines, two-thirds of the nobility of Flanders and Hainaut languished in French prisons. Jim Bradbury describes the debilitating effect of Bouvines on Flanders, and the humiliation of Ferrand in Paris in *Philip Augustus. King of France. 1180–1223* (London, 1998), pp. 312–13.
75. Bradbury, *Philip Augustus*, p. 313.
76. According to Warnkoenig, Philip refrained from confiscating the fief because Ferrand, officially merely the baillif of the county, was guilty of treason. He did not hold Jeanne, the countess of Flanders, responsible for her husband's actions. Warnkoenig, *Histoire de la Flandre*, p. 230.
77. According to de Cant, most Flemish nobles were released between March, 1215 and October, 1217. De Cant, *Jeanne et Marguerite de Constantinople*, p. 69.
78. The text of the treaty of Paris, signed October 24, 1214, is published in Teulet, *Trésor des Chartes*, no. 1088, p. 407. The charter was sealed by the countess and fifteen witnesses, including Sibylle of Wavrin, Arnould of Audenarde, and Gérard of Jauche, who would become some of her strongest supporters. According to the terms of the treaty, she was instructed to grant Jean of Nesles, Sohier of Ghent, "and all the other men of the king" [et omnes alii homines domini regis] all the lands they had forfeited during the revolt. See also Dept, *Les Influences Anglaise*, p. 125.

2 Wielding Power: 1214–80

1. Linda Mitchell, "The Lady is a Lord," *Historical Reflections/Réflexions Historique* 18 (1992): 71–98, p. 78: "Thirteenth-century England behaved in a patriarchal fashion while exhibiting all the requirements of a hierarchic society. Distinctions of inherited status took precedence over gender, despite legal and social restrictions on female public action. This could provide the opportunity for de facto, unregulated female action on a broad scale and with

important social significance." In other words, as long as women were eligible to inherit authority, the possibility of female power continued to exist.
2. See William Mendel Newman, *Les Seigneurs de Nesle in Picardie (XIIe–XIIIe siècle). Leurs Chartes et Leur Histoire. Étude sur la Noblesse Régionale Ecclésiastique et Laïque*, vol. 1 (Philadelphia, 1971).
3. This suspicion is confirmed by Dept, *Les Influences Anglaise et Francaise dans le Comté de Flandre au Début du XIIIe Siècle* (Paris, 1928), p. 125. The severity of Ferrand's punishment was rivaled only by that meted out to Renaud de Dammartin, the count of Boulogne. While Jeanne was eventually able to secure Ferrand's release, Renaud's wife, Ida, was never successful. Renaud, whose relationship with Philip was much more complicated than Ferrand's, died in prison in 1227. See Henri Malo, *Un Grand Feudataire. Renaud de Dammartin et la Coalition de Bouvines* (Paris, 1898).
4. While a slight increase is notable, these numbers pale in comparison to Jeanne's activity as a patron after 1220, as discussed in later chapters. In 1219, the total number of charters issued by the countess reached twenty-two. This number would continue to climb until her death in 1244.
5. Scholars who have relied on the chronicle of Jacques de Guyse identify Matilda, the dowager countess, as the primary instigator, arguing that she coerced a reluctant Bouchard into marriage with Marguerite in order to prevent the young heiress from leaving Flanders and Hainaut. However, it is difficult to rely on de Guyse because of his tendency to incorporate popular legends into his chronicle. Various discussions of the marriage are available, the most reliable being that of Theo Luykx, *Johanna van Constantinopel. Gravin van Vlaanderen en Henegouwen, haar Leven (1199/1200–1244), haar Revgeering (1205–1244), vooral in Vlaanderen* (Antwerp, 1946), pp. 206–208. Some historians suggest that the marriage was instigated by the ten-year-old Marguerite, who seduced the dashing and charismatic Bouchard. It is difficult to imagine that the forty-year-old Bouchard was less than a willing and complicit participant in the events. See L.A. Warnkoenig, *Histoire de la Flandre et de ses Institutions Civiles et Politiques jusqu'a l'Annee 1309* (Bruxelles, 1835), p. 235. David Nicholas identifies Philip Augustus as the instigator of the marriage. However, no cite is included for this information. David Nicholas, *Medieval Flanders* (New York, 1992), p. 156. The most comprehensive account of the marriage and the later civil wars that resulted is provided by Charles Duvivier, *Les Influences Française et Germanique en Belgique au XIII siècle, La Querelle des d'Avesnes et des Dampierres jusqu'a la mort des de Jean d'Avesnes*, 2 vols. (Bruxelles, 1894). Much of his argument regarding the extent of Marguerite's complicity and the questions concerning legitimacy that later emerged relies on the testimony provided in the depositions of 1246. However, such testimony is provided primarily by the Avesnes themselves and their supporters, most notably Thierry de la Hamaide. In the absence of any corroborating documentation, I am hesitant to accept this version of events. The discussion here relies primarily on charter evidence, but does incorporate some information from various chronicles to illustrate the range of views on this subject, which fostered sentiment in opposition to both countesses.

6. The charter issued from Ghent on April 3, 1214, conveyed Jeanne and Ferrand's promise to investigate the claims advanced by Bouchard regarding Marguerite's inheritance. Alexandre Teulet, Joseph de Laborde, Elie Berger, and Henri Francois Delaborde, eds., *Layettes du Trésor des Chartes* (Paris, 1863–75), no. 1067, p. 398. One would expect that with such a wealthy and potentially powerful heiress, negotiations regarding the dowry would have occurred prior to the marriage, rather than two years after. Marguerite's consent would not have been sufficient for a canonically valid marriage since she was only ten, and hence still considered a minor in most thirteenth-century courts. In addition, according to the terms of the treaty of Pont de l'Arche, Philip Augustus had the right to approve the marriages of both Jeanne and Marguerite; his formal approval would have been conveyed in an official document. Duvivier says that no consent other than Marguerite's was needed since both she and Bouchard were younger children without "patrimoine personnel." However, this is not true of Marguerite, who stood to inherit the dower of Matilda, a not insignificant portion of land, as evidenced by the charter issued in 1235 dividing Marguerite's inheritance equally among her seven sons from both of her marriages. Duvivier, *Les Influences Française*, no. xxxvii, pp. 51–53.
7. The account of the marriage is provided by the Avesnes in a memoire addressed to King Louis IX in order to establish the marriage as legitimate and their position as heirs to Marguerite as countess of Flanders and Hainaut. The complete text is provided by Duvivier, *Les Influences Française*, no. xcvi, pp. 144–65. The original resides in the Archives Nationales, Paris, J 540.
8. It has been argued that absence of official opposition immediately following the marriage in 1212 is evidence of Jeanne and Ferrand's approval. However, events may have precluded an immediate response. Any action would have required the involvement of Ferrand, who was embroiled in his vendetta against Philip Augustus. It wasn't until the treaty of Paris was signed in October 1214 that Jeanne was free to turn her full attention to her sister's marriage. Hence, her appeal to the Fourth Lateran Council in 1215 would not have come as a surprise to her contemporaries, but rather would have been viewed as a logical, and in a sense timely, response to events. This conclusion is advanced by Luykx, *Johanna van Constantinopel*, p. 206 and Kervyn de Lettenhove, *Histoire de Flandre*, vol. 1 (Bruxelles, 1847), p. 210.
9. Duvivier, *Les Influences Française*, p. 57.
10. The traditionally pro-French stance of the Avesnes family suggests that Bouchard's appointment may have been instigated by Philip Augustus. According to Dept, Jacques of Avesnes was one of only a handful of Flemish nobles receiving French money fiefs in 1200. Dept, *Les Influences Anglaise*, p. 75. Even Kervyn de Lettenhove, who argues for the validity of the marriage, believes that Jeanne and Ferrand were unaware of the marriage until after it had occurred. Kervyn de Lettenhove, *Histoire de Flandre*, p. 210.
11. According to Duvivier, Bouchard replaced Nicolas de Condé, who had been named in 1210. The fact that Bouchard himself was removed from the

office as early as November 22, 1213 and replaced by Gérard of Jauche lends support to the theory that the wedding occurred without the consent of the count and countess. Duvivier, *Les Influences Française*, p. 56.
12. Teulet, *Trésor des Chartes*, no. 1155, pp. 424–25.
13. Innocent stated that the ecclesiastical council originally convened to settle the issue had found the evidence of Bouchard's perfidy convincing, indisputable proof of his status as a subdeacon and cantor. It is possible that Innocent is referring to a charter of 1205, in which Bouchard was identified as a canon of Laon. Bouchard was also granted a prebend in the cathedral of Tournai by Philip of Alsace. Teulet, *Trésor des Chartes*, no. 1156, p. 425.
14. It is interesting to note Innocent's repeated use of the word "*puella*" to describe Marguerite, rather than "*mulieram*," employed earlier by the archbishop of Rheims. It was perhaps a deliberate attempt to emphasize her extreme youth at the time of the marriage. Teulet, *Trésor des* Chartes, no. 1156, p. 425.
15. After listing Bouchard's crimes, Honorius repeated the sentence issued by his predecessor. Teulet, *Trésor des Chartes*, no. 1233, p. 446.
16. Mouskes cites the complicity of Sohiers of Wavre as well, who "guarded" Marguerite during her stay at the chateau of Houffalize. Philippe Mouskes, *Chronique Rimée*, ed. Baron de Reiffenberg (Bruxelles, 1836), v. 23226–23233, p. 410. From the text of the bull issued by Honorius, it is evident that Bouchard's supporters had successfully located priests who were willing to perform mass in spite of the excommunication. Teulet, *Trésor des Chartes*, no. 1342, p. 479.
17. Mouskes, *Chronique Rimée*, v. 23207–23220, p. 409. According to Mouskes, Bouchard, freed from prison in 1221, journeyed to Rome to appeal to the pope. Although initially unwilling to grant his forgiveness, the pope ordered Bouchard to wander the holy land as a destitute pilgrim. Bouchard proceeded to perform his penance, remaining in Syria until 1223. However, when he returned to Flanders to claim his bride and family, he discovered that she had since remarried: Mouskes, *Chronique Rimée*, v. 23280–23293, p. 412. It is clear that Bouchard lived well into the thirteenth century, as attested by a charter issued in January 1246, which challenged the division of Marguerite's inheritance that had occurred in 1234. Bouchard was listed among those appealing the division of Marguerite's inheritance in 1234. Teulet, *Trésor des Chartes*, no. 5404, p. 591.
18. Scholars have cited a donation made in 1234 by Marguerite to the abbey of Flines, in which she requests prayers for B., her lord and husband, as proof of her continued attachment to Bouchard. However, scrutiny of the original charters, available in Archives Départementales du Nord (ADN), Lille, prove that in published version, the letter G. has been mistaken for a B. Marguerite was, in fact, requesting prayers for her husband William, or Guillaume, not Bouchard. I have been unable to identify a single charter issued by Marguerite that contains a request for prayers on behalf of her first husband. However, in the archives of the abbey of Flines alone, dozens of

charters can be found, all issued after 1234, which mention G. or W., "quondam domini et mariti mei" [once my lord and husband]. This includes the actual foundation charter of the abbey, issued in October, 1234: "Ego M., quod pro remedio anime mea et domini W. de Dampetra, quondam mariti mei, necnon et omnium antecessorum meorum, locum qui dicitur Honor Beate Marie, situm prope villam de Orchies, in diocese Tornacensi, cum omnibus appendiciis suis, contuli in elemosinam Beato Bernardo et ordini Cysterciensi." Édouard Hautcoeur, ed., *Cartulaire de l'Abbaye de Flines* (Lille, 1874), no. 12 (October 9, 1234), p. 10.

19. Mouskes states that the two surviving Avesnes children were placed in the custody by William's brother, Archambaud of Dampierre, for seven years. Mouskes, *Chronique Rimée*, v. 28166–28181, pp. 583–84. If Mouskes's chronology is correct, and the boys were entrusted to Archambaud in 1224, following the collapse of the revolt of the False Baldwin, they would have remained in prison until 1232. Since it was William of Dampierre's brother who retained custody of the boys, it seems logical to conclude that William and Marguerite were initially responsible for placing them in prison. Why they were eventually released in 1232 remains a mystery.

20. Archives Départementales du Nord (ADN), Lille, Inventaire Chronologique et detaillé des chartres de la Chambre des Comptes à Lille 2157 H51, no. 347.

21. The initial conflict and its resolution were recorded in two separate charters, the first dated Easter 1221, and the second sometime later in April of the same year. ADN, Lille, Inv. Chron., 2187 H51, no. 350; Inv. Chron., 2187 H51, no. 351. In issuing his verdict, Jean of Nesle stipulated that the inhabitants of Audenarde and Pamele be exempted from the tax; Inv. Chron., 2187 H51, no. 399.

22. The purchase occurred on October 28, 1218. Dept suggests that this maneuver was intended to neutralize the influence of the pro-French party in Flanders and to bolster the strength of the pro-English towns, whose autonomy was previously hampered by the traditional prerogatives of the castellans. Dept, *Les Influences Anglaise*, p. 148.

23. ADN, Lille, Inv. Chron., 2187 H51, no. 316. After this date, Michel of Harnes disappears from the witness lists of charters issued by the countess, replaced by a variety of other men and women. One of the witnesses of this act was Hellin of Wavrin, the senechal of Flanders.

24. ADN, Lille, Inv. Chron., 2187 H51, no. 432.

25. Teulet, *Trésor des Chartes*, no. 1497 (January 7, 1222). See also Newman, *Les Seigneurs de Nesle*, p. 39. Luykx dates the resignation of Jean of Nesle to 1224 rather than 1222. Luykx, *Johanna van Constantinopel*, p. 149.

26. While Luykx suggests that Jean of Nesle willingly sold the castellany to the countess to raise funds, Newman rejects this explanation, citing a lack of corroborating evidence. Newman, *Les Seigneurs de Nesle*, p. 39.

27. These three men appear as witnesses in a number of important documents issued by Jeanne in the years after Ferrand's death as well, including the

charter recording the terms of her daughter Marie's marriage to Robert of Artois. Teulet, *Trésor des Chartes*, no. 2388; (June 1235), p. 294.
28. ADN, Lille, Inv. Chron., 2187 H51, no. 308.
29. ADN, Lille, Inv. Chron., 2187, H51, no. 397. She stipulated that the exemption not be granted to the children of these individuals, who would be expected to pay the customary taxes owed to her after the death of their parents.
30. Warnkoenig, vol. 3, no. 13, p. 254; Inv. Chron., 2187 H51, no. 315; no. 349.
31. Alphonse Wauters, ed., *Table Chronologique des Chartes et Diplômes Imprimées Concernant l'Histoire de la Belgique* (Brussels, 1903–12), no. xi, p. 478.
32. Dept, *Les Influences Anglaise*, p. 148.
33. R.L. Wolff provides the most detailed account of these events. See R.L. Wolff, "Baldwin of Flanders and Hainaut, First Latin Emperor of Constantinople: His Life, His Death and Resurrection, 1171–1225," *Speculum* 27 (1952): 281–322.
34. The hermit claimed that as Baldwin IX, he had escaped from the prison of Ionnitsa, only to be enslaved by Syrians. He persuaded a group of visiting German merchants to buy his freedom. In order to explain his failure to reveal his identify prior to this date, the false Baldwin claimed that his experience had left him skeptical of power and authority and more inclined toward the peace and solitude he found in the forest of Glançon.
35. Geneviève de Cant, *Jeanne and Marguerite de Constantinople, Comtesses de Flandres et de Hainaut au XIIIe siècle* (Brussels, 1995), p. 105. The rebellion was particularly strong in the city of Valenciennes, and attracted supporters primarily from the county of Hainaut, including Bouchard of Avesnes. See Luykx, *Johanna van Constantinopel*, pp. 213–24. Wolff, erroneously in my opinion, attributes the initial success of the imposter to the people's frustration under the rule of "two unstable and self-willed women." See R.L. Wolff, "Baldwin of Flanders and Hainaut," pp. 300–301.
36. L.A. Warnkoenig, *Histoire de la Flandre*, p. 237. Henry III, attempting to manipulate the situation to his own advantage, made overatures of peace to the imposter, addressing him as Baldwin, and proffering an alliance. Henry obviously viewed this as an occasion to weaken Flanders, whose relationship with England had deteriorated after the death of John I and the solidification of French control following Bouvines. The letter was sent from London on April 11, 1225.
37. Duvivier, *Les Influences Française*, p. 169.
38. Dept, *Les Influences Anglaise*, p. 172.
39. Teulet, *Trésor des Chartres*, no. 53 (June 1225).
40. Gabrielle Spielgel, *Romancing the Past*, p. 52: "Since Bouvines, Jeanne had been counseled and supervised by royal baillis but had maintained a semblance of comital authority and autonomy. Louis' campaign in Flanders in 1225 forced her to acknowledge her total dependence on the French king, thus destroying even the illusion of an independent Flanders."
41. Dept, *Les Influences Anglaise*, p. 165. In a brief sketch of Jeanne's life, Lucienne Mazenod suggests that she initially refused to pay Ferrand's

ransom, preferring to keep him in prison so that she could maintain control of Flanders. However, there is no evidence provided to substantiate this claim. All of the available evidence presents Jeanne as extremely dedicated in her efforts to secure her husband's release. See Lucienne Mazened, ed., *Les femmes célèbres*, vol. 1 (N.p., 1960), p. 303. He is perhaps relying on de Meersseman, who argues that Jeanne actually conspired to keep Ferrand in prison, prefering sole control of Flanders and Hainaut to the shared rule that would result from his release. He cites Jeanne's failure to act prior to 1223 as evidence for his argument. However, he omits the numerous sources which prove that Jeanne was acting on Ferrand's behalf long before 1223. J. de Meersseman, "Étude Historique sur Jeanne de Constantinople, Comtesse de Flandre," *Annales de la Societe d'Emulation pour l'histoire et des Antiquites de la Flandre Occidentale*, vol. 2 (Bruges, 1841).

42. This charter cites a total of 29,000 *livres* borrowed from various sources. These loans were guaranteed by Blanche, the countess of Troyes, and her son Thibaut, count of Champagne, and were borrowed expressly for Ferrand's release. Published in Édouard le Glay, *Histoire de Jeanne, de Constantinopla, Comtesse de Flandre et de Hainaut* (Lille, 1841), pp. 67–68.

43. According to Le Glay, Jeanne also enlisted the services of the bishops of Tournai, Cambrai and Thérouanne, to no avail. Le Glay, *Histoire de Jeanne*, p. 66.

44. Karen Nicholas has suggested that Philip's refusal may have been prompted by his desire to prevent the countess from producing an heir in the hopes that upon her death, he could seize direct control of the counties. Karen Nicholas, "Countesses as Rulers in Flanders," in *Aristocratic Women in Medieval France*, ed. Theodore Evergates (Philadelphia, 1999), pp. 111–37. Although Philip had pursued similar policies successfully in regards to other fiefs in his kingdom, the presence of Marguerite complicated the matter as it applied to Flanders. As long as Jeanne remained childless, the county was destined to pass to her sister, her legitimate successor as countess. It could only revert to the French crown if no heir was present. Louis does seem to have adopted his father's policy of assimilating the fiefs of his most powerful vassals through marriage, as indicated by the betrothal of Jeanne's daughter Marie to his brother Robert in 1235. However, the situation as it existed in 1224, prior to the birth of any children to the count and countess, were not conducive to such machinations. Marie was not born until after Ferrand's return. The terms of the marriage are outlined in detail by Luykx, *Johanna van Constantinopel*, pp. 326–28.

45. According to Warnkoenig, the first draft of the treaty of Melun was produced prior to Louis VIII's death. However, the nobles of Flanders and Hainaut refused to comply, citing the exorbitant payment of 50,000 *livres parisis* stipulated by the terms of the treaty. After Louis's death, Louis IX agreed to lower the ransom, suggesting a more acceptable payment of 25,000 *livres parisis*. However, it is difficult to determine the accuracy of Warnkoenig's statement due to the absence of corroborating evidence. See Warnkoenig, *Histoire de la Flandre*, p. 233. Élie Berger attributes Louis IX's

willingness to free Ferrand to the intervention of his mother, Blanche of Castile. Blanche was related to Ferrand, and could have possibly formed a relationship with Jeanne during the young countess' residence at the royal court from 1208 to 1212. Élie Berger, *Histoire de Blanche de Castille: Reine de France* (Paris, 1895), p. 330.
46. Jeanne and Ferrand vowed to uphold the terms of the treaty, to remain loyal vassals of Louis, to provide military service when required, and to prohibit construction of any new fortresses south of the Escaut. The 50,000 *livres* were to paid in two installments, the first at the time of Ferrand's release. Published in Teulet, *Trésor des Chartes*, no. 1762, p. 77.
47. Her progress is noted by Luykx, and it provides evidence of Jeanne's commitment to liberate her husband as soon as possible. Between December 14 and December 31, Jeanne traveled to four different towns in Flanders, collecting signatures from each government. She returned to Paris in December 31, signed the treaty with Louis IX and Blanche, collected Marguerite's guarantee on January 2, the guarantee of the échevins of Douai on January 5, and returned to Paris in January 6, the date of Ferrand's official liberation. Luykx, *Johanna van Constantinopel*, pp. 259–60.
48. Teulet, *Trésor des Chartes*, no. 1897 (December 1226), p. 111.
49. Duvivier, *Les Influences Française*, p. 96.
50. The chronicler of Tours stated that Pierre asked Innocent IV to annul Jeanne and Ferrand's marriage so that he could marry the countess. Luykx, *Johanna van Constantinopel*, p. 249. David Nicholas suggests that the marriage to Pierre was actually instigated by Philip. This seems unlikely considering Philip's relationship to and noted suspicion of the duke of Brittany; Nicholas, *Medieval Flanders*, p. 155. According to Henri Pirenne, the possibility of an alliance between Flanders and Brittany forced Louis into action: "Louis VIII n'eut d'autre moyen pour empêcher la réalisation de ce plan, qui eut suscite contre la couronne une formidable puissance féodale, que de délivrer le vaincu de Bouvines." Henri Pirenne, *Histoire de Belgique* (Brussels, 1929), p. 236.
51. Jean Richard, *Saint Louis. Crusader King of France*, trans. Jean Birrell (Cambridge, 1992), p. 15.
52. Baldwin, *The Government of Philip Augustus*, p. 271.
53. Careful exploitation of the feudal right of wardship appears to have been part of the systematic policy pursued by Philip Augustus in his campaign to consolidate control of his vassals and centralize authority in France. See Baldwin, *The Government of Philip Augustus*, p. 271.
54. Teulet, *Trésor des Chartes*, no. 2491 (April 12, 1237), p. 336; no. 2492 (April 12, 1237), p. 336. See also Luykx, *Johanna von Constantinopel*, pp. 329–31.
55. Two of Marguerite's Dampierre children held the title of count during her rule. The eldest son, William, performed homage to Louis IX in the 1250s, but he died unexpectedly at a tournament in Trazegnies in 1251. He was succeeded as count by his brother Guy, who performed homage to the king of France in 1252. However, Guy remained in a supporting role in affairs until Marguerite's abdication in 1278, when he assumed complete control

of Flanders. All of the charters I have examined that were issued jointly by Marguerite and her sons follow the formula of listing her name and title first, followed by theirs. For example, a charter issued in June 1248 to the town council of Ghent begins "Margareta Flandriae et Hainoniae comitissa et Willelmus ejus filius comes et dominus de Dampetra" [Marguerite, countess of Flanders and Hainaut and William her son, count and lord of Dampierre]. Warnkoenig, *Histoire de la Flandre*, vol. 3, no. 23, pp. 276–77. The inscription on his seal reflects his subordinate status. Although he has adopted the title of count of Flanders, he identifies himself as the "son of the countess" on the *contre-sceau* [reverse side].

56. If Marguerite's marriage to Bouchard was considered valid, Jean of Avesnes would have succeeded as ruler of the two counties upon his mother's death. However, according to canon law, as enforced by the papacy, children of invalid marriages were considered illegitimate, and dismissed in favor of legitimate heirs. This principle was obviously in effect in Flanders from the twelfth century. If illegitimate children were valid candidates, William of Thy-le-Chateau, the son of Philip of Alsace, would have succeeded as count instead of his half-sister, Marguerite. Naturally, extenuating circumstances affected the papacy's enforcement of the rule, which was far from consistent. See Georges Duby, *Medieval Marriage. Two Models from Twelfth-Century France*, trans. Elborg Forster (Baltimore, 1978).
57. This agreement must have been made prior to the birth of Jeanne's youngest child, Marie, who later entered the abbey of Flines as a Cistercian nun. The agreement was confirmed by Louis IX. Published in Le Glay, *Histoire de Jeanne*, pp. 195–99.
58. De Cant, *Jeanne et Marguerite de Constantinople*, p. 190.
59. According to some accounts, Jean of Avesnes actually presented himself to the king at Peronne, where he appealed to Louis to reconsider the succession. An altercation ensued between Jean of Avesnes and William of Dampierre, which culminated in a hostile exchange of words and the abrupt departure of Jean of Avesnes. Whether or not this exchange actually occurred is impossible to determine. However, Louis's arbitration of 1246 suggests that the decision was appealed by Jean of Avesnes. See Warnkoeing, *Histoire de la Flandre*, p. 245.
60. De Cant, *Jeanne et Marguerite de Constantinople*, p. 190.
61. De Cant, *Jeanne et Marguerite de Constantinople*, p. 194.
62. Kervyn de Lettenhove, *Histoire de Flandre*, p. 249.
63. De Cant, *Jeanne et Marguerite de Constantinople*, p. 200.
64. On April 28, the Avesnes formally named their representatives. The Dampierres soon followed, announcing theirs on June 17. Kervyn de Lettenhove, *Histoire de Flandre*, p. 250.
65. Early reports suggest that Flemish losses at Westkappelle rivaled those of Bouvines. However, it is necessary to account for the medieval tendency toward exaggeration. For example, Matthew Paris states that Marguerite's army lost 50,000 men. However, Matthew Paris, ensconced within the walls of the abbey of Saint-Albans, can hardly be considered a reliable

source for events that occurred across the channel. For instance, the battle of Westkappelle is reported by Matthew as occurring in the year 1254, rather than 1252. In addition, Matthew Paris seldom refrained from sharing his personal opinion of individuals, and his portrayal of Marguerite is particularly vicious: "In the same year, a great slaughter of men, horses, and cattle took place in the provinces adjoining Flanders and Germany, and it was believed that more than forty thousand fighting men were slain. Like Troy, which was said to have been destroyed with its inhabitants through a woman, so this deadly slaughter was caused by a woman, namely, the countess of Flanders." See *The Chronicles of Matthew Paris*, trans. Robert Vaughn (Gloucester, 1984), p. 30.

66. Teulet, *Trésor des Chartes*, no. 4290, p. 320.
67. Jean's younger brother Baldwin of Avesnes abstained from engaging in the dynastic conflict that had consumed his elder brother, and Jean of Avesnes's son and successor Jean II was a minor at the time of his father's death.
68. Louis required Marguerite to pay Charles 160,000 *livres tournois* in compensation for his services. The sum was dispensed over the course of thirteen years, with Marguerite receiving a receipt for full payment in 1271. See Jean Dunbabin, *Charles I of Anjou. Power, Kingship and State-Making in Thirteenth-Century Europe* (New York, 1998), p. 38.
69. Wielding a sword is cited by Duby as a central image associated with power in the Middle Ages, and the primary obstacle women faced in their attempt to rule: "I prefer to evoke a concrete image, a symbolic object, the better to enter into the thought of the men of whom I speak. . .This object is the sword. *Potestas*, the power to command and to punish, the duty of preserving the peace and justice, was exercised by the sword such as one solemnly entrusted to the lord's son when he came to power and held unsheathed before him when he fulfilled his function." Georges Duby, "Women and Power," in *Cultures of Power: Lordship, Status and Process in 12th-Century Europe*, ed. Thomas N. Bisson (Philadelphia, 1995), pp. 69–85, p. 73.
70. Theresa Earenfight discusses the challenges posed to the government of Maria of Castile, identifying them not as the result of opposition to a woman's rule per se, but rather as stemming from opposition to her as the king's lieutenant. Theresa Earenfight, "Maria of Castile, Ruler or Figurehead? A Preliminary Study in Aragonese Queenship," *Mediterranean Studies* 4 (1994): 46–61, especially pp. 60–61.
71. Duby quotes a letter from Bernard of Clairvaux to Melisende, queen of Jerusalem, which provides insight into what some members of medieval society believed about the relationship between women and *potestas*. Duby, "Women and Power," p. 78.
72. Jane Schulenberg, "Female Sanctity: Public and Private Roles, ca. 500–1100," in *Women and Power in the Middle Ages*, ed. Mary Erler and Maryanne Kowaleski (Athens, 1988), pp. 102–125, especially p. 105. According to Schulenberg, the distinction between public and private, which she describes as redundant in the early medieval period, became increasingly delineated in the eleventh and twelfth centuries, with the emergence of

formal institutions of government. Public power passed from aristocratic families to the bureaucratic officials employed in the king's service.
73. Joanne McNamara and Suzanne Wemple, "The Power of Women Through the Family," in *Women and Power in the Middle Ages*, ed. Mary Erler and Maryanne Kowaleski (Athens, 1988), pp. 83–101; p. 5: "The success of the aristocracy as a class in adjusting itself to this broad political change was accomplished largely at the expense of the aristocratic women. As the families were resisting princely encroachment upon their rights by insisting upon the indivisibility of the patrimony, the economic rights of women were restricted. Concurrently as rulers slowly developed an impersonal machinery for government, queens and empresses, as well as ladies on a somewhat more modest level, were excluded from public life." They do note that this process occurred more gradually in France, and women were never categorically excluded from inheritance, particularly in cases of absence of male heir. Pauline Stafford presents a similar trajectory of women's power, which, she argued, reached a nadir in the twelfth century with the "shift away from household politics toward greater bureaucratization in Western Europe." See Pauline Stafford, *Queens, Concubines and Dowagers, The King's Wife in the Early Middle Ages*, 2nd. rev. ed. (London, 1998), p. 195. In the revised edition of this important work, Stafford suggests that the views about the relegation of women presented earlier may need to be amended in light of more recent studies. Kimberly LoPrete challenges this narrative of women's marginalization: "When practitioners of this emerging history of mentalités turned to the noble family and women. . . the social models erected posited a deterioration in noblewomen's status until they were systematically marginalized in the eleventh and twelfth centuries." LoPrete, "Historical Ironies in the Study of Capetian Women," in *Capetian Women*, ed. Kathleen Nolan (New York, 2003), pp. 271–86, p. 273.
74. LoPrete, "The Gender of Lordly Women: The Case of Adela of Blois," in *Pawns or Players? Studies on Medieval and Early Modern Women*, ed. Christine Meek and Catherine Lawless (Dublin, 2003), p. 110.
75. For a more detailed discussion of seals and their meaning for medieval nobles, see Brigitte Bedos-Rezak, "Women, Seals, and Power in Medieval France, 1150–1350," in *Women and Power in the Middle Ages*, pp. 61–82. Depictions of Jeanne's seal can be found in Maurice Vanhaeck, ed., *Cartulaire de l'Abbaye de Marquette* (Lille, 1937).
76. For the terms of this dispute, see Warnkoenig, *Histoire de la Flandre*, vol. 3, no. 15 (1223), pp. 436–37.
77. Édouard de Coussemaker, ed., *Inventaire Analytique et Chronologique des Archives de la Chambre des Comptes à Lille* (Lille, 1865), no. 574 (1233), p. 233.
78. Illustrations of both of these seals are available in Hautcoeur, *Cartulaire de l'Abbaye de Flines*, p. 491.
79. Teulet, *Trésor des Chartes*, no. 3223 and no. 3224 (March 1245), p. 548.
80. In light of her ability to translate the authority she inherited into actual power, it is not surprising that her sons identified themselves in relation to

their mother on their own seals, overt recognition that their own position was derived from her. According to Amy Livingstone, the use of seals by aristocratic women was one of the primary indications that were "recognized participants in the power relationships that defined the medieval world." See Amy Livingstone, "Powerful Allies and Dangerous Adversaries. Noblewomen in Medieval Society," in *Women in Medieval Western European Culture*, ed. Linda E. Mitchell (New York, 1999), pp. 7–30, especially p. 24.
81. See Alan M. Stahl, "Coinage in the Name of Medieval Women," in *Medieval Women and the Sources of Medieval History*, ed. Joel T. Rosenthal (Athens, 1990), pp. 321–41, especially p. 321.
82. Lori J. Walters, "The Image of Blanchefleur in Montpellier BI, sect. méd. H 249," in *The Manuscripts of Chrétien de Troyes*, ed. Keith Busby, Terry Nixon, Alison Stones, and Lori Walters, 2 vols. (Amsterdam, 1993), pp. 437–55. Walters concludes that "Manessier's refashioning of Blanchefleur as a strong, dignified, and chaste ruler-a fitting likeness of Jeanne herself-surely helped the poet win favor at the royal court," p. 445. See also Lori J. Walters, "Jeanne and Marguerite de Flandre as Female Patrons," *Dalhousie French Studies* 28 (1994): 15–27. Reliance on certain modern sources has resulted in the presence of some factual errors in this discussion of Jeanne and Marguerite. However, it provides a detailed discussion of their literary patronage.
83. June Hall McCash, "The Cultural Patronage of Medieval Women: An Overview," in *The Cultural Patronage of Medieval Women*, ed. McCash (Athens, 1996), pp. 1–49, p. 21. Jeanne also commissioned a translation of a *Vita Sanctae Marthae* during the early years of her reign. Mary D. Stanger, "Literary Patronage at the Medieval Court of Flanders," *French Studies* 11 (1957): 214–29.
84. Richard, *Saint Louis*, p. 12.

3 Securing Power through Religious Patronage

1. This understanding of her obligation as a ruler was not unique, as suggested by William Chester Jordan's discussion of the various ways piety informed Louis IX's approach to governance. See W.C. Jordan, "Isabelle of France and Religious Devotion at the Court of Louis IX," in *Capetian Women*, ed. Kathleen Nolan (New York, 2003), pp. 209–224.
2. In the words of Miriam Shadis, "the goals of patronage and politicking were to establish self and family-as well as to please God." Miriam Shadis, "Piety, Politics, and Power: The Patronage of Leonor of England and Her Daughters Berenguela of Leon and Blanche of Castile," in *The Cultural Patronage of Medieval Women*, ed. June Hall McCash (Georgia, 1996), p. 213.
3. Joel T. Rosenthal warns against attempts to distinguish between secular and sacred concerns since "the medieval mind (and social conscience) made no distinction between an eventual sacerdotal and a social end of charity." Joel T. Rosenthal, *The Purchase of Paradise. Gift Giving and the Aristocracy, 1307–1485* (London, 1972), pp. 9–10. For a similar discussion, see Emma

Cownie, *Religious Patronage in Anglo-Norman England, 1066–1135* (Woodbridge, 1998), pp. 3–10.
4. See Shadis, "Piety, Politics, and Power," p. 216; Victoria Chandler, "Politics and Piety: Influences on Charitable Donations during the Anglo-Norman period," *Revue Benedictine* 90 (1980): 63–72, p. 64.
5. Cownie, *Religious Patronage*, pp. 7–8.
6. Édouard Hautcoeur, ed., *Cartulaire de l'Abbaye de Flines* (Lille, 1874), no. 7 (May 1234), pp. 6–7.
7. Jean Francois Foppens, ed., *Diplomatum Belgicorum Nova Collectio sive Supplementum ad Opera Diplomatica Auberti Miraei*, vol. 3 (Brussels, 1734), no. 117, p. 585. Marguerite's generosity allowed the abbey to amass a patrimony wealthy enough to sustain 100 choir nuns and 18 *conversae*, as determined by Philippe, abbot of Clairvaux, in response to a papal bull issued by Clément IV in 1270. Hautcoeur, *Cartulaire de l'Abbaye de Flines*, no. 173 (June 18, 1270), pp. 184–86.
8. See Adriaan Verhulst, *The Rise of Cities in North-West Europe* (Cambridge, 1999) and David Nicholas, "Of Poverty and Primacy: Demand, Liquidity, and the Flemish Economic Miracle, 1050–1200," *American Historical Review* 96 (1991): 17–41.
9. The difficulties encountered by the Flemish nobility are chronicled by H.E. Warlop, *The Flemish Nobility Before 1300*, 4 vols. (Kortrijk, 1975–76) and Gabrielle Spiegel, *Romancing the Past. The Rise of Vernacular Prose Historiography in Thirteenth-Century France* (Berkeley, 1993), p. 27.
10. In this charter, Marguerite approved the sale of a fief held by P. Walter of Gistel to the abbey of Vaucelles for the sum of 3,750 *livres*. The text of the charter clearly indicates that Walter was forced to sell the land in order to alleviate the burden of his current debts. Warlop, *The Flemish Nobility*, vol. 1, p. 282.
11. Warlop, *The Flemish Nobility*, vol. 1, p. 292.
12. Spiegel, *Romancing the Past*, p. 33. John Baldwin also notes the importance of the Artois in the battle between France and Flanders. John Baldwin, *The Government of Philip Augustus. Foundations of French Royal Power in the Middle Ages* (Berkeley, 1986), p. 24.
13. See Jim Bradbury, *Philip Augustus, King of France. 1180–1223* (London, 1998), pp. 312–13. For the complete text of the treaty of Paris see Alexandre Teulet, Joseph de Laborde, Élie Berger, and Henri Francois Delaborde, eds., *Layettes du Trésor des Chartes*, vol. 1 (Paris, 1863), no. 1088, p. 407.
14. This list excludes the abbeys of Ravensberg (1194–1205), Blendeques (1186–1206), Brayelle (1196–1250), and Fontenelles (1212). Although also located along the southern periphery near Lille, these abbeys were all founded prior to 1214.
15. Hautcoeur, *Cartulaire de l'Abbaye de Flines*, no. 117 (July 1258), pp. 119–20; no. 28 (July 1242), pp. 29–30; no. 89 (January 1250), pp. 79–80.
16. Hautcoeur, *Cartulaire de l'Abbaye de Flines*, no. 173 (June 18, 1270), pp. 184–86.
17. Patrick Geary, *Phantoms of Remembrance. Memory and Oblivion at the End of the First Millennium* (Princeton, 1994), pp. 141–44.

18. Janet Burton, *The Monastic Order in Yorkshire, 1069–1215* (Cambridge, 1999), p. 123. See also Cownie, *Religious Patronage*, pp. 7–8 and Robin Fleming, "Monastic Lands and England's Defense in the Viking Age," *English Historical Review* 100 (1985): 247–65.
19. See most notably Stephen D. White, *Custom, Kinship and Gifts to Saints: The Laudatio Parentum in Western France, 1050–1150* (Chapel Hill, 1988).
20. Ferdinand van de Putte, ed., *Chronicon et cartularium abbatiae sancti Nicolai Furnensis*, (Bruges, 1849), no. 97 (1241), p. 99.
21. Alphonse Wauters, ed., *Table Chronologique des Chartes et Diplômes Imprimés Concernant l'Histoire de la Belgique*, vol. 4 (Brussels, 1903–12), no. 123 (June 1246), p. 448.
22. According to Milis, the exact circumstances regarding the affiliation of the abbey to Arrouaise remain unknown. However, at the time of affiliation, the foundation supported seven canons. Ludo Milis, *L'Ordre des Chanoines Réguliers d'Arrouaise. Son Histoire et son Organization de la Fondation de l'Abbaye (vers 1090) à la fin des Chapitres Annuels (1471)* (Bruges, 1969), p. 153.
23. Georges Callewaert, ed., *Chartes Anciennes de l'Abbaye de Zonnebeke* (Bruges, 1925), no. 41 (February 9, 1218), p. 46; no. 45 (March 1219), p. 51; no. 53 (January 1222), p. 55.
24. According to Milis, despite the affiliation of the abbey to Arrouaise in 1132, several secular canons remained in residence until 1164–65, indicating a gradual transition to the Order. Milis, *Arrouaise*, p. 152. In both of these documents, the countesses arranged for arbitration of disputes involving the abbey and a third party. Paris, Bibliothèque Nationale, *Cartulaire de l'Abbaye de Saint-Calixte de Cysoing*, Coll. Flandre, vol 73, 147r–149v (March 1218); Lille, Archives Départementales du Nord (ADN) 38 H 14/52 (November 18, 1262). The first confirmation involved a sale made by the abbey to Arnoud, seigneur of Cysoing, Lille, ADN 38 H 71/342 (May 1, 1253). The second involved land at Bruille, sold by Baudouin de la Fosse to the abbey, Lille, ADN 38 H 68/330 (January 14, 1268).
25. Lille, ADN 38 H 48/254 (January 30, 1251).
26. Wauters, *Table Chronologique*, vol. 4, p. 347.
27. *Chronicon et Cartularium abbatiae sancti Nicolai Furnensis*, pp. 96–97 and Wauters, *Table Chronologique*, vol. 4, p. 352 and 354.
28. Lille, ADN, Inventaire Chronologique et detaillé des charters de la Chambre des Comptes à Lille 2157 H 51, no. 1421. Marguerite expressly retained all judicial rights connected with the land in question.
29. Lille, ADN, Inv. Chron., 2157 H 51, no. 1477, pp. 583–84.
30. Georges Callewaert, ed., *Chartes Anciennes de l'Abbaye de Zonnebeke* (Bruges, 1925), no. 44 (February 26, 1219), p. 50.
31. Léopold van Hollebeke, ed., *L'Abbaye de Nonnenbossche, de l'ordre de St. Benoît, près d'Ypres (1101–1796)* (Bruges, 1865), no. 35, (April 1, 1220), p. 98.
32. Léopold Van Hollebeke, ed., *Cartulaire de l'Abbaye de Saint-Pierre de Loo (1093–1794)* (Bruxelles, 1870), no. 38 (July 17, 1220), pp. 43–44.

33. E. Feys and A. Nelis, eds., *Les Trois Cartulaires de la Prévoté ou Abbaye de Saint-Martin à Ypres* (Bruges, 1880), no. 189 (May 31, 1255), p. 128; no. 192 (June 1255), p.130; no. 197 (October 23, 1255), p. 132.
34. E. Feys and Nelis, *Cartulaires de Saint-Martin*, no. 79 (December 1213), p. 59; no. 93 (May 1218), pp. 66–67; no. 134 (May 1235), p. 91; no. 145 (July 1237), p. 97; no. 185 (November 25, 1253), pp. 124–25; no. 227 (May 1263), p. 152; no. 230 (February 13, 1264), p. 153.
35. Lille, ADN, 10 H 160/2516 (Jan 1240); 10 H 210/3442 (1260).
36. J. de Smet, ed., *Cartulaire de Cambron* (Brussels, 1869), no. 20 (November 1254), pp. 456–57; no. 6 (April 1243), pp. 647–48; no. 42 (May 1273), pp. 465–67; no. 19 (July 1250), p. 658; no. 21 (July 1257), pp. 437–38.
37. Van Hollebeke, *L'Abbaye de Nonnenbossche*, no. 35 (April 1, 1220), p. 98.
38. Lille, ADN, Inv. Chron, 2187 H51, no. 635 (July 1236).
39. Lille, ADN, 10 H 210/3442 (1260).
40. Lille, ADN, 1 H 65/738 (May 9, 1265).
41. E. Feys and A. Nelis, *Cartulaires de Saint-Martin*, no. 153 (June 1240), pp. 102–103.
42. E. Feys and A. Nelis, *Cartulaires de Saint-Martin*, no. 19, pp. 59–60.
43. Lille, ADN, B 404/808 (December 4, 1244). This difficulty is primarily the result of the loss of the community's archives. However, scholars concur that Marguerite was the initial founder of the convent at Bergues, and generally date the foundation to the early 1240s. See Alphonse de Laroière, "Notice sur le Couvent des Dominicains à Bergues (Saint-Winoc)," *Bulletin du Comité Flamand de France* 4 (1870): 348–84, especially p. 350.
44. Hellin de Commines, who later served as Marguerite's confessor, was appointed the first prior of the community. Marie-Dominique Chapotin, *Histoire des Dominicains de la Province de France. Le Siècle des Fondations* (Paris, 1898), p. 346. Also G.G. Meersseman, "Les Débuts de l'Ordre des Frères-Prêcheurs dans le Comté de Flandre (1224–1280)," *Archivum Fratrum Praedicatorum* 17 (1947): 54–76.
45. G.G. Meersseman, "Jeanne de Constantinople et les Frères Prêcheurs," *Archivum Fratrum Praedicatorum* 19 (1949): 122–68, p. 139.
46. The final conditions of foundation were included in a charter issued by Jeanne in October 1233, published in Meersseman, "Jeanne de Constantinople," p. 161.
47. Meersseman, "Jeanne de Constantinople," p. 161. However, this agreement did include the stipulation that the parish church retain the right to perform funeral services for all individuals who requested burial among the friars.
48. This charter, issued by Marguerite in conjunction with her son Guy, stipulated that the friars separate their land from that retained by the countess with a cloister, and it granted them permission to build a bridge to span the canal that divided the land of the chateau from that of the meadow. I.L.A. Diegerick, ed., *Inventaire Analytique et Chronologique des Chartes et Documents Appartenant Aux Archives de la Ville d'Ypres* (Bruges, 1853–68), no. 106 (September 1, 1268), p. 91. See also Henri Marie Iweins, "Monographie du couvent des Frères-Precheurs à Ypres (1267–1797)," *Annales de la Société*

Historique, Archéologique et Littéraire de la Ville d'Ypres et de l'Ancienne West-Flandre 3 (1865): 41–192.
49. According to de Meersseman, the canons of Saint-Martin obtained a letter from pope Urban IV prohibiting all mendicants from establishing foundations in the parishes of Saint-Martin or Saint-Jacques. See de Meersseman, "Les Débuts de l'Ordre des Frères Prêcheurs," p. 74.
50. Wauters, *Table Chronologique*, vol. 4 (January 1275), p. 457; (February 1275), p. 458.
51. Lille, ADN, 16 G 17/166 (March 14, 1274). The nuns had already received several grants of land from Marguerite, including several fiefs in the parish of Foumielles, acquired by the countess on their behalf. Lille, ADN, 130 H 5/45 (May 1272).
52. Marguerite makes reference to this donation in a charter issued two years after the original grant. George Descamps, *Notre-Dame du Val-des-Écoliers prieuré ensuite abbaye de Chanoine Reguliérs, OSA à Mons (1252–1769)* (Mons, 1885), no. 1 (August 1252), pp. 275–76.
53. Descamps, *Val-des-Écoliers*, no. 4 (August 31, 1252), p. 278.
54. This charter contains Marguerite's request for the bishop's assent to the foundation, and it specifies the size and value of the land in question. Descamps, *Val-des-Écoliers*, no. 2 (August 19, 1252), pp. 276–77.
55. Descamps, *Val-des-Écoliers*, no. 6 (November 18, 1252), pp. 279–80.
56. Joseph-Marie Canivez, ed., *Statuta Capitulorum generalium ordinis Cisterciensis*, vol. 2, ed. Canivez (Louvain, 1933), no. 66 (1236), p. 168. The abbots of Villiers, Val-Saint-Lambert, and Grandpré were assigned the task of inspecting the abbey to ensure an adequate endowment.
57. Joseph-Marie Canivez, *L'Ordre de Cîteaux en Belgique. Des Origines (1132) aux XVIeme Siècle* (Forges-lez-Chimay, 1926), p. 367.
58. Canivez, *Statuta Capitulorum*, vol. 1, no. 62 (1241), p. 242.
59. For a discussion of the political significance of the actions of patrons, see Emma Cownie, "Religious Patronage at Post-Conquest Bury St. Edmonds," *Haskins Society Journal* 7 (1997): 1–9. The actions of the countesses in this respect were certainly not without precedent. For example, Penelope Johnson has exposed the family strategies of the counts of Anjou, who utilized donations to the monastery of La Trinité, Vendôme, as a way of "establishing, consolidating, and extending their own political power" in a frequently contested region in France. See Penelope Johnson, *Prayer, Patronage and Power: The Abbey of La Trinité, Vendôme, 1032–1187* (New York, 1981), p. 30 and "Agnes of Burgundy: An Eleventh-Century Woman as Monastic Patron," *Journal of Medieval History* 15 (1989): 93–104. Janet Burton correlates foundation activity with the precariousness of the patron's political position, which would certainly apply to the countesses. Burton describes foundation activity as part of "a self-conscious expression of their status in society, a need which increased in times of tenurial and political insecurity." See Burton, *The Monastic Order in Yorkshire*, p. 193.

NOTES 157

60. David Nicholas, "Of Poverty and Primacy: Demand, Liquidity and the Flemish Economic Miracle, 1050–1200," *American Historical Review* 96 (1991): 17–41.
61. *Inventaire analytique des Archives de Lille*, no. 583 (November 1233), p. 236; Paris, BN, MS latin, 10967 (Cartulaire de Marquette), f. 22r.
62. Maurice Vanhaeck, ed., *Cartulaire de l'Abbaye de Marquette*, no. 963 (1248) (Lille, 1937), p. 391.
63. Paris, Bibliothèque nationale de France, Collection Flandre et Artois (Titres de l'abbaye de Ravensberg), November 1227.
64. Hautcoeur, *Cartulaire de l'Abbaye de Flines*, vol. 1, no. 36 (April 1244), pp. 36–37; vol. 2, no. 179 (October, 1271), p. 191.
65. Rijksarchief Bruges, no. bl. 6717 (December 1241).
66. Pastoralism made it possible for Cistercian nuns not only to avoid reliance upon lay brothers which their father abbeys may have been reluctant to provide, but they also avoided the contradiction inherent in the practice of manual labor and the Order's insistence on strict enclosure for women. Louis Lekai, *The Cistercians: Ideals and Reality* (Kent, OH, 1977), p. 353.
67. Charles Piot, ed., *Cartulaire de l'Abbaye d'Eename* (Bruges, 1881), no. 268 (May 1247), pp. 238–39.
68. I.L.A. Diegerick, ed., *Inventaire Analytique et Chronologique des Chartes et Documents appartenant aux Archives de L'Ancienne Abbaye de Messines* (Bruges, 1853–68), no. 104 (January 1256), p. 59.
69. Lille, ADN, 33 H 56/998.
70. Benjamin Guérard, ed., *Cartulaire de l'Abbaye de Saint-Bertin* (Paris, 1841), no. 642 (May 1223), p. 280.
71. Lille, ADN, 10 H 210 (August 1256).
72. Lille, ADN, 27 H 18/285 (February 11, 1271).
73. Auguste van Lokeren, ed., *Chartes et Documents de l'Abbaye de Saint-Pierre au Mont Blandin à Gand (630–1599)* (Gand, 1868), no. 677, p. 317; no. 755, p. 336.
74. Lille, ADN, 1 H 324 (July 1275).
75. Wauters, *Table Chronologique*, vol. 4 (July 1233), p. 175.
76. The family's renunciation was made in the presence of "Symon" and "other laybrothers" of the abbey. Lille, ADN, 30 H 33/648 (February 1235); 30 H 33/651 (January 11, 1242).
77. Lille, ADN, 33 H 48/730.
78. J. de Smet, ed., *Cartulaire de Cambron* (Brussels, 1869), no. 20 (November 1254), pp. 456–57. Marguerite forbade the erection of any other mills in the specified area.
79. Smet, *Cartulaire de Cambron*, no.135, pp. 145–46.
80. Lille, ADN, 1 H 260/2837 (August 1242).
81. Wauters, *Table Chronologique*, vol. 4 (December 25, 1226), p. 25; Édouard Hautcoeur, ed., *Cartulaire de l'Église Collegiale de Saint-Pierre de Lille* (Lille, 1894), no. 171 (July 24, 1221), p. 162.
82. Wauters, *Table Chronologique*, vol. 3 (May 16, 1212), p. 359.

83. Rijksarchief Gent, Inv. 20 (August 1241), f. 236. The loan, guaranteed by Egidius van Brugge, was to be repaid with funds from the countess's grainery at Veurne.
84. For reclamation in the Low Countries, see William Tebrake, "Rural Society and Drainage Institutions in Late-Medieval Holland," in *La Société rurale et les institutions gouvernementales au Moyen Age. Actes du Colloque de Montréal, 13–15 Mai, 1993*, ed. John Drendel (1995), pp. 149–60 and William Tebrake, *Medieval Frontier Culture and Ecology in Rijnland* (College Station, TX, 1985). For Flanders in particular, see Adriaan Verhulst, *Histoire du Paysage Rural en Flandre de l'époque Romaine au XVIIIe siècle* (Bruxelles, 1966).
85. Verhulst distinguishes between two types of polders in maritime Flanders. "Polders anciens" were those that required little manual labor to build, and generally were subject to reclamation in the eleventh and twelfth centuries. "Polders moyens" were located along the coast in the north, the area targeted for reclamation by the countesses in the thirteenth century, and required a significant amount of effort and expense before they could be transformed into pasture or arable land. See Verhulst, *Histoire du Paysage Rural*, p. 28.
86. Bryce Lyon, "Medieval Real Estate Development and Freedom," *American Historical Review* 63 (1957): 47–61, especially p. 51.
87. The geography of the area also complicated reclamation attempts. See Verhulst, *Histoire du Paysage Rural*, pp. 49–57.
88. Boudelo's endowment, which was largely the product of the patronage of Jeanne and Marguerite, consisted almost exclusively of land along the northern coast of Flanders near the polders. The abbey received a total of five grants of land from Jeanne, of which four were *wastine*, or wasteland. According to Michel, Boudelo was responsible for much of the reclamation that occurred in northern Flanders. See Édouard Michel, *Abbayes et Monastères de Belgique. Leur Importance et leur rôle dans le développement du Pays* (Brussels, 1923), p. 111. Michel's conclusion is supported by the number of donations of *wastine* made to the abbey of Boudelo by the countesses, including twelve *bonniers* near the parish of Sint-Katherina-Sinaai made in 1219, and *wastine* sold to the abbey for 356 *livres* in March 1223. Cyriel Vleeschouwers, ed., *Het Archief van de Abdij van Baudelo te Sinaai-Waas en te Gent* (Brussels, 1983), no. 20 (October 9, 1219), pp. 181–82; no. 32 (March 4, 1223), p. 188.
89. For the location of these holdings see Foppens, *Opera Diplomatica*, vol. 3, no. 163 (1276), p. 131. Verhulst describes the role played by Ter Doest in the clearance of these lands in Verhulst, *Histoire du Paysage Rural*, p. 111.
90. The land was sold for a total of 180 *livres*, Wauters, *Table Chronologique*, vol. 4 (May 20, 1243), p. 393.
91. Ferdinand van de Putte and Charles Carton, eds., *Chronique de l'Abbaye de Ter Doest* (Bruges, 1845), no. 9 (June 1273), p. 56.
92. See Louis Lekai, *The White Monks* (Okauchee, 1957), p. 211.
93. Édouard de Coussemaker, *Inventaire analytique des Archives de Lille*, no. 631 (January 1235), p. 256.

94. Vanhaek, *Cartulaire de l'Abbaye de Marquette*, no. 9 (June 1228), pp. 7–8.
95. *Cartulaire de l'Abbaye de Marquette*, no. 220 (October 1265), pp. 211–12.
96. Wauters, *Table Chronologique*, vol. 4, p. 403.
97. *Cartulaire de l'Abbaye de Marquette*, no. 58 (September 1233), pp. 46–47; no. 125 (December 1244), p. 110.
98. *Cartulaire de l'Abbaye de Marquette*, no. 151 (July 1248), pp. 136–37; no. 156 (January 1249), pp. 146–47.
99. *Cartulaire de l'Abbaye de Marquette*, no. 236 (September 11, 1269), pp. 226–27.
100. Hautcoeur, *Cartulaire de l'Abbaye de Flines*, no. 2, doc. 147 (January 26, 1265), p. 160–61; no. 190 (September 1276), p. 213.
101. Rijksarchief Gent, fonds Oosteeklo, Inv. 31 (Cartularium), no. 14 (February 1250).
102. Ferdinand van de Putte, ed., *Speculum Beatæ Mariæ Virginis ou Chronique et Cartulaire de l'Abbaye de Groeninghe* (Bruges, 1872), no. 7 (1265), pp. 13–15.
103. Rijksarchief Gent, fonds Nieuwenbos (Cartularium), Inv. 50, 1250.
104. Theo Luykx, *Johanna van Constantinopel, Gravin van Vlaanderen en Henegouwen, haar Leven (1199/1200–1244), haar Revgeering (1205–1244), vooral in Vlaanderen* (Antwerp, 1946), no. 6 (July 10, 1217), p. 530; no. 26 (1227), pp. 555–56; no. 11 (October 1219), p. 542; no. 14 (October 1253), p. 573. The location of this land, near Ghent, suggests that it was most likely a combination of marsh and wasteland, requiring drainage, or at least diking, and then clearance.
105. Rijksarchief Gent, fonds Doornzele, July 1251.
106. Rijksarchief Gent, fonds Oosteeklo, Inv. 31, Cartularium: Fundatieboek van Oost Eecloo, doc. 14 (February 1250).
107. Rijksarchief Gent, fonds Oosteeklo (Cartularium) doc. 19bis (May 1266).
108. In the past, scholars have posited the existence of a general reluctance among communities of Benedictines to engage in reclamation as a key factor contributing to their economic decline during this period, citing the extensive capital necessary for projects of this magnitude and the reticence of the monks and nuns themselves to undertake such labor-intensive activity. See Georges Duby, *Rural Economy and Country Life in the Medieval West*, trans. Cynthia Poston (Columbia, SC, 1968), p. 70. Verhulst also cites Saint-Bavon and Mont Blandin and mentions Oudenbourg and Saint-André as instrumental in what he categorizes as the "Third Phase" of reclamation in Flanders, which began under the direction of Jeanne, and involved the less fertile land of the north. Verhulst, *Histoire du Paysage Rurale*, 106. For a more specific discussion of the efforts of the nuns of Bourbourg see Michel Mollat, "Les Hôtes de l'Abbaye de Bourbourg," *Melanges d'Histoire du Moyen Age dedies a la memoire de Louis Halperin* (Paris, 1951), pp. 513–21.
109. Rijksarchief Gent, Inv. 20 (November 19, 1215), E116; (November 19, 1217), F117; (September 1236), F199.
110. Van Lokeren, *Chartes et Documents de l'Abbaye de Saint-Pierre au Mont Blandin*, no. 466 (August 1221), p. 246; no. 475 (21 Mars 1224), pp. 48–49; no. 610 (December 1249), p. 291.

111. *Cartulaire d'Eename*, no. 165 (May 1228), pp. 133–34; no. 164 (May 1228), 133.
112. *Cartulaire d'Eename*, no. 312 (January 1275), pp. 284–85.
113. *Cartulaire d'Eename*, no. 293 (February 1250), p. 263.
114. Rijksarchief Bruges, no. bl. 7404 (February 1251); Rijksarchief Bruges, no. bl. 7413 (October 1252).
115. Rijksarchief Bruges, no. bl. 7115 (July 14, 1256).
116. Paris, BN, MS lat. 9920 (1244), 22r.
117. Paris, BN, Collection Flandre et Artois, vol. 193 (March 1260); Octave Delepierre, *Précis analytique des documents que renferme le dépôt des archives de la Flandre-occidentale à Bruges* (Bruges, 1840–42), no. 96 (January 3, 1269), p. 58; Paris, Bibliothèque Nationale, Collection Flandre et Artois, vol. 193 (February 1272).
118. The relationship between mendicants and towns was so pronounced that Jacques LeGoff suggested that the number of mendicant foundations in a region could be used as a determinate of the level of urbanization. Although LeGoff's thesis has been modified to a certain degree, it nevertheless recognizes the relationship that existed between towns and the mendicant orders which emerged during the late twelfth and early thirteenth century, and the impact of these developments on society. Jacques LeGoff, "Ordres Mendiants et Urbanisation dans la France Médiévale," *Annales, Économies, Sociétés, Civilisations* 4 (1970): 924–46. See more recently Octaaf Mus and Paul Trio, "L'Implantation des Ordres Mendiants dans l'Agglomération Yproise Durant le XIIIe Siècle," *Les Moines Dans La Ville. Actes du colloque de Lille*, vol. 7 (1996): 177–84.
119. Lille, ADN, 40 H 556/1343C (May 1243).
120. The historiography of the beguines is fairly complex, in part due to their later condemnation by the church. Once considered by scholars as complexes established to provide shelter for poor and unmarried women, beguinages are now more accurately viewed as pious institutions from their inception, inhabited by women who choose a life of celibacy and poverty, if only temporarily. See Penelope Galloway, "Discreet and Devout Maidens: Women's Involvement in Beguine Communities in Northern France, 1200–1500," in *Medieval Women and Their Communities*, ed. Diane Watt (Toronto, 1997), pp. 92–115, and more recently the study by Walter Simons, *Cities of Ladies. Beguine Communities in the Medieval Low Countries, 1200–1565* (Philadelphia, 2001).
121. Rijksarchief Gent, fonds Sint-Elisabethbegijnhof (1269).
122. Jean Bethune, ed., *Cartulaire du Béguinage de Sainte-Élisabeth à Gand* (Bruges, 1883), no. 22 (May 21, 1269), p. 321.
123. Lille, ADN, 162 H 1/2 (October 26, 1276).
124. Two examples of her personal involvement include the beguinage of Champfleury and that of Ypres. Lille, ADN, 30 H 17/268; Foppens, *Opera Diplomatica*, vol. 4 (January 1270), pp. 253–54.
125. The beguinages established in Germany seldom resembled the *curtis beguinage* of Flanders. The numerous beguinages described by Philipps in

NOTES 161

his detailed study of medieval Strasbourg consist primarily of a handful of women sharing a house in the midst of the secular community. See Dayton Phillips, *Beguines in Medieval Strasburg* (Stanford, 1941).
126. Lille, ADN, Inv. Chron., 2187 H 51, no. 578 (September 1233); no. 622 (September 1235); Foppens, *Opera Diplomatica*, vol. 4, no. 111 (1233), p. 93; Inv. Chron., no. 576 (September 1233); Lille, ADN, 186 H 14/2 (August 1233).
127. Édouard Hautcoeur, ed., *Cartulaire de l'Église Collegiale de Saint Pierre de Lille* (Lille, 1894), no. 257 (April 1237), pp. 231–33.
128. Lille, ADN, Inv. Chron., 2187 H 51, no. 349.
129. Foppens, *Opera Diplomatica*, vol. 4, no. 81 (September 1233), p. 236.
130. Foppens, *Opera Diplomatica*, vol. 4, no. 109 (1265), p. 684.
131. Édouard de Coussemaker, ed., *Inventaire Analytique et Chronologique des Archives de la Chambre des Comptes à Lille* (Lille, 1865), no. 717 (1240), p. 294.
132. L.A. Warnkoenig, *Histoire de la Flandre et de ses Institutions Civiles et Politiques jusqu'a l'Année 1309*, vol. 3 (Bruxelles, 1835), no. 20 (June 1235), p. 268.
133. Lille, ADN, Inv. Chron., 2187 H 51, no. 906. The agreement stipulated that any surplus be used to provide the things necessary for the celebration of mass.
134. June Hall McCash, "The Cultural Patronage of Medieval Women. An Overview," in *The Cultural Patronage of Medieval Women*, ed. June Hall McCash (Athens, 1996), pp. 1–49, especially p. 1.
135. Penelope Johnson, "Agnes of Burgundy: An Eleventh-Century Woman as Monastic Patron," *Journal of Medieval History* 15 (1989): 93–104.
136. Shadis, "Piety, Politics and Power," p. 202: "The royal women of medieval France and Castile used patronage as a way to cultivate political power and authority. Diffusing the boundaries between the public and the private, they developed patronage projects with the specific goals of building and reinforcing their own power and that of their family or lineage."

4 Translating Secular Power into Spiritual Gains

1. Maurice Vanhaeck, ed., *Cartulaire de l'Abbaye de Marquette* (Lille, 1937), no. 82 (May 1236), pp. 66–74. This charter confirms the foundation and lists a range of donations made since it was established in 1224, many of which were granted by Jeanne and her husband Ferrand. Ferrand's involvement in the original foundation was expressly mentioned although at the time he was still in prison. Presumably Jeanne consulted with her husband during his incarceration.
2. The house was bequeathed to the nuns of Marquette after Jeanne's death in 1244. Archives Départementales du Nord, Lille, 33 H 3/61 (December 1233). Permission was granted in response to Jeanne's petition directly to Gregory IX. Vanhaeck, *Cartulaire de l'Abbaye de Marquette*, no. 71 (April 17, 1236), pp. 63–64. Ferrand's heart was interred in the cathedral of Noyon, while his body was taken to Marquette to be buried alongside their daughter Marie. Geneviève de Cant, *Jeanne et Marguerite de Constantinople, Comtesses de Flandre et de Hainaut u XIIIe siècle* (Brussels, 1995), p. 156.

3. Édouard Hautcoeur, ed., *Cartulaire de l'Abbaye de Flines*, vol. 1 (Lille, 1874), no. 12, p. 10.
4. Hautcoeur, *Cartulaire de l'Abbaye de Flines*, no. 45, p. 93.
5. Megan McLaughlin discusses the values of such *arengae*, or preambles to charters, to modern historians. See Megan McLaughlin, *Consorting with Saints: The Ideology of Prayer for the Dead in Early Medieval France* (Ithaca, 1994), p. 179.
6. Burton discusses the motives that prompted patrons as well as the difficulty of deciphering such motives from charters in her extensive study of foundations in Yorkshire. Janet Burton, *The Monastic Order in Yorkshire, 1069–1215* (Cambridge, 1999) p. 139. See also Ludo Milis, *Angelic Monks and Earthly Men: Monasticism and its Meaning to Medieval Society* (Woodbridge, 1992), pp. 87–91.
7. Jean Francois Foppens, ed., *Diplomatum Belgicorum Nova Collection sive Supplementum ad Opera Diplomatica Auberti Mirae*, vol. 3 (Brussels, 1734), no. 33 (July 1239), pp. 586–87.
8. Foppens, *Opera Diplomatica*, vol. 4, no. 136 (August 1252), pp. 114–15. Also printed in George Descamps, *Notre-Dame du Val-des-Écoliers prieuré ensuite abbaye de Chanoines Réguliers, OSA à Mons* (Mons, 1885), no. 1 (August 1252), pp. 275–76.
9. This concept is discussed by Christopher Holdsworth in a brief but informative study of the various practices that characterized medieval patronage of religious communities. Christopher Holdsworth, *The Piper and the Tune: Medieval Patrons and Monks* (Reading, 1991). See also André Vauchez, *The Laity in the Middle Ages. Religious Beliefs and Devotional Practices*, trans. Margery J. Schneider (Notre Dame, 1993) and the very compelling study by Megan McLaughlin, *Consorting with Saints*, p. 128.
10. Foppens, *Opera Diplomatica*, vol. 4, no. 95 (January 13, 1234), p. 310. The money was to assist in the construction of buildings necessary for the friars.
11. Foppens, *Opera Diplomatica*, vol. 3, no. 24 (1234), pp. 582–83.
12. See Vauchez, *The Laity in the Middle Ages*.
13. For the role of founder, its significance and the ensuing obligations see Emma Cownie, *Religious Patronage, 1066–1135* (Woodbridge, 1998), p. 186.
14. Jane Martindale discusses the implications of the deliberation, which would have accompanied the act of foundation. See Jane Martindale, "Monasteries and Castles: the Priories of St-Florent de Saumur in England after 1066," in *England in the Eleventh Century*, ed. Carola Hicks (Stamford, 1992), pp. 135–57.
15. See appendix 1 for a list of all of the religious and monastic communities included in quantitative analysis for this study.
16. There are a variety of studies that address the history of the Cistercian Order and its incursion into the Low Countries. See Joseph-Marie Canivez, *L'Ordre de Cîteaux en Belgique des Origines (1132) au XXme siècle*, 2nd ed. (Forges-lez-Chimay, 1926); Also Erin Jordan, "Prayers, Patronage and Polders: Assessing Cistercian Foundations in Thirteenth-Century Flanders and Hainaut," *Cîteaux: Commentarii cistercienses* 53 (2002): 99–126.

17. BN, Paris, Latin MS 10967 (Cartulaire de l'Abbaye de Marquette), f. 22r; Vanhaeck, *Cartulaire de l'Abbaye de Marquette*, no. 54 (1232), pp. 43–44.
18. For a more detailed discussion of the holdings of Flines see Édouard Hautcoeur, *Histoire de l'Abbaye de Flines* (Paris, 1874).
19. Theo Luykx, *Johanna van Constantinopel, Gravin van Vlaanderen en Henegouwen, haar Leven (1199/1200–1244), haar Revgeering (1205–1244), vooral in Vlaanderen* (Antwerp, 1946), no. 6 (July 10, 1217), p. 535; no. 9 (January 1219), p. 537; no. 11 (October 1219), p. 538.
20. The foundation of Bijloke, initiated in 1228, was confirmed in 1233, after the death of Ferrand. Cyriel Vleeschouwers, ed., *Het archief van de Abdij von Baudelo te Sinaai-Waas en te Gent* (Brussels, 1983), no. 61 (1228), p. 190. The community was initially associated with a hospital in the city of Ghent. After the nuns were transferred to their new residence at Bijloke, the hospital buildings were granted to the Dominicans. Vleeschouwers, *Het archief van de Abdij von Baudelo*, no. 70 (November 1233), p. 207; Foppens, *Opera Diplomatica*, vol. 4, no. 27 (October 1228), p. 584; no. 37 (May 1243), p. 593.
21. Alphonse de Vlaminck, ed., *Cartulaire de l'Abbaye de Zwyveke-lez-Termonde* (Gand, 1869), no. 23 (November 1230), pp. 21–22.
22. See Canivez, *Les Cistercians en Belgique*, p. 482. After their disastrous experience in the first location, the majority of the nuns abandoned the community. Marguerite, however, was able to locate new recruits, who were installed in the new foundation after it was secured from the encroachment of the sea. For the foundation of the abbey see Luce Knockaert, "De Stichting der Cistercienzerinnen Abdij ter Hagen Onder Axel (1236)," *Cîteaux in de Nederlanden* 9 (1958): 121–31.
23. Léopold Devillers, "Chronique de l'Abbaye d'Épinlieu," *Annalectes pour servir à l'Histoire Ecclésiastique de la Belgique* 15 (1878): 161–86, no. 1 (November 25, 1217), pp. 178–79.
24. Foppens, *Opera Diplomatica*, vol. 4, no. 32 (December 1237), p. 587. Jeanne's role in the foundation of Hemelsdale is mentioned in a charter issued by the bishop of Therenburgh in 1241, Ferdinand Van de Putte and Charles Carton, eds., *Chronique et Cartulaire de l'Abbaye de Hemelsdale* (Bruges: 1858), no. 12, p. 52; no. 19, pp. 59–60.
25. Joseph-Marie Canivez, ed., *Statuta Capitulorum generalium ordinis Cisterciensis ab anno 1116 ad annum 1786*, vol. 2 (Louvain, 1933), no. 27 (1234), p. 132. The confirmation of 1234 appears in Alphonse Wauters, ed., *Table Chronologique des Chartes et Díplomes Imprimés Concernant l'Histoire de la Belgique*, vol. 4 (1903–12), p. 216.
26. Canivez, S*tatuta Capitulorum*, vol. 2 (1232), (1234), (1236), and (1240).
27. For information on the beguines in the Low Countries, see Walter Simons, *Cities of Ladies. Beguine Communities in the Medieval Low Countries, 1200–1565* (Philadelphia, 2000). For the actions of the countesses on behalf of beguine communities specifically, see Erin Jordan, "The Countesses of Flanders and the *Curtis Beguinage*: Challenging Traditional Restrictions of

Religious Women in Thirteenth-Century France," *Proceedings of the Western Society for French History* 29 (2001): 21–30.

28. Jean Bethune, ed., *Cartulaire du Beguinage de Sainte-Elisabeth à Gand* (Bruges, 1883), no. 4 (May 14, 1242), p. 3; Rijksarchief Gent, Inv. 20 (August 1242), fol. 239. Saint-Bavon also conceded the right to erect a chapel.
29. A charter issued in 1262 by the bishop of Tournai refers to the role played by the countesses in the foundation of the abbey. Foppens, *Opera Diplomatica*, vol. 4 (1262), pp. 685–86; Marguerite's involvement in the beguinage of Douai is reflected in a charter issued by her in December 1245. Archives Départementales du Nord (AND), Lille, 1 G 91/211.
30. Foppens, *Opera Diplomatica*, vol. 4, no. 128 (February 1242), p. 108.
31. ADN, 162 H 1/1.
32. This is the date cited by most scholars. However, Gratien argues that the first wave of transfers began earlier, around 1230. P. Gratien, *Histoire de la Foundation et de l'Evolution de l'Ordre des Frères Mineurs au XIIIe siècle* (Paris, 1928), p. 158.
33. Information regarding the convent in Mons is taken from P. Fulgence Thyrion, *Les Frères-Mineurs à Valenciennes au XIIIe siècle* (Valenciennes, 1913), p. 179.
34. The transfer was facilitated by the city of Bruges, and the new convent was built with funds donated by local merchants. See J.H.R. Moorman, *Medieval Franciscan Houses* (New York, 1983), p. 91. However, Moorman's dating of this transaction seems to be incorrect. Moorman argues that the first friars were present by 1221, and the transfer occurred in 1233. Simons suggests that the first foundation did not occur until 1227, with the transfer occurring in 1246, a scenario supported by the documents published by Luykx. Jeanne, Ferrand, and Marguerite are mentioned in the document describing the transfer. Luykx, *Johanna van Constantinopel*, no. 81 (March, 1246), pp. 614–45. Marguerite also gave the Franciscans of Bruges the relic of the left hand of St. Marguerite of Antioch, apparently still covered in skin. See Thyrion, *Les Frères-Mineurs à Valenciennes*, p. 179.
35. Simons questions the traditional version of Franciscan settlement in Ghent, arguing that the transfer of the community to the heart of the city occurred in 1226–27, rather than 1256, as suggested by Moorman, *Medieval Franciscan Houses*, p. 200. Simons identifies Arnulf II of Gavere as the founder of the second community, rather than Jeanne and Ferrand. Walter Simons, *Bedelordekloosters in het Graafschap Vlaanderen* (Brugge, 1987), pp. 33–40.
36. Wauters, *Table Chronologique*, vol. 4 (August 21, 1250), p. 597. Simons, *Bedelordekloosters*, pp. 41–44.
37. These dates indicate the year when the foundation was officially accepted by the General Chapter of the Dominican Order. Small communities of friars were generally present prior to their formal acceptance into the Order, as noted where relevant in the discussion of individual foundations. The history of individual foundations can be found in Simons, *Bedelordekloosters*.
38. This donation, made with the approval of Walter, bishop of Tournai, was officially made in 1228. Foppens, *Opera Diplomatica*, vol. 3, no. 103 (1228), p. 88.

NOTES 165

39. This initial residence was given to the friars prior to 1227 by Zegher Parys, a bourgeois of Ghent. G.G. Meersseman, "Les Débuts de l'Ordre des Frères Prêcheurs dans le Comté de Flandre (1224–1280)," *Archivum Fratrum Praedicatorum* 17 (1947): 54–76, especially p. 69. See also Simons, *Bedelordekloosters*, pp. 72–73.
40. According to Simons, Dominican friars were present in Bruges as early as 1228, six years before formal foundation occurred. Simons, *Bedelordekloosters*, pp. 75–77. Foppens, *Opera Diplomatica*, vol. 3, no. 95 (January 13, 1234), p. 310.
41. Marie-Dominique Chapotin, *Histoire des Dominicains de la Province de France. Le Siècle des Fondations* (Paris, 1898), p. 201.
42. Chapotin, *Histoire des Dominicains*, p. 201.
43. G.G. Meersseman, "Jeanne de Constantinople et les Frères Prêcheurs," *Archivum Fratrum Praedicatorum* 19 (1949): 122–68, especially p. 148.
44. Meersseman, "Jeanne de Constantinople," p. 139. The final conditions of foundation were included in a charter issued by Jeanne in October 1233, published in Meersseman, "Jeanne de Constantinople," p. 161. However, this agreement did include the stipulation that the parish church retain the right to perform funeral services for all individuals who requested burial among the friars.
45. A. Desplanque, C.C. Dehaisnes, and Jules Finot, eds., *Inventaire Sommaire des Archives départementales anterieurs à 1790, Nord*, 8 vols. (Lille, 1865–1895), vol. 1, p. 308. It is difficult to assign a date to the initial foundation of the Dominican convent in the town of Bergues. A small group of friars clearly resided in the town prior to the promulgation of Jeanne's will in 1244, in which the countess granted 100 *solidi* to the local clergy to compensate them for any loss of revenue incurred because of the friars.
46. This donation was made on November 29, 1244, less than a week before Jeanne's death. Chapotin, *Histoire des Dominicains*, p. 69.
47. I.L.A. Diegerick, ed., *Inventaire Analytique et Chronologique des Chartes et Documents Appartenant aux Archives de la Ville d'Ypres* (Bruges, 1853–68), no. 110 (1269), p. 97; Foppens, *Opera Diplomatica*, vol. 3, no. 156 (June 1275), pp. 129–30; ADN, 16 G 17/166 (March 14, 1274).
48. Rijksarchief Bruges, no. bl. 9651: In the charter issued in October 1215, Jeanne stipulated that the canons of the community "observe a canonical life according to the rule of Saint Augustine and following the institutes of the Order of Arrouaise."
49. *Chartes du Chapitre de Saint-Waudru de Mons*, ed. Léopold Devillers (Brussels, 1899), no. 9 (November 1252), p. 264. Marguerite donated a "manse" to the canons, and secured approval of the neighboring community of canonesses of Saint-Waudru.
50. ADN, 49 H 3/8 (October 1261). Marguerite confirmed several donations made to the abbey, including an annual rent of twenty *sous* granted by her sister. ADN, 49 H 3/11 (November 1265). For a more detailed discussion of Victorine cannoness, who remain rather elusive figures in the historical record, see Erin Jordan, "The Success of the Order of Saint Victor: A Comparative

Study of the Patronage of Canonical Foundations in Thirteenth-Century Flanders and Hainaut," *Revue d'Histoire Ecclésiastique* 96 (2001): 5–33.
51. For the history of the abbey of Eeckhout and Marguerite's involvement, see N.N. Huyghebaert, "Origines et Rapports des Deux Monastères Brugeois de St. Berthélemy de l'Eeckhout et de Saint-Trond," *Augustiniana* 19 (1969): 257–90. Ursmer Berlière, ed., *Monasticon Belge*, vol. 3 (Bruges, 1890), p. 1033.
52. A. Bonvarlet, "Notice sur le couvent des Dominicans à Bergues," *Bulletin du Comité Flamand de France* 4 (1866–68): 348–84.
53. Burton, *The Monastic Order*, "The seeming innocuousness of the *pro anima* clause in charters masks the enormity of medieval humanity's fear of retribution; and the development of the doctrine of purgatory fast-growing in the twelfth century, added an extra incentive to secure vicarious intercession" p. 182.
54. The most useful works on this topic remain Stephen D. White's *Custom, Kinship and Gifts to Saints: The Laudatio Parentum in Western France 1050–1150* (Chapel Hill, 1988) and Barbara Rosenwein, *To Be the Neighbor of St. Pete: The Social Meaning of Cluny's Property, 909–1049* (Ithaca, 1989).
55. Vanhaeck, *Cartulaire de l'Abbaye de Marquette*, no. 13 (August 1228), p. 10.
56. Vanhaeck, *Cartulaire de l'Abbaye de Marquette*, no. 10 (June 1228), p. 8: ". . . propter nostrarum ac antecessorum et successorum nostrorum remedium animarum." [for the remedy of our souls and for our ancestors and successors].
57. Foppens, *Opera Diplomatica*, vol. 1, no. 104 (1228), p. 88: ". . .pro animarum nostrarum et antecessorum nostrorum remedio. . . ." ["for the remedy of our souls and those of our ancestors and successors"].
58. Bethune, *Cartulaire du Beguinage de Sainte-Elisabeth*, no. 13 (September 1245), pp. 10–11. ". . .pro salute anime nostre ac pro animabus antecessorum et successorum" ["for the safety of our soul and for the souls of ancestors and successors"].
59. *Inventaire des archives d'Ypres*, no. 106 (1268), p. 91.
60. ADN, 130 H 5/47 (1274): ". . .nous avons donne et donnoi pour diu et en aumosne as dites suers de notres dites nouvelle abbaye. . .pour le salut des ames de nous de nos ancilleurs et de nos successeurs. . ." [we have given and give for good and in aims to said sisters of ours said new abbey. . .for the safety of the souls of us and our ancestors and successors].
61. See Cownie, *Religious Patronage* (Woodbridge, 1998), pp. 7–10.
62. Joel T. Rosenthal, *The Purchase of Paradise, Gift Giving and the Aristocracy, 1307–1485* (London, 1972), p. 124. His sentiments are echoed by McLaughlin, who argues that the presence of an individual's name in a charter conveying a donation was rarely, if ever, simply a result of formula, but rather a clear indication of a personal connection to the donor. McLaughlin, *Consorting with Saints*, p. 143.
63. Rijksarchief Bruges, no. 11.152 (January 12, 1220).
64. Vanhaeck, *Cartulaire de l'Abbaye de Marquette*, no. 80 (May 1236), p. 65.
65. Édouard de Coussemaker, ed., *Inventaire Analytique et Chronologique des Archives de la Chambre des Comptes à Lille* (Lille, 1865), no. 866 (1245), p. 354.
66. ADN, 127 H 30/215 (July 22, 1249).
67. Foppens, *Opera Diplomatica*, vol. 4, no. 95 (January 13, 1234), p. 310.

NOTES

68. Wauters, *Table Chronologique*, vol. 4, p. 139 and p. 578.
69. ADN, Lille, Inv. Chron., no. 1437, pp. 569–70.
70. ADN, Lille, Inv. Chron., no. 1044, pp. 424–25.
71. ADN, Lille, Inv. Chron., no. 1383, p. 547.
72. Holdsworth, *The Piper and the Tune*, p. 7. Also C.H. Lawrence, *Medieval Monasticism. Forms of Religious Life in Western Europe in the Middle Ages* (New York, 1984), p. 69.
73. ADN, 38 H 28/108 (March 1223).
74. Bethune, *Cartulaire du Beguinage de Saint Elisabeth*, no. 3 (October 1236), pp. 2–3.
75. Vanhaeck, *Cartulaire de l'Abbaye de Marquette*, no. 51 (July 1232), pp. 37–38; no. 102 (1263), p. 83; no. 68 (1245), p. 50.
76. Hautcoeur, *Cartulaire de l'Abbaye de Flines*, no. 143 (September 1263), pp. 155–57. This abbey was also the recipient of Marguerite's rather sizable collection of relics, left to the community after her death, which included teeth of Saint Peter and Saint Paul. Hautcoeur, *Cartulaire de l'Abbaye de Flines*, no. 201 (May 1278), p. 222.
77. Wauters, *Table Chronologique*, vol. 4, pp. 80.
78. Vanhaeck, *Cartulaire de l'Abbaye de Marquette*, no. 214 (November 1263), pp. 206–207; E. Brouette, ed., *Recueil des Charters et Documents de l'Abbaye du Val-Saint-Georges à Salzinnes* (Achel, 1971), no. 121 (July 1252), pp. 151–52.
79. The pittance was to be paid for with a rent of forty *sous* purchased by Marguerite from the abbey of Nonnenbosch. Vanhaeck, *Cartulaire de l'Abbaye de Marquette*, no. 246 (September 1271), p. 236.
80. Vanhaeck, *Cartulaire de l'Abbaye de Marquette*, no. 125 (December 1244), p. 110; no. 71 (April 17, 1236), pp. 63–64.
81. ADN, Lille, Inv. Chron., no. 1330, p. 529.
82. Jeanne and Marguerite were not alone in preferring the prayers of Cistercians, as discussed by J.C. Ward, "Fashions in Monastic Endowment: The Foundations of the Clare Family, 1066–1314," *Journal of Ecclesiastical History* 32 (1981): 427–51. See also Cownie, *Religous Patronage*, p. 192; Constance Berman, "Fashions in Monastic Patronage: The Popularity of Supporting Cistercian Abbeys for Women," *Proceedings of the Western Society for French History* 17 (1990): 36–45; McLaughlin, *Consorting with Saints*, p. 130.
83. The relationship between the spirituality of particular monastic orders and society has been examined in regards to the mendicants by Lester Little and Barbara Rosenwein. However, in their study of the changes in society which prompted changes in spirituality, they did not explictly address the period between the decline of the Benedictine monasticism and the rise of the Dominicans and Franciscans, i.e., the period of Cistercian expansion. It is my belief that the Cistercians formed a bridge between the two chronological and conceptual periods described by Little and Rosenwein. The position of the Cistercians in this type of spiritual continuum explains the particular attraction they exerted on patrons during the late twelfth and thirteenth centuries. See Lester Little and Barbara Rosenwein, "Social Meaning in the Monastic and Mendicant Spritualities," *Past and Present* 63 (1986): 4–32.

84. Wauters, *Table Chronologique*, vol. 4, p. 303.
85. Canivez, S*tatuta Capitulorum*, vol. 2 (1232), p. 94 (1234), p. 129 (1244), p. 330.
86. Perhaps the most interesting aspect of this surge of Cistercian women's foundations was that it occurred in spite of the Order's attempts in the 1220s to stymie the incorporation of additional houses of nuns. The incredible influx of female foundations into the Order during the first few decades of the thirteenth century had taxed the Order's ability to provide the necessary male personnel, particularly monks needed to conduct services and hear confession. For the position of the women within the Order, see Brigitte Degler-Spengler, "The Incorporation of Cistercian Nuns into the Order in the Twelfth and Thirteenth Centuries," in *Hidden Springs: Cistercian Monastic Women: Medieval Religious Women*, 3:1, ed. John A. Nichols and Lillian Thomas Shank (Kalamazoo, 1995), pp. 85–134; Constance H. Berman, *The Cistercian Evolution* (Philadelphia, 2000), pp. 40–45; and Roger de Ganck, "The Cistercian Nuns of Belgium in the Thirteenth Century," *Cistercian Studies Quarterly* 5 (1970): 169–87. The efforts of Jeanne and Marguerite to secure the aid of lay brothers for female foundations is discussed by Reinhard Schneider, *Vom Klosterhaushalt zum Stadt- und Staatshaushalt: Der Zisterziensische Beitrag* (Stuttgart, 1994).
87. These figures are based upon the total number of charters issued by Jeanne or Marguerite to female Cistercian foundations (356) and the total number of charters issued to male Cistercian foundations (120).
88. Requests for pittances to be distributed to the nuns of Marquette were made on several occasions, see Vanhaeck, *Cartulaire de l'Abbaye de Marquette*, no. 125 (December 1244), p. 110; no. 214 (November 1263), pp. 206–207; no. 246 (September 1271), p. 236; no. 254 (November 1273), pp. 243–44, and to the nuns of Groeninghe, Ferdinand Van De Putte, ed., *Speculum Beatae Mariae Viriginis ou Chronique et Cartulaire de l'Abbaye de Groeninghe* (Bruges, 1872), no. 10 (1236), pp. 11–13. Anniversary masses were requested from Nieuwenbos, Notre-Dame-des-Près, Épinlieu, Bijloke, and Groeninghe, among others.
89. Jeanne gave a rent of four *livres*, ten *deniers* to fund a pittance for the monks of Ter Doest, Archives du Grand Séminaire de Bruges, fonds Ter Doest, no. 692 (July 1236). Jeanne and Ferrand donated rents to Aulne, requesting masses in return, Foppens, *Opera Diplomatica*, vol. 3, no. 107 (1229), pp. 391–92. In 1276, Marguerite requested several masses from the monks of Ter Doest, Foppens, *Opera Diplomatica*, vol. 3, no. 158 (April 1263), pp. 130–31.
90. Hautcoeur, *Cartulaire de l'Abbaye de Flines*, no. 172 (November 1273), pp. 194–206.
91. This claim is made by Lawrence, who proffers it as an explanation for the subordinate role assumed by women and their communities in medieval monastic life. See Lawrence, *Medieval Monasticism*, p. 219. The importance of masses in attracting patrons is also discussed by Burton, *The Monastic Order*, p. 146. Recent studies of patronage which de-emphasize the role of prayers and focus instead upon a more sweeping connection between the founder and the community suggest that our understanding of the role of

intercessory masses in attracting patrons may need further examination. See in particular McLaughlin, *Consorting with Saints*, p. 129. See also Berman, who suggests that patrons did believe women's prayers to be as effective as men's in securing salvation: "It is perhaps impossible to determine why in the early thirteenth century the foundation of houses for Cistercian nuns were seen as an appropriate pious activity, particularly for great ladies of the time, but founders' intentions are clear. While there has been a tendency for modern historians of medieval religious life to dismiss the importance of religious women by discounting the efficacy of their prayers, thirteenth-century founders thought differently." Berman, "Abbeys for Cistercian Nuns in the Ecclesiastical Province of Sens: Foundation, Endowment, and Economic Activities of the Earlier Foundations," *Revue Mabillon* 73 (1997): 83–113, p. 89.

92. Arguments about the efficacy of prayers are often predicated upon the wealth of an individual community. In other words, if patrons valued the prayers of women and men equally, they would have directed donations equally, and there would be little discrepancy in the wealth of men's and women's communities. However, I would argue that the difference in size was perhaps more a result of the function of Cistercian abbeys, rather than a product of the indifference of patrons to women's prayers. In attempting to evaluate differences in the way men's and women's prayers were regarded by patrons, it is also necessary to account for regional difference, as well as the individual position of the patron. Clearly, in Flanders, Cistercian women's houses outnumbered those for men, suggesting that while the number of donations to men's and women's houses would have been the same, they were divided up amongst the women's houses, resulting in fewer donations per foundation. Obviously these questions require further consideration and will hopefully be examined in much more detail at a later date. See Burton, *The Monastic Order*, p. 146.

93. Beatrice was married to Marguerite's eldest son from her second marriage, William of Dampierre, who appears in charters as count of Flanders until his death in 1251. Instead of returning to her father's domain in Brabant, Beatrice remained in Flanders, supported by a sizable dowry conferred on her by Marguerite after William's death.

94. The extent of their efforts are discussed in detail in Berman, "Fashions in Monastic Patronage," pp. 36–45.

95. Sally Thompson, *Women Religious: The Founding of English Nunneries After the Norman Conquest* (Oxford, 1991), p. 171.

96. Jeanne and Marguerite were certainly not alone in their propensity to direct donations to Cistercian foundations, as discussed by McLaughlin, *Consorting with Saints*, p. 130.

97. For an explanation of the nature of the spirituality of these women and how it was influenced by Cistercian theology see De Ganck, "The Cistercian Nuns of Belgium in the Thirteenth Century," pp. 176–86.

98. Although most of the women who appear in thirteenth-century hagiography were living in the diocèse of Liège, located in the county of Brabant,

their proximity to the countesses and Flanders may account for the interest displayed by Jeanne and Marguerite in Cistercian women as avenues to salvation. For a more detailed discussion of these spiritual currents see Simone Roisin, "L'Efflorescense Cistercienne et le Courant Féminin de Piété au XIIIe siècle," *Revue Histoire Ecclésiastique* 39 (1943): 345–68 and "Réflexions sur la culture intellectuelle en nos Abbaye Cisterciennes Médiévales," in *Miscellanea Historica in Honorem Leonis van der Essen: Universitatis Catholicae in oppido Lovaniensi iam annos XXV professoris* (Brussels, 1947), pp. 245–56. Also see Brenda Bolton, "Some Thirteenth Century Women in the Low Countries. A Special Case?" *Nederlands Archief voor Kerkgeschiedenis* 61 (1981): 7–29.

99. According to Lekai, Cistercian convents during this period were "the most influential centers of the new spirituality inaugurated by St. Bernard." Louis Lekai, *The White Monks* (Okauchee, WI, 1957), p. 243.
100. Ritamary Bradley, "Love and Knowledge in *Seven Manners of Loving*," in *Hidden Springs*, p. 362.
101. Edmund Mikkers, "Meditations on the Life of Alice of Schaerbeek," in *Hidden Springs*, p. 397.
102. Thomas Renna discusses the attempt by Cistercian writers to accommodate the virtue of charity as a result of the new emphasis placed upon good works and the active way in the thirteenth century. See Thomas Renna, "Hagiography and Feminine Spirituality in the Low Countries," *Cîteaux* 39 (1988): 287–95. See also Caroline Walker Bynum, *Jesus as Mother: Studies in the Spirituality of the High Middle Ages* (Berkeley, 1982).
103. The appeal of such a connection to patrons is discussed at length by McLaughlin, *Consorting with Saints*, p. 130.
104. For the increasing importance of crusade and pilgrimage in medieval secular religion, see Vauchez, *The Laity in the Middle Ages*, pp. 45–50.
105. Regine Pernoud, *Blanche of Castile* (New York, 1975), p. 214. The argument here is not about women's participation in pilgrimage generally but is specific to women in positions of authority.
106. Lambert argues that Francis differed from his predecessors because he viewed the life of Christ as the primary model of conduct, rather than the lives of the apostles. Malcolm Lambert, *Franciscan Poverty. The Doctrine of the Absolute Poverty of Christ and the Apostles in the Franciscan Order, 1210–1323* (London, 1961), p. 58. Also C.H. Lawrence, *The Friars. The Impact of the Early Mendicant Movement on Western Society* (London, 1994), pp. 15–25 and Richard Emery, *The Friars in Medieval France* (New York, 1962), p. 1.
107. Little offers a concise yet consummate discussion of the differences between the friars and the Benedictines, and the ability of both to appeal to the society that surrounded them. See Lester Little, *Religious Poverty and the Profit Economy in Medieval Europe* (Ithaca, 1978), p. 199.
108. This stipulation, a product of the General Chapter of 1220, facilitated expansion of the Order, and certainly allowed the Dominicans to avoid many of the problems encountered by the Franciscans concerning the

contradiction between their pastoral mission and their restrictions on ownership of property. See Brenda Bolton, *The Medieval Reformation* (New York, 1983), p. 78, and Little, *Religious Poverty*, pp. 156–57.
109. By adhering to a more flexible stance regarding ownership of property, the Dominicans advocated an interpretation of the *vita apostolica* that was consistent with Jeanne's understanding of the nature and function of patronage. As a patron of considerable means, the countess targeted the most pious communities, whom she associated with the most efficacious prayers. In light of Franciscan reluctance to accept donations, she clearly turned her attention to their rivals, the Dominicans, who proved much less reticent to participate in the traditional patronage exchange, yet promised equally potent prayers.
110. The way of life envisioned by Francis of Assisi was intended to adhere as rigidly as possible to the model established by Christ and his apostles. For Francis, poverty was not merely a means to an end, but rather an end in and of itself, the primary goal of Franciscan life. See Gratien, *l'Ordre des Frères Mineurs au XIIIe siècle* and J.R.H. Moorman, *A History of the Franciscan Order from its Origins to the Year 1517* (Oxford, 1968).
111. According to Bennett, "poverty played but a subordinate and accessory part" in the way of life envisioned by Dominic. R.F. Bennett, *The Early Dominicans. Studies in Thirteenth-Century Dominican History* (Cambridge, 1937), p. 31. In contrast to Dominic, Francis viewed preaching as merely one aspect of the apostolic life, secondary in importance to the observation of poverty. Little, *Religious Poverty*, p. 162. See also Lawrence, *Medieval Monasticism*, p. 243.
112. In particular, manual labor was dispensed with, and the time spent on the liturgy and the divine office was to be limited to prevent interference with preaching and preparation for preaching. Lawrence, *Medieval Monasticism*, p. 253. Bennett suggests that Dominic's preoccupation with preaching even led him to approve the neglect of liturgical activities if deemed necessary. Bennett, *The Early Dominicans*, p. 26.
113. The majority of Franciscan foundations for women were established in Southern Europe. The Order's female branch never attained the same level of popularity in the North. During the lifetime of Saint Clare, forty-seven communities had been established in Italy, nine in Spain, five in Germany, and only four in France. Gratien, *l'Ordre des Frères Mineurs au XIIIe siècle*, p. 580.
114. The founder of the community at Bruges, Ermentrudis van Keulen, was present in Bruges as early as 1240, living as a holy woman in the city. However, the actual community did not form until 1255–56. It transferred to a second location in 1260–61. Simons, *Bedelordekloosters*, pp. 126–27. The community at Langemark was initially inhabited by sisters who had traveled from Bruges and were installed in a temporary dwelling near the Friars. In 1258, they received a considerable donation of property at Rosendale from Margareta, the widow of Jan Boudraven, thus facilitating the construction of a secure, permanent dwelling. See H. Lippens, "L'Abbaye des Clarisses d'Ypres aux XIIe et XIVe siècles," *Revue d'histoire*

Franciscaine 7 (1930): 297–330. For a more concise history of the foundation, see Simons, *Bedelordekloosters*, pp. 128–29.
115. The land was given in return for an annual rent of nine *deniers*. Foppens, *Opera Diplomatica*, vol. 4, no. 150 (1266), p. 126.
116. Lippens, "L'Abbaye des Clarisses d'Ypres," no. 4 (1269), pp. 308–309; no. 10 (1273), p. 311.
117. Meersseman, "Jeanne de Constantinople," p. 160.

Conclusion

1. Kimberly A. LoPrete, "The Gender of Lordly Women: the Case of Adela of Blois," in *In Pawns or Players? Studies on Medieval and Early Modern Women*, ed. Christine Meek and Catherine Lawless (Dublin, 2003), pp. 90–110, especially p. 91: "Either the woman under discussion is cast as the singular exception who proves the rule of every other woman's powerlessness or she is said to have been perceived and treated by her contemporaries as an honorary man."
2. Joan Wallach Scott, "Is Female to Male as Nature is to Culture?" in *Feminism and History*, ed. Joan Wallach Scott (Oxford, 1996), pp. 90–91: "Thus I think we would do better to use these polarities (domestic and public) only when our historical evidence supports them, and not assume that they always represent the fundamental meanings that society sees in the sexes."
3. Linda E. Mitchell, *Portraits of Medieval Women. Family, Marriage and Politics in England, 1225–1350* (New York, 2003), p. 134: "The conflict might arise between competing cultural norms within a given society and historical analysis exterior to it. In other words, civilizations might have conflicting conceptions of gender embodied in their cultures, the historian might privilege one conception over another and thereby fail to acknowledge both the validity of the other conception and the prevalence of interior conflict."
4. LoPrete, "The Gender of Lordly Women," p. 110.
5. Janet Nelson, "The Problematic in the Private," *Social History*, 15 (1990): 355–64, p. 363. Nelson, although directing her criticism Duby, challenges the fundamental distinction posed by scholars regarding public and private spheres and its feasibility as a model for medieval society. In this respect, her discussion is extremely useful and questions she poses can be integrated into a wider dialogue concerning this issue.
6. See most recently Sharon Farmer, *Surviving Poverty in Medieval Paris. Gender, Ideology and the Daily Lives of the Poor* (Ithaca, 2002) and Ruth Mazo Karras, *From Boys to Men. Formations of Masculinity in Late Medieval Europe* (Philadelphia, 2003).
7. Carol Clover, "Regardless of Sex: Men, Women, and Power in Early Northern Europe," *Speculum* 68 (1993): 363–87, especially p. 371.

BIBLIOGRAPHY

Primary Sources: Manuscripts

Bruges: Rijksarchief

No. bl. 7405, Abdij Spermalie
No. bl. 7406, Abdij Spermalie
No. bl. 7441, Abdij Spermalie
No. bl. 7002, Saint-Andries-lez-Bruges
No. bl. 7391, Saint-Andries-lez-Bruges
No. bl. 7377, Saint-Andries-lez-Bruges
No. bl. 7185, Saint-Andries-lez-Bruges
No. bl. 7187, Saint-Andries-lez-Bruges
No. bl. 7411, Saint-Andries-lez-Bruges
No. bl. 7413, Saint-Andries-lez-Bruges
No. bl. 7419, Saint-Andries-lez-Bruges
No. bl. 7423, Saint-Andries-lez-Bruges
No. bl. 7115, Saint-Andries-lez-Bruges
No. bl. 7427, Saint-Andries-lez-Bruges
No. bl. 7435, Saint-Andries-lez-Bruges
No. bl. 7222, Saint-Andries-lez-Bruges
No. bl. 7333, Saint-Andries-lez-Bruges
No. bl. 11416 Dominicans-Ypres
No. bl. 11466, Abdij Mesen
No. bl. 9176, Abdij Nonnenbossche
No. bl. 9177, Abdij Nonnenbossche
No. bl. 6680, Abdij Oudenbourg
No. bl. 6681, Abdij Oudenbourg
No. bl. 6697, Abdij Oudenbourg
No. bl. 6708, Abdij Oudenbourg
No. bl. 6711, Abdij Oudenbourg
No. bl. 6717, Abdij Oudenbourg
No. bl. 6724, Abdij Oudenbourg
No. bl. 6735, Abdij Oudenbourg
No. bl. 6738, Abdij Oudenbourg
No. bl. 6768, Abdij Oudenbourg
No. bl. 9651, Abdij Zoetendale

No. bl. 7390, Abdij Zoetendale
No. bl. 11.152, Abdij Zoetendale
No. bl. 6084, Abdij Saint-Bertin
No. bl. 12018, Begijnhof de Wijngaard

Lille, Archives Départementales du Nord

1H non côté, Anchin
3H non côté, Saint-Sepulcre
5H non côté, Hasnon
8H non côté, Saint-André du Cateau
9H non côté, Liesses
10H non côté, Marchiennes
26H non côté, Saint-Saulve
27H non côté, Saint-Pierre de Loos
28H non côté, Vaucelles
30H non côté, Notre-Dame-des-Près
33H non côté, Marquette
38H non côté, Sainte-Calixte de Cysoing
40H non côté, Saint-Jean-Baptiste de Valenciennes
41H non côté, Sainte-Élisabeth de Valenciennes
51H non côté, Beaulieu
127H non côté, Dominicans, Lille
130H non côté, Abbiette
162H non côté, Sainte-Élisabeth de Lille

Paris: Bibliothèque Nationale

Collection Dom Grenier, vol. 101, Saint-André du Cateau
Collection Flandre
vol. 73, Sainte-Calixte de Cysoing
vol. 46, Hôpitaux Comtesse
Collection Flandre et Artois
vol. 230, Ravensberg
vol. 66
Latin MS 10167, Bonne-Ésperance
Latin MS 17675, Cartulaire de l'Abbaye de Brayell d'Annai
Latin MS 9920, Cartulaire de Notre-Dame de Bourbourg
Latin MS 10969, Cartulaire de Notre-Dame du Cambrai
Latin MS 9124, Cartulaire du Comté de Flandre
Latin MS 10967, Cartulaire de l'Abbaye de Marquette

Ghent: Rijksarchief

O.7, Boudelo
O.8, Boudelo
O.20, Boudelo

O.206, Boudelo
O.19, Boudelo
Cartulaire A, Boudelo
Cartulaire B, Boudelo
fonds de Ter Hagen, n. 2, Ter Hagen
D 90, Drogen
Inv. Lavaut 50, Nieuwenbos
Inv. 31bis, Oosteeklo
Inv. 20F, Saint-Baafs en Bisdom

Primary Sources: Printed Material

Backmund, Norbert, ed. *Monasticon Praemonstratense.* Straubing: C. Attenkofersche Buchdruckerei, 1952.

Beaunier, Dom, ed. *Recueil Historique, Chronologique, et Topographique des Archevêchez, Evêchez, Abbayes et Prieurés de l'Ancienne France.* Paris: Ligugé, 1906.

Berlière, Ursmer, ed. *Monasticon Belge.* 11 vols. Bruges: Gembloux, 1890.

Bethune, Jean, ed. *Cartulaire du Béguinage de Sainte-Élisabeth à Gand.* Bruges: Aimé-Zuttere, 1883.

le Breton, Guillaume. "Gesta Philippi August." In *Oeuvres de Rigord et de Guillaume le Breton,* ed. Henri-Francois Delaborde. Vol. 1. Paris: Librarie Renouard, 1882.

Callewaert, Georges, ed. *Chartes Anciennes de l'Abbaye de Zonnebeke.* Bruges: Plancke, 1925.

de Coussemaker, Édouard, ed. *Inventaire Analytique et Chronologique des Archives de la Chambre des Comptes à Lille.* 2 vols. Lille: M. Quarré, 1865.

de Coussemaker, Ignatius, ed. *Cartulaire de l'Abbaye de Bourbourg.* Lille: Imrp. V. Ducoulombier, 1859.

———.*Cartulaire de l'Abbaye de Cysoing et de ses Dépendances.* Lille: Des clée et de Brouwer, 1886.

Jacques de Guyse. *Annales Hanonienses.* Ed. M. de Fortia d'Urbain. Paris: Sautelet, 1831.

Delaborde, H.F., and Charles Petit-Dutaillis, eds. *Recueil des Actes de Philippe Auguste.* 4 vols. Paris: Imprimere Nationale, 1916–79.

Delepierre, Octave. *Précis analytique des documents que renferme le dépôt des archives de la Flandre-occidentale à Bruges.* Bruges: Vandecastede Werbrouck, 1840–42, no. 96 (January 3, 1269).

Demarquette, Albert, ed. *Cartulaire et Abbesses de la Brayelle d'Annai.* Lille: Ducoulombier, 1885–86.

Denis du Péage, D, ed. *Documents sur le Béguinage de Lille.* Lille: Impr. SILIC, 1942.

Devillers, Léopold, ed. *Chartes du Chapitre de Saint-Waudru de Mons.* Brussels: Kiessling et Cie., 1899.

———. "Chronique de l'Abbaye d'Épinlieu." *Annalectes pour servir à l'Histoire Ecclésiastique de la Belgique* 15 (1878): 161–86.

Dhondt, J., ed. *Bijdrage tot het cartularium van Mesen (1065–1334).* Brussels: Palais des Academies, 1941.

Diegerick, I.L.A., ed. *Inventaire Analytique et Chronologique des Chartes et Documents Appartenant aux Archives de l'ancienne abbaye de Messines*. Bruges: De Zuttere, 1876.

——. *Inventaire Analytique et Chronologique des Chartes et Documents Appartenant aux Archives de la Ville d'Ypres*. 7 vols. Bruges: De Zuttere, 1853–68.

Finot, Jules, ed. *Inventaire Sommaire des Archives Hospitalières de Lille antérieures à 1790*. Lille: L. Danel, 1892.

Foppens, Jean Francois, ed. *Diplomatum Belgicorum Nova Collectio sive Supplementum ad Opera Diplomatica Auberti Miraei*. 5 vols. Brussels: Francisci Foppens, 1734.

de Ghellinck, A., ed. *Cartulaire de l'Abbaye de Beaulieu*. Bruges: Plancke, 1894.

Gilliodts-van-Severen, L., ed. *Inventaire des Archives de la Ville de Bruges*. Bruges: E. Gailliard, 1871–76.

Guérard, Benjamin, ed. *Cartulaire de l'Abbaye de Saint-Bertin*. Paris: Imprimerie Royale, 1841.

Haignère, Daniel, ed. *Les Chartes de Saint-Bertin d'après le Grand Cartulaire de Dom Charles-Joseph Dewitte*. 2 vols. Saint-Omer: H. d'Homont, 1866.

Hautcoeur, Édouard, ed. *Cartulaire de l'Abbaye de Flines*. Lille: M. Quarré, 1874.

——. *Cartulaire de l'Église Collegiale de Saint-Pierre de Lille*. Lille: M. Quarré, 1894.

d'Herbomez, Armand, ed. *Chartes de l'Abbaye de Saint-Martin de Tournai*. Bruxelles: M. Hayez, 1898–1910.

Lavant, J.B., ed. *Inventaire des Archives de l'Abbaye de la Byloke, 1164–1807*. Gand, 1881.

Matthew Paris. *Chronica Majora*. Ed. Richard Vaughan. Cambridge: University of Cambridge Press, 1958.

Mouskes, Philippe. *Chronique Rimée*. Ed. Baron de Reiffenberg. Bruxelles: M. Hayez, 1836.

Musseley, Charles, ed. *Inventaire des Archives de la Ville de Courtrai*. 2 vols. Courtrai: Musseley, 1854–58.

Petit, Roger, ed. *Inventaire des Archives du Prieure du Val-des-Écoliers à Houffalize*. Brusells: Archives générales du Royaume, 1971.

Piot, Charles, ed. *Cartulaire de l'Abbaye d'Eename*. Bruges: De Zuttere-van Kersschaver, 1881.

Pruvost, Alexandre, ed. *Chronique et Cartulaire de l'Abbaye de Bergues-Saint-Winoc*. 2 vols. Bruges: Vandescasteele-Werbrouck, 1875–78.

Saint-Génois, Jules Ludger Dominique Ghislain, ed. *Inventaire Analytique des Chartes des Comtes de Flandre, avant l'avènement des princes de la maison de Bourgogne, autrefois déposées au Chateau de Rupelmonde, et conservées aujourd'hui aux archives de la Flandre-Orientale*. Ghent: de Vanryckegem-Hovaere, 1843–46.

Serrure, Gérard, ed. *Cartulaire de Saint-Bavon*. Gand: Annoot-Braeckman, 1836.

de Smet, J., ed. *Cartulaire de Cambron*. Brusells: M. Hayez, 1869.

Teulet, Alexandre, Joseph de Laborde, Elie Berger, and Henri-Francois Delaborde, eds. *Layettes du Trésor des Chartes*. 5 vols. Paris: Plon, 1863–1909.

Van de Putte, Ferdinand, ed. *Chronicon et cartularum abbatiae sancti Nicolai Furnensis*. Bruges: Vandecasteele-Werbrouck, 1849.

——. *Chronica et cartularum monasterii de Dunis*. Bruges: Société d'Emulation de Bruges, 1864–67.

———. *Speculum Beatae Mariae Virginis ou Chronique et Cartulaire de l'Abbaye de Groeninghe*. Vandescasteele-Werbrouck, 1872.

Van de Putte, Ferdinand, and Charles Carton, eds. *Chronica Abbatiae Warnestoniensis, ordinis canonicorum regularum S. Augustini ex actis quibusdam monasterii et ex auctoribus collectum*. Bruges: Société d'Emulation de Bruges, 1852.

———. *Chronique de l'Abbaye de Ter Doest*. Bruges: Vandecasteele-Werbrouck, 1845.

———. *Chronique et Cartulaire de l'Abbaye de Hemelsdale*. Bruges: Vandecasteele-Werbrouck, 1858.

Van Hollebeke, Léopold, ed. *L'Abbaye de Nonnenbossche, de l'ordre de St. Benoît, près d'Ypres (1101–1796)*. Bruges: Vandecesteele-Werbrouck, 1865.

———, ed. *Cartulaire de l'Abbaye de Saint-Pierre de Loo (1093–1794)*. Bruxelles: M. Hayez, 1870.

Van Lokeren, Auguste, ed. *Chartes et Documents de l'Abbaye de Saint-Pierre au Mont Blandin à Gand (630–1599)*. Gand: H. Hoste, 1868.

Van Overstraeten, Daniel, ed. *Inventaire des Archives de l'Abbaye de Ghislinghien*. Brussels: Archives générales du Royaume, 1976.

Vanhaeck, Maurice, ed. *Cartulaire de l'Abbaye de Marquette*. S.I.L.I.C., vol. 46, Lille, 1937.

de Vlaminck, Alphonse, ed. *Cartulaire de l'Abbaye de Zwyveke-lez-Termonde*. Gand: C. Annott-Braekman, 1869.

Vleeschouwers, Cyriel, ed. *Het archief van de Abdij van Boudelo te Sinaai-Waas en te Gent*. Brussels: Ruisbroekstraat, 1983.

Wauters, Alphonse, ed. *Table Chronologique des Chartes et Diplômes Imprimés Concernant l'Histoire de la Belgique*. 11 vols. Brussels: Librairie Kiessling et Cie., P. Imbreghts, 1903–12.

Wellens, Robert, ed. "Les Archives de l'abbaye de bethleem ou de belian à Mesvin-lez-mons." *Archives et bibliothèques de Belgique* 35 (1964): 186–225.

———. *Inventaire des Archives de l'Abbaye Cistercienne d'Épinlieu*. Brussels: Archives Générales du Royaume, 1970.

Secondary Works

Arnould, E. "Histoire de l'Abbaye de Beaupré sur la Lys." *Comité Flamand de France* 16 (1887): 215–347.

Auberger, Jean-Baptiste. *L'Unanimité cistercienne primitive: Mythe ou réalité*. Achel: Éditions sine Parvulos VBVB, 1986.

Baldwin, John. *The Government of Philip Augustus. Foundations of French Royal Power in the Middle Ages*. Berkeley: University of California Press, 1986.

Becquet, Jean. *Vie Canoniale en France aux XIe-XIIe siécles*. London: Variorum Reprints, 1985.

Bedos-Rezak, Brigitte. "Women, Seals and Power in Medieval France, 1150–1350." In *Women and Power in the Middle Ages*. Ed. Mary C. Erler and Maryanne Kowaleski. Athens, GA: University of Georgia Press, 1988, pp. 85–97.

Bennett, R.F. *The Early Dominicans. Studies in Thirteenth-Century Dominican History*. Cambridge: Cambridge University Press, 1937.

Berger, Élie. *Histoire de Blanche de Castille: Reine de France.* Paris: Thorin et Fils, 1895.

Berlière, Ursmer. "La Fondation de l'Abbaye de Épinlieu." *Revue Benedictine* 9 (1982): 381–93.

——. "Les Monastères doubles aux XIIe et XIIIe siècles." *Memoires de l'Academie Royale de Beligique, Classe des Lettres et des Sciences Morales et Politiques* 18 (1923): 3–32.

——. "Le Nombre des Moines dans les Anciens Monastères." *Revue Benedictine* 41 (1929): 231–61; 42 (1930): 18–42.

Berman, Constance H. "Abbeys for Cistercian Nuns in the Ecclesiastical Province of Sens: Foundation, Endowment, and Economic Activities of the Earlier Foundations." *Revue Mabillon* 73 (1997): 83–113.

——. *The Cistercian Evolution.* Philadelphia: University of Pennsylvania Press, 2000.

——. "Cistercian Women and Tithes." *Cîteaux* 49 (1998): 95–128.

——. "Economic Practices of Cistercian Women's Communities: A Preliminary Look." In *Speculum Studiosorum: Studies in Honor of Father Louis J. Lekai, OCSO.* Ed. John R. Sommerfeldt. Kalamazoo, MI: Cistercian Publications, 1993, pp. 15–32.

——. "Fashions in Monastic Patronage: The Popularity of Supporting Cistercian Abbeys for Women." *Proceedings of the Western Society for French History* 17 (1990): 36–45.

——. *Medieval Agriculture, the Southern-French Countryside, and the Early Cistercians: A Study of Forty-three Monasteries.* Transactions of the American Philosophical Society 76, 5. Philadelphia: American Philosophical Society, 1986.

——. "Men's Houses, Women's Houses: The Relationship Between the Sexes in Twelfth-Century Monasticism." In *The Medieval Monastery.* Ed. Andrew MacLeish. Minneapolis: University of Minnesota Press, 1988, pp. 43–52.

——. "Women as Donors and Patrons to Southern-French Monasteries in the Twelfth and Thirteenth Centuries." In *Worlds of Medieval Women: Creativity, Influence, Imagination.* Ed. Constance H. Berman, Judith Rice Rothschild, and Charles W. Connell. Morgantown: West Virginia University Press, 1985, pp. 53–68.

Bolton, Brenda. *The Medieval Reformation.* New York: Homes and Meier, 1983.

——. "Some Thirteenth-Century Women in the Low Countries. A Special Case?" *Nederlands Archief voor Kerkgeschiendis* 61 (1981): 7–29.

——. "*Vitae Matrum*: A Further Aspect of the Frauenfrage." In *Medieval Women.* Ed. Derek Baker. Studies in Church History: Subsidia, 1. Oxford: Blackwell, 1978, pp. 253–72.

Bonnard, Fourrier. *Histoire de l'abbaye royale et de l'ordre des chanoines réguliers de Saint Victor de Paris.* Paris: A. Savaete, 1904–08.

Bouchard, Constance Brittain. *Holy Entrepreneurs: Cistercians, Knights and Economic Exchange in Twelfth-Century Burgundy.* Ithaca: Cornell University Press, 1991.

Bradbury, Jim. *Philip Augustus. King of France. 1180–1223.* New York: Longman, 1998.

Brooke, Christopher. *The Monastic World, 1100–1300.* New York: Random House, 1974.

Brooke, Rosalind. *The Coming of the Friars*. London: George Allen and Unwin, 1975.
Bur, Michel. "Rôle et Place de la Champagne dans le Royaume au Temps de Philippe Auguste." In *La France de Philippe Auguste. Le Temps des Mutations.* Ed. R.H. Bautier. Paris: Éditions du Centre nationale de la recherche scientifique, 1982, pp. 237–54.
Burton, Janet. *The Monastic Order in Yorkshire, 1069–1215.* Cambridge: Cambridge University Press, 1999.
———. *Monastic and Religious Orders in Britain, 1100–1300.* Cambridge: Cambridge University Press, 1994.
———. "Yorkshire nunneries in the Middle Ages: recruitment and resources." In *Government, Religion, and Society in Northern England 1000–1700.* Ed. Keith J. Stringer, John C. Appleby, and Paul Dalton. Stroud: Sutton Publishing, 1997, pp. 104–216.
Bynum, Caroline Walker. *Holy Feast, Holy Fast.* Berkeley: University of California Press, 1982.
———. *Jesus as Mother: Studies in the Spirituality of the High Middle Ages.* Berkeley: University of California Press, 1982.
Canivez, Joseph-Marie. *L'Ordre de Cîteaux en Belgique des Origines (1132) aux XXme Siècle.* Forges-lez-Chimay: V. Cantineau, 1926.
———, ed. *Statuta Capitulorum generalium ordinis Cisterciensis ab anno 1116 ad annum 1786.* vol. 2. Louvain: Bureaux de la Revue, 1933.
de Cant, Geneviève. *Jeanne and Marguerite de Constantinople, Comtesses de Flandre et de Hainaut au XIIIe siècle.* Bruxelles: Racine, 1995.
Cantor, Norman. "The Crisis of Western Monasticism, 1050–1130." *American Historical Review* 66 (1960): 47–67.
Capentier, B. "Le Béguinage Sainte-Elisabeth de Valenciennes, de sa foundation au XVIe siècle." *Mémoires du Cercle archéologique historique de Valenciennes* 4 (1959): 95–192.
Carson, Patricia. *The Fair Face of Flanders.* Ghent: E. Story Scientia, 1969.
Celis, G. "De Begijnhoven in Oost-Vlaanderen. Geschiedkundige studie." *Oostvlaamsche Zanted* 4 (1929): 88–94.
Chapotin, Marie-Dominique. *Histoire des Dominicains de la Province de France. Le Siècle des Fondations.* Paris: Imprimerie Nationale, 1898.
Cheyette, Fredric. *Ermengard of Narbonne and the World of the Troubadours.* Ithaca: Cornell University Press, 2001.
Chorley, P. "The Cloth Exports of Flanders and Northern France during the Thirteenth Century: A Luxury Trade?" *Economic History Review* 40 (1987): 349–79.
Clover, Carol J. "Regardless of Sex: Men, Women and Power in Early Northern Europe." *Speculum* 68 (1993): 364–88.
Cooke, E. "Donors and Daughters: Shaftesbury Abbey's Benefactors Endowments and Nuns." *Anglo-Norman Studies* 12 (1984): 29–45.
Cottineau, Laurent-Henri. *Répertoire topo-bibliographique des Abbayes et Prieurés.* 3 vols. Macon: Protat, 1935–38.

Cownie, Emma. *Religious Patronage in Anglo-Norman England, 1066–1135*. Woodbridge: Boydell, 1998.

———. "Religious Patronage at Post-Conquest Bury St. Edmunds." *Haskins Society Journal* 7 (1997): 1–9.

Daly, Lowrie. *Benedictine Monasticism. Its Formation and Development through the Twelfth Century*. New York: Sheed and Ward, 1965.

Davies, Wendy, and Paul Fouracre, eds. *Property and Power in the Early Middle Ages*. Cambridge: Cambridge University Press, 1995.

Degler-Spengler, Brigitte. "The Incorporation of Cistercian Nuns into the Order in the Twelfth and Thirteenth Century." In *Hidden Springs: Cistercian Monastic Women: Medieval Religious Women* 3:1. Ed. John A. Nichols and Lillian Thomas Shank. Kalamazoo, MI: Cistercian Publications, 1995, pp. 85–134.

Dept, Gaston G. *Les Influences Anglaise et Française dans le comté de Flandre au Debut du XIIIe Siècle*. Paris: Edward Champion, 1928.

Dereine, Charles. "Vie Commune, Régle de Saint Augustin et Chanoines Réguliers au XIe siècle." *Revue d'histoire Ecclésiastique* 41 (1946): 365–406.

Derville, Alain. "Dîmes, Rendements du Blé et 'Revolution Agricole' dans le Nord de la France au Moyen Age." *Annales, Économies, Sociétés, Civilisations* 42 (1987): 1411–32.

Descamps, George. *Notre-Dame du Val-des-Écoliers prieuré ensuite abbaye de Chanoines Réguliers, OSA à Mons (1252–1769)*. Mons: Dequesne-Masquillier, 1885.

Despy, Georges. "Les Chapitres des Chanoinesses Noble en Belgique au Moyen Age." *Federation archéologique et historique de Belgique* 35 (1955): 169–79.

Dickinson, John Compton. *The Origins of the Austin Canons and their Introduction in England*. London: SPCK, 1950.

Donkin, Robert. *The Cistercians. Studies in the Geography of Medieval England and Wales*. Toronto: Pontifical Institute of Medieval Studies, 1978.

———. "The Site Changes of Medieval Cistercian Monasteries." *Geography* 44 (1959): 251–58.

Duby, Georges. *The Early Growth of the European Economy*. Ithaca, NY: Cornell University Press, 1974.

———. *A History of Private Life*. Ed. Philippe Aries and Georges Duby. Cambridge: Belknap Press, 1988.

———.*The Legend of Bouvines. War, Religion and Culture in the Middle Ages*. Trans. Catherine Tihany. Berkeley: University of California Press, 1990.

———. *Medieval Marriage. Two Models from Twelfth-Century France*. Trans. Elborg Forster. Baltimore: Johns Hopkins University Press, 1978.

———. *Rural Economy and Country Life in the Medieval West*. Trans. Cynthia Poston. Columbia, SC: University of South Carolina Press, 1968.

———. "Women and Power." In *Cultures of Power: Lordship, Status and Process in 12th Century Europe*. Ed. Thomas N. Bisson. Philadelphia: University of Pennsylvania Press, 1995, pp. 69–85.

Dunbabin, Jean. *France in the Making, 843–1180*. 2nd edition. Cambridge: Oxford University Press, 2000.

Duvivier, Charles. *Les Influences Française et Germanique en Belgique au XIIIe siècle, La Querelle des d'Avesnes et des Dampierres jusqu'a la mort de Jean d'Avesnes (1257)*. 2 vols. Brussels: C. Marquardt, 1894.

Earenfight, Theresa. "Maria of Castile, Ruler or Figurehead? A Preliminary Study in Aragonese Queenship." *Mediterranean Studies* 4 (1994): 45–61.

Emery, Richard. *The Friars in Medieval France.* New York: Columbia University Press, 1962.

van Engen, John. "The 'Crisis of Cenobitism' Reconsidered: Benedictine Monasticism in the Years 1050–1150." *American Historical Review* 66 (1960): 47–67.

Erens, A. "Les Soeurs dans l'Ordre de Prémontré." *Analecta Praemonstratensia* 5 (1929): 5–29.

Erler, Mary C., and Maryanne Kowaleski, eds. *Gendering the Master Narrative. Women and Power in the Middle Ages.* Ithaca: Cornell University Press, 2003.

———. *Women and Power in the Middle Ages.* Athens: University of Georgia Press, 1988.

Esser, Kajetan. *Origins of the Franciscan Order.* Chicago: Franciscan Herald Press, 1970.

van Ette, Aloïs. *Les Chanoines Réguliers de Saint Augustin.* Cholet, France: Imprimerie Farré et Freulon, 1953.

Evergates, Theodore. *Feudal Society in the Bailliage of Troyes under the Counts of Champagne, 1152–1284.* Baltimore: Johns Hopkins University Press, 1975.

———, trans. and ed. *Feudal Society in Medieval France. Documents from the County of Champagne.* Philadelphia: University of Pennsylvania Press, 1993.

———, ed. *Aristocratic Women in Medieval France.* Philadelphia: University of Pennsylvania Press, 1999.

Farmer, Sharon. *Surviving Poverty in Medieval Paris. Gender, Ideology and the Daily Lives of the Poor.* Ithaca: Cornell University Press, 2002.

Fenster, Thelma S., and Clare A. Lees, eds. *Gender in Debate From the Early Middle Ages to the Renaissance.* New York: Palgrave, 2002.

Feys, E., and A. Nelis, eds. *Les Trois Cartulaires de la Prévoté ou Abbaye de Saint-Martin à Ypres.* New York: Zuttere, 1880.

Fletcher, Anthony. *Gender, Sex and Subordination in England, 1500–1800.* New Haven: Yale University Press, 1995.

de Fontette, Micheline. *Les Religieuses à l'age Classique du Droit Canon.* Paris: Librairie Philosopher J. Vrin, 1967.

Freed, John. *The Friars and German Society in the Thirteenth Century.* Cambridge, MA: Medieval Academy of America, 1977.

———. "Urban Development and the 'Cura Monialium' in Thirteenth-Century Germany." *Viator* 3 (1972): 311–27.

Galloway, Penelope. " 'Discreet and Devout Maidens': Women's Involvement in Beguine Communities in Northern France, 1200–1500." In *Medieval Women and Their Communities.* Ed. Diane Watt. Toronto: University of Toronto Press, 1997, pp. 92–115.

de Ganck, Roger. "The Cistercian Nuns in Belgium in the Thirteenth Century Seen Against the Background of the Second Wave of Cistercian Spirituality." *Cistercian Studies Quarterly* 5 (1970): 169–87.

———. "The Integration of Nuns in the Cistercian Order, Particularly in Belgium." *Cîteaux: Commentarii cistercienses* 35 (1984): 235–47.

Ganshof, F.L. *La Flandre sous la Premiers Comtes.* Vol. 1. Brussels: La Renaissance du Livre, 1943.

Geary, Patrick. *Phantoms of Remembrance. Memory and Oblivion at the End of the First Millennium.* Princeton: Princeton University Press, 1994.

Genicot, Léopold. *Histoire de la Walloonie.* Toulouse: Édouard Privat, 1973.

———. *L'Économie Rurale Namuroise au Bas Moyen Age.* Brussels: Éditions Nauwelaerts, 1982.

Gilchrist, Roberta. *Gender and Material Culture: The Archeology of Religious Women.* London: Routledge, 1994.

Giroud, Charles. *L'Ordre des Chanoines Réguliers de Saint-Augustin et ses Diverses Formes de Régime Interne.* Martigny: Éditions du Grand-Saint-Bernard, 1961.

Glissen, John. "Le Privilége de Masculinité dans le droit coutumier de La Belgique et du nord de la France." *Revue du Nord* 43 (1961): 201–216.

Godding, Philippe. *Le droit privé dans les Pays-Bas méridionaux du 12e au 18e siède.* Brussels: Imprimerie J. Duclout, 1987.

———. "Le droit au service du patrimoine familial: Les Pays-Bas Méridionaux (12e–18e siècles)." In *Marriage, Property and Succession.* Ed. Lloyd Bonfield. Berlin: Duncker and Humblot, 1992, pp. 15–35.

Goffin, Louis. *Ferrand de Portugal, Comte de Flandre et de Hainaut.* Lisbon: Academia Das Cienias de Lisoba Biblioteca de Altos Estudos, 1967.

Gold, Penny Schine. *The Lady and the Virgin. Image Attitude and Experience in Twelfth Century France.* Chicago: University of Chicago Press, 1985.

Goldberg, P.J.P. *Constructions of Widowhood and Virginity in the Middle Ages.* New York: St. Martin's, 1999.

———. *Woman is a Worthy Wight: Women in English Society, c. 1200–1500.* Phoenix Mill, UK: Alan Sutton Publishing, 1992.

———. *Women in Medieval English Society.* Stroud: Sutton Publishing, 1992.

Golding, Brian J. "Burials and benefactions: an aspect of monastic patronage in thirteenth-century England." In *England in the Thirteenth Century, Proceedings of the 1984 Harlaxton Symposium.* Ed. W.M. Ormrod. Harlaxton: Boydell and Brewer, 1985, pp. 64–75.

———. *Gilbert of Sempringham and the Gilbertine Order, c. 1130–1300.* Oxford: Clarendon Press, 1995.

Gosse, M. *Histoire de l'Abbaye et de l'Ancienne Congrégation des Chanoines Réguliers d'Arrouaise.* Lille: Léonard Danel, 1786.

Gratien, P. *Histoire de la Fondation et de l'Évolution de l'Ordre des Frères Mineurs au XIIIe siècle.* Paris: Société S. François d'Assise, 1928.

Greven, Joseph. *Die Anfänge Der Beginen.* Munster: Aschendorffsche Verlagsbuchhandlung, 1912.

Grundmann, Herbert. *Religious Movements in the Middle Ages.* Trans. Steven Rowan. Notre Dame, IN: University of Notre Dame Press, 1995.

———. "Zur Geschichte der Beginen im 13. Jahrhundert." *Archiv Für Kulturgesch* 21 (1931): 296–320.

Hallam, Elizabeth M., and Everard, Judith, eds. *Capetian France. 987–1328.* 2nd edition. New York: Longman, 2001.

Harrison, Dick. *The Age of Abbesses and Queens: Gender and Political Culture in Early Medieval Europe.* Lund, Sweden: Nordic Academic Press, 1998.

Heene, Katrien. "Gender and Mobility in the Low Countries: Traveling Women in Thirteenth-Century Exempla and Saint's Lives." In *The Texture of Society. Medieval Women in the Southern Low Countries.* Ed. Ellen E. Kittell and Mary A. Suydam. New York: Palgrave, 2004, pp. 31–49.

Heinrich, Mary Pia. *The Canonesses and Education in the Early Middle Ages.* Washington, DC, [s.n.], 1924.

de Hemptinne, Thérèse. "Vlaanderen en Henegouwen onder de ergenamen van de Boudewyns, 1070–1244." *Algemene Geschiedenis der Nederlanden* 1 (1977): 372–98.

Herlihy, David. *Opera Muliebra.* New York: McGraw Hill, 1990.

Hicks, Carola, ed. *England in the Eleventh Century.* Stamford: Paul Watkins, 1992.

Hill, Bennett. *English Cistercian Monasteries and their Patrons in the Twelfth Century.* Urbana, IL: University of Illinois Press, 1968.

Hinnebusch, William. *The Dominicans. A Short History.* New York: Alba House, 1975.

———. "Poverty in the Order of Preachers." *Catholic Historical Review* 45 (1959): 436–53.

Holdsworth, Christopher. *The Piper and the Tune: Medieval Patrons and Monks.* Reading: University of Reading Press, 1991.

Humphrey, Patricia. "Ermesenda of Barcelona: The Status of her Authority." In *Queens, Regents and Potentates.* Ed. Theresa M. Vann. Dallas: Academia, 1993, pp. 15–35.

Huyghebaert, N.N. "Origines et Rapports des Deux Monastères Brugeois de St. Berthélemy de l'Eeckhout et de Saint-Trond." *Augustiniana* 19 (1969): 257–90.

Jansen, Douglas C. "Women and Public Authority in the Thirteenth Century." In *Queens Regents and Potentates.* Ed. Theresa M. Vann. Dallas: Academia, 1993, pp. 91–103.

Johns, Susan M. *Noblewomen, Aristocracy and Power in the Twelfth-Century Anglo-Norman Realm.* Manchester: University of Manchester Press, 2003.

Johnson, Penelope. "Agnes of Burgundy: An Eleventh-Century Woman as Monastic Patron." *Journal of Medieval History* 15 (1989): 93–104.

———. *Equal in Monastic Profession.* Chicago: University of Chicago Press, 1991.

———. *Prayer, Patronage and Power: The Abbey of La Trinité, Vendôme, 1032–1187.* New York: New York University Press, 1981.

Jordan, Erin L. "Prayers, Patronage and Polders: Assessing Cistercian Foundations in Thirteenth-Century Flanders and Hainaut." *Cîteaux: Commentarii cistercienses* 53 (2002): 99–126.

———. "The Countesses of Flanders and the *Curtis Beguinage*: Challenging Traditional Restriction of Religious Women in Thirteenth-Century France." *Proceedings of the Western Society for French History* 29 (2001): 33–44.

Jordan, William Chester. "Isabelle of France and Religious Devotion at the Court of Louis IX." In *Capetian Women.* Ed. Kathleen Nolan. New York: Palgrave, 2003, pp. 209–224.

Karras, Ruth Mazo. *From Boys to Men. Formations of Masculinity in Late Medieval Europe.* Philadelphia: University of Pennsylvania Press, 2003.

Kervyn de Lettenhove, B. *Histoire de Flandre.* Vol. 1. Bruxelles: St. Lebegue, 1847.

Kittell, Ellen. *From ad Hoc to Routine. A Case Study in Medieval Bureaucracy.* Philadelphia: University of Pennsylvania Press, 1991.

Kittell, Ellen, and Suydam, Mary A., eds. *The Texture of Society. Medieval Women in the Southern Low Countries*. New York: Palgrave, 2004.

Knockaert, Luce. "De Stichting der Cistercienzerinnen Abdij ter Hagen Onder Axel (1236)." *Cîteaux in de Nederlanden* 9 (1958): 121–31.

Koebner, Richard. "The Settlement and Colonization of Europe." In *Cambridge Economic History of Europe*. Vol. 3. Ed. M.M. Postan. Cambridge: Cambridge University Press, 1963.

Labande, Edmond-René. "Les filles d'Aliénor d'Aquitaine: étude comparative." *Cahiers de civilisation medievale* 29 (1986): 101–112.

Labarge, Margaret Wade. *A Small Sound of the Trumpet*. London: Hamish Hamilton, 1986.

Lambert, Malcolm. *Franciscan Poverty. The Doctrine of the Absolute Poverty of Christ and the Apostles in the Franciscan Order, 1210–1323*. London: SPCK, 1961.

Laplane, Henri. *L'Abbaye des Clairmarais après des Archives*. St. Omer, 1863.

Lauwers, M., and Walter Simons. "Les Communautés Béguinales à Tournai du XIIIe au Xve siècle." *Tornacum* 3 (1988): 103–124.

Lawrence, C.H. *The Friars. The Impact of the Early Mendicant Movement on Western Society*. London: Longman, 1994.

———. *Medieval Monasticism. Forms of Religious Life in Western Europe in the Middle Ages*. London: Longman, 1984.

Lebecq, Stéphane. "Les Cisterciens de Vaucelles en Flandre maritime au XIIIe Siècle." *Revue du Nord* 54 (1972): 371–85.

Leclercq, Jean. *Women and Saint Bernard of Clairvaux*. Trans. Marie-Bernard Saïd. Kalamazoo, MI: Cistercian Publications, 1989.

Le Glay, Édouard. *Histoire des Comtes de Flandre*. Paris: Société Saint Augustine, 1843.

———. *Histoire de Jeanne de Constantinople, Comtesse de Flandre et de Hainaut*. Lille: Vanackere, 1841.

LeGoff, Jacques. "Ordres Mendicants et Urbanisation dans la France Médiévale." *Annales, Économies, Sociétés, Civilisations* 25 (1970): 924–46.

Lekai, Louis. *The Cistercians. Ideal and Reality*. Kent, OH: Kent State University Press, 1977.

———. *The White Monks*. Okauchee, WI: Our Lady of Spring Bank Press, 1957.

Linot, Jules. "Histoire de la Fondation des Frères Mineurs de Valenciennes." *France Franciscaine* 3 (1914): 45–89.

Lippens, F.H. "L'Abbaye des Clarisses d'Ypres aux XIIIe et XIVe siècles." *Revue d'histoire Franciscaine* 7 (1930): 297–330.

———. "Les Frères Mineures à Gand du XIIIe au XIVe siècle." *France Franciscaine* 13 (1930): 219–59.

Little, Lester. *Religious Poverty and the Profit Economy in Medieval Europe*. Ithaca, NY: Cornell University Press, 1978.

Little, Lester, and Barbara Rosenwein. "Social Meaning in the Monastic and Mendicant Spiritualities." *Past and Present* 63 (1986): 4–32.

Livingstone, Amy. "Kith and Kin: Kinship and Family Structure of the Nobility of Eleventh-and Twelfth-Century Blois-Charters." *French Historical Studies* 20 (1997): 419–58.

———. "Noblewomen's Control of Property in Early Twelfth-Century Blois-Chartres." *Medieval Prosopography* 18 (1995): 55–72.

———. "Powerful Allies and Dangerous Adversaries. Noblewomen in Medieval Society." In *Women in Medieval Western European Culture*. Ed. Linda E. Mitchell. New York: Garland, 1999, pp. 7–30.

Lloyd, T.H. *The English Wool Trade in the Middle Ages*. Cambridge: Cambridge University Press, 1982.

Longère, Jean. *L'Abbaye Parisienne de Saint-Victor au Moyen Age*. Biliotheca Victorina 1. Paris: Brepols, 1991.

LoPrete, Kimberly A. "Adela of Blois and Ivo Chartres: Piety, Politics and the Peace in the Diocese of Chartes." In *Anglo-Norman Studies XIV: Proceedings of the Battle Conference*. Ed. Marjorie Chibnall. Woodbridge, 1992.

———. "The Gender of Lordly Women: The Case of Adela of Blois." In *Pawns or Players? Studies on Medieval and Early Modern Women*. Ed. Christine Meek and Catherine Lawless. Dublin: Four Courts Press, 2003, pp. 90–110.

———. "Historical Ironies in the Study of Capetian Women." In *Capetian Women*. Ed. Kathleen Nolan. New York: Palgrave, 2003, pp. 271–86.

Luykx, Theo. *Atlas Historique et Culturel de la Belgique*. Bruxelles: Elsevier, 1959.

———. *De grafelije financiele Bestuursinstellingen en het grafelijke patrimonium in Vlaanderen tijdens de regering van Margareta van Constantinople (1244–1278)*. Brussels: Palais der Academien, 1961.

———. "Gravin Johanna van Constaninople en de godsdienstige vrouwen-begegingen in Vlaanderen gedurende de eerste helft der XIII de eeuw." *Ons Geestelyk Erf* 17 (1943): 5–30.

———. *Johanna van Constantinopel, Gravin van Vlaanderen en Henegouwen, haar Leven (1199/1200–1244), haar Revgeering (1205–1244), vooral in Vlaanderen*. Antwerp: N.V. Standaard, 1946.

Lyon, Bryce. "Medieval Real Estate Development and Freedom." *American Historical Review* 63 (1957): 47–61.

Mahn, Jean-Berthold. *L'Ordre cistercienne et son gouvernement de origines au milieu du XIIIe siècle (1098–1265)*. Paris: Boccard, 1945.

Martindale, Jane, ed. *Status, Authority and Regional Power. Aquitaine and France, 9th to 12th Centuries*. Aldershot, Great Britain: Variorum, 1997.

Maurer, Helen E. *Margaret of Anjou. Queenship and Power in Late Medieval England*. Suffolk: Boydell, 2003.

Mazenod, Lucienne. *Les Femmes Célebres*. Tome I. Paris: Editions d'art, 1960.

McCash, June Hall, ed. *The Cultural Patronage of Medieval Women*. Athens, GA: University of Georgia Press, 1996.

———. "Marie de Champagne and Eleanor of Aquitaine: A Relationship Reexamined." *Speculum* 54 (1979): 698–711.

McDonnell, Ernest. *Beguines and Beghards in Medieval Culture, with Special Emphasis on the Belgian Scene*. New Brunswick: Rutgers University Press, 1954.

McLaughlin, Megan. *Consorting with Saints: The Ideology of Prayer for the Dead in Early Medieval France*. Ithaca: Cornell University Press, 1994.

Meersseman, G.G. "Les Frères Prêcheurs et le Movement dévôt en Flandre au XIIIe siècle." *Archivum Fratrum Praedicatorum* 18 (1948): 69–130.

———. "Jeanne de Constantinople et les Frères Prêcheurs." *Archivm Fratrum Praedicatorum* 19 (1949): 122–68.

———. "Le Débuts de l'Ordre des Frères-Prêcheurs dans le Comté de Flandre (1224–1280)." *Archivum Fratrum Praedicatorum* 17 (1947): 54–76.

De Mersseman, J. "Études Historique sur Jeanne de Constantinople, Comtesse de Flandre." *Annales de la Societe d'Émulation pour l'histoire et des Antiquités de la Flandre Occidentale*. Vol. 2. Bruges: Vandescasteele-Werbrouck, 1840, pp. 73–87, pp. 109–132; 1841, pp. 15–52, pp. 281–330.

Michel, Édouard. *Abbayes et Monastères de Belgique. Leur Importance et leur rôle dans le développement du Pays*. Brussels: G. Van Oest et Cie., 1923.

Mikkers, Edmund. "The Spirituality of Cistercian Nuns: A Methodological Approach." In *Hidden Springs: Cistercian Monastic Women: Medieval Religious Women* 3:2. Ed. John A. Nichols and Lillian Thomas Shank. Kalamazoo, MI: Cistercian Publications, 1995, pp. 525–42.

———. "Meditations on the Life of Alice of Schaerbeek." In *Hidden Springs: Cistercian Monastic Women: Medieval Religious Women* 3:2. Ed. John A. Nichols and Lillian Thomas Shank. Kalamazoo, MI: Cistercian Publications, 1995, pp. 395–414.

Milis, Ludo. *Angelic Monks and Earthly Men: Monasticism and its Meaning to Medieval Society*. Woodbridge, Suffolk, 1992.

———. "De Kerk Tussen de Gregoriaanse hervorming en Avignon." *Algemene Geschiedenis der Nederlanden* 3 (1982): 166–211.

———. *L'Ordre des Chanoines Réguliers d'Arrouaise. Son Histoire et son Organization de la Fondation de l'Abbaye (vers 1090) à la fin des Chapitres Annuels (1471)*. Bruges: De Tempel, 1969.

Mitchell, Linda E. *Portraits of Medieval Women. Family, Marriage and Politics in England, 1225–1350*. New York: Palgrave, 2003.

———. "The Lady is a Lord." *Historical Reflections/Réflexions Historiques* 18 (1992).

Mollat, Michel. "Les hôtes de l'abbaye de Bourbourg." *Melanges d'histoire du Moyen Age, dediés à la memoire de Louis Halphen*. Paris: Presses Universitaires de France, 1951.

Moorman, J.H.R. *A History of the Franciscan Order from its Origins to the Year 1517*. Oxford: Clarendon Press, 1968.

———. *Medieval Franciscan Houses*. New York: Franciscan Institute, 1983.

de Moreau, Édouard. *Histoire de l'Église en Belgique*. 5 vols. Brussels: L'Édition Universelle, 1945–52.

Neel, Carol. "The Origins of the Beguines." *Signs* 14 (1989): 321–41.

Newman, William Mendel. *Les Seigneurs de Nesle in Picardie (XIIe-XIIIe siécle). Leurs Chartes et Leur Histoire. Étude sur la Noblesse Régionale Ecclésiastique et Laïque*. 2 vols. Philadelphia: American Philosophical Society, 1971.

Nicholas, David. *Medieval Flanders*. New York: Longman, 1992.

———. "Of Poverty and Primacy: Demand, Liquidity and the Flemish Economic Miracle, 1050–1200." *American Historical Review* 96 (1991): 17–41.

Nicholas, Karen. "Countesses as Rulers in Flanders." In *Aristocratic Women in Medieval France.* Ed. Theodore Evergates. Philadelphia: University of Pennsylvania Press, 1999, pp. 111–37.

———. "Women as Rulers: Countesses Jeanne and Marguerite of Flanders." In *Queens, Regents and Potentates.* Ed. Theresa Vann. Dallas: Academia, 1993, pp. 52–71.

Nimal, H. *Les Béguinages.* Nivelles: Lanneau et Despret, 1908.

Ollivier, R.P. *Le Grand Béguinage de Gand.* Paris: P. Lethielleux, 1903.

Parisse, Michel, ed. *Les Religieuses en France au XIIIe siècle.* Nancy: Presses Universitaires de Nancy, 1985.

Pernoud, Régine. *Blanche of Castile.* Trans. Henry Noel. New York: Coward, McCann and Geoghegan, 1975.

Petit-Dutaillis, Charles. *The Feudal Monarchy in France and England from the Tenth to the Thirteenth Century.* Trans. E.D. Hunt. New York: Barnes and Noble, 1966.

Philippen, L.J.M. *De Begijnhoven, Oorsprong, geschiendis, inrichting.* Antwerp: Ch. and H. Courtin, 1918.

Phillips, Dayton. *Beguines in Medieval Strasbourg.* Stanford: Stanford University Press, 1941.

Pirenne, Henri. *Economic and Social History of Medieval Europe.* London: Routledge and Kegan Paul, 1936.

———. *Histoire de Belgique.* Brussels: Maurice Lamertin, 1929.

Powicke, Maurice. *The Loss of Normandy, 1189–1204.* Manchester: Manchester University Press, 1960.

Renna, Thomas. "Hagiography and Feminine Spirituality in the Low Countries." *Cîteaux* 39 (1988): 287–95.

Richard, Jean. *Les ducs de Bourgogne et la Formation su Duché du XIe au XIVe siècle.* Paris: Société des Belles Lettres, 1954.

———. *Saint Louis. Crusader King of France.* Trans. Jean Birrell. Cambridge: Cambridge University Press, 1992.

Roehl, Richard. "Plan and Reality in a Medieval Monastic Economy: The Cistercians." *Studies in Medieval and Renaissance History* 9 (1972): 83–114.

Roisin, Simone. "L'éfflorescence Cistercienne et le Courant Féminine de Piété au XIIIe siècle." *Revue d'Histoire Ecclésiastique* 39 (1943): 342–78.

———. "Réflexions sur la culture intellectuelle en nos Abbaye Cisterciennes Médiévales." In *Miscellanea Historica in Honorem Leonis van der Essen: Universitatis Catholicae in oppido Lovaniensi iam annos XXV professoris.* Brussels: Éditions Universitaires, 1947.

Rosaldo, Michelle Zimbalist. "Women, Culture and Society: A Theoretical Overview." In *Women, Culture and Society.* Ed. Rosaldo and Louise Lamphere. Stanford: Stanford University Press, 1974, pp. 17–42.

Rosenthal, Joel T. *Patriarchy and Families of Privilege in Fifteenth-Century England.* Pennsylvania: University of Pennsylvania Press, 1991.

———. *The Purchase of Paradise. Gift Giving and the Aristocracy, 1307–1485.* London: Routledge and Kegan Paul, 1972.

Rosenwein, Barbara. *To Be the Neighbor of St. Peter: The Social Meaning of Cluny's Property, 909–1049.* Ithaca: Cornell University Press, 1989.

Samaran, M. Charles, ed. *Recueil des Actes de Philippe Auguste*, 4 vols. Paris: Imprimerie Nationale, 1966.

Schmitz, Philibert. *L'Histoire de l'Ordre de Saint Benoît*. 7 vols. Liège: Éditions de Maredsous, 1948–56.

Schneider, Reinhard. *Vom Klosterhaushalt zum Stadt-und Staatshaushalt*. Stuttgart: Anton Hiersemann, 1994.

Schulenberg, Jane. "Female Sanctity: Public and Private Roles, ca. 500–1100." In *Women and Power in the Middle Ages*. Ed. Mary C. Erler and Maryanne Kowaleski. Athens: University of Georgia Press, 1988, pp. 102–125.

Scott, Joan Wallach. "Gender: A Useful Category of Historical Analysis." In *Feminism and History*. Ed. Joan Wallach Scott. Oxford: Oxford University Press, 1986, 152–86.

Serbat, L. "L'église des Frères-Mineurs à Valenciennes." *Revue d'histoire Franciscaine* 2 (1925): 141–77.

Shadis, Miriam. "Blanche of Castile and Facinger's 'Medieval Queenship': Reassessing the Argument." In *Capetian Women*. Ed. Kathleen Nolan. New York: Palgrave, 2003, pp. 137–62.

———. "Piety, Politics and Power: The Patronage of Leonor of England and her Daughters Berenguela of Leon and Blanche of Castile." In *The Cultural Patronage of Medieval Women*. Ed. June Hall McCash. Athens: University of Georgia Press, 1996, pp. 102–134.

Shadis, Miriam, and Constance Hoffman Berman. "A taste of the Feast: Reconsidering Eleanor of Aquitaine's Female Descendants." In *Eleanor of Aquitaine. Lord and Lady*. Ed. Bonnie Wheeler and John C. Parsons. New York: Palgrave, 2003. pp. 177–211.

Showalter, Elaine, ed. *Speaking of Gender*. New York: Routledge, 1989.

Simons, Walter. *Stad en Apostolaat. De vestigig van de bedelorden in het graafschap Vlaanderen (ca. 1225–1350)*. Brussels: Paleis der Academiën, 1987.

———. *Bedelordekloosters in het Graafschap Vlaanderen*. Brugge: Jan Cobbaut, 1987.

———. "The Beguine Movement in the Southern Low Countries: A Reassessment." *Bulletin von het Belgische Historisch Instituut te Rome* 59 (1989): 63–105.

———. "Begynen en begarden in het middeleeuwse douai." *De Franse Nederlanden. Les Pays-Bas Francais* 17 (1992): 180–97.

———. *Cities of Ladies. Beguine Communities in the Medieval Low Countries, 1200–1565*. Philadelphia: University of Pennsylvania Press, 2001.

Sivéry, Gérard. "Les Débuts de l'économie cyclique et de ses crises dans les bassins scaldiens et mosans, fin du XIIe et début du XIIIe siècle." *Revue du Nord* 64 (1982): 667–81.

———. *L'Économie du royaume de France au siècle de Saint Louis (vers 1180–1315)*. Lille: Presses Universitaires, 1984.

Southern, R.W. *The Making of the Middle Ages*. New Haven: Yale University Press, 1953.

———. *Western Society and the Church in the Middle Ages*. London: Penguin Books, 1970.

Spiegel, Gabrielle. *Romancing the Past. The Rise of Vernacular Prose Historiography in Thirteenth-Century France*. Berkeley: University of California Press, 1993.

Stafford, Pauline. *Queen Emma and Queen Edith. Queenship and Women's Power in Eleventh-Century England.* Oxford: Blackwell, 1997.

———. *Queens, Concubines and Dowagers. The Kings Wife in the Early Middle Ages.* London: Leicester University Press, 1998.

Stranger, Mary. "Literary Patronage at the Medieval Court of Flanders." *French Studies* 11 (1957): 214–29.

Stuard, Susan Mosher. "The Chase after Theory: Considering Medieval Women." *Gender and History* 4 (1992): 135–46.

———. "The Dominion of Gender or How Women Fared in the High Middle Ages." In *Becoming Visible. Women in European History*. Ed. Renate Bridenthal, Claudia Koonz, and Susan Stuard. Boston: Houghton Mifflin, 1987, pp. 129–52.

———. *Women in Medieval Society*. Philadelphia: University of Pennsylvania Press, 1976.

Tabuteau, Emily Zack. *Transfers of Property in Eleventh-Century Norman Law*. Chapel Hill: University of North Carolina Press, 1988.

Tebrake, William. "Reclamation of Land." In *Dictionary of the Middle Ages*. Vol. 10. Ed. Joseph Strayer. New York: Scribner and Sons, 1962, pp. 272–79.

———. *Medieval Frontier Culture and Ecology in Rijnland*. College Station, TX: Texas A and M University Press, 1985.

Thompson, Sally. *Women Religious: The Founding of English Nunneries After the Norman Conquest*. Oxford: Clarendon Press, 1991.

Thompson, Victoria. *Power and Border Lordship in Medieval France. The County of the Perche, 1000–1226*. Suffolk: Boydell, 2002.

———. "Women, Power and Protection in Tenth and Eleventh Century England." In *Medieval Women and the Law*. Ed. Noël James Menuge. Suffolk: Boydell, 2000, pp. 1–18.

Thyrion, P. Fulgence. *Les Frères-Mineurs à Valenciennes au XIIIe siècle*. Valenciennes: G. et Veuve P. Girad, 1913.

Tyson, Diana B. "Patronage of French Vernacular History Writers in the Twelfth and Thirteenth Centuries." *Romania* 100 (1979): 180–222.

Vandermaesen, Maurice. "Vlaanderen en Henegouwen onder het Huis van Dampierre, 1244–1384." *Algemene Geschiedenis der Nederlanden* 2 (1982): 400–414.

Van Werveke, H. "The Economic Policies of Government: The Low Countries." In *Cambridge Economic History of Europe*. Vol. 3. Ed. M.M. Postan. Cambridge: Cambridge University Press, 1963.

Varenbergh, Émile. *Histoire des Rélations Diplomatiques entre le Comté de Flandre et l'Angleterre au Moyen Age*. Brussels: C. Muquardt, 1874.

Vauchez, André. *The Laity in the Middle Ages. Religious Beliefs and Devotional Practices*. Trans. Margery J. Schneider. Notre Dame: University of Notre Dame Press, 1993.

Vaughn, Robert, trans. *The Chronicles of Matthew Paris*. Gloucester: A. Sutton, 1984.

Verheijen, Luc. *La Règle de Saint Augustin. I: Tradition Manuscrit. II: Recherches historiques*. Paris: Études Augustiniennes, 1967.

Verhulst, Adriaan. *Histoire du Paysage Rurale en Flandre de l'époque Romaine au XVIIIe siècle*. Bruxelles: La Renaissance du livre, 1966.

———. *De Sint-Baafsabdij te Gent en Haar Grondbezit (VII-XIV Eeuw)*. Brussels: Palais der Academien, 1958.

Verlinden, O. "Markets and Friars." In *Cambridge Economic History of Europe*. Vol. 3. Ed. M.M. Postan. Cambridge: Cambridge University Press, 1963.

Vicaire, M.H. *L'Imitation des apôtres: Moines, chanoines, mendiants (IVe-XIIIe siècle)*. Paris: Les editions du cerf, 1963.

Walker, Sue Sheridan. "Free Consent and the Marriage of Feudal Wards in Medieval England." *Journal of Medieval History* 8 (1982): 123–34.

——. ed. *Wife and Widow in Medieval England*. Ann Arbor, MI: University of Michigan Press, 1993.

——. "Wrongdoing and Compensation: The Pleas of Wardship in 13th and 14th century England." *Journal of Legal History* 9 (1988): 267–307.

Walters, Lori J. "The Image of Blanchefleur in Montpellier BI, sect. méd. H 249." In *The Manuscripts of Chrétien de Troyes*. Ed. Keith Busby, Terry Nixon, Alison Stones, and Lori Walters, 2 vols. Amsterdam: Rodopi, 1993.

——. "Jeanne and Marguerite de Flandre as Female Patrons."*Dalhousie French Studies* 28 (1994): 15–27.

Ward, J.C. "Fashions in Monastic Endowment: The Foundations of the Claire Family, 1066–1314." *Journal of Ecclesiastical History* 32 (1981): 427–51.

Wardrop, J. *Fountains Abbey and its Benefactors, 1132–1300*. Suffolk: Cistercian Publications, 1987.

Warlop, H.E. *The Flemish Nobility Before 1300*, 4 vols. Kortrijk: G. Desmet-Huysman, 1975–76.

Warnkoenig, L.A. *Histoire de la Flandre et de ses Institutions Civiles et Politiques jusqu'a l'Année 1309*, 5 vols. Bruxelles: M. Hayez, 1835.

Waugh, Scott L. *The Lordship of England: Royal Wardships and Marriages in English Society and Politics 1217–1327*. Princeton: University of Princeton Press, 1988.

Weber, Max. *The Theory of Social and Economic Organization*. Trans. A.M. Henderson and Talcott Parsons. New York: Free Press, 1947.

Wemple, Suzanne. *Women in Frankish Society. Marriage and the Cloister, 500–900*. Philadelphia: University of Pennsylvania Press, 1981.

White, Stephen D. *Custom, Kinship and Gifts to Saints: The Laudatio Parentum in Western France 1050–1150*. Chapel Hill: University of North Carolina Press, 1988.

Wolff, R.L. "Baldwin of Flanders and Hainaut, First Latin Emperor of Constantinople: His Life, Death, and Resurrection, 1171–1225." *Speculum* 27 (1952): 281–322.

Wood, Susan. *English Monasteries and their Patrons in the Thirteenth Century*. Oxford: Oxford Historical Series, 1955.

Ziegler, Johanna. "The *curtis beguinages* in the Southern Low Countries and Art Patronage: Interpretation and Historiography." *Bulletin de l'Institute historique Belge de Rome* 57 (1987): 31–70.

INDEX

Anchin, abbey of, 75, 76, 118
Arnould of Audenarde, 40, 42–43
authority vs. power, 2, 4, 10, 22–24, 30, 37–38, 56–58, 112–115

Baldwin IX, count of Flanders
 alliance with England, 26–27, 28
 death of, 3, 11, 17
 Fourth Crusade, 2–3
 struggle with France, 2
Bauduin d'Avesnes, 7
Bauduin Ninove, 7
Beatrice of Brabant, 51
Beaupré-sur-la-Lys, abbey of, 65–66, 119
beguines
 comital patronage of, 82, 93–94
 role in secular community, 81–82
Bijloke, abbey of, 79, 92, 119
Blanche of Castile, 47, 52, 104
Bonham, abbey of, 65, 119
Bouchard of Avesnes
 bailiff of Hainaut, 40, 42
 inheritance settlement, 51
 marriage to Marguerite, 4, 31–32, 39–40
Boudelo, abbey of, 78, 119
Bourbourg, abbey of, 80, 118
Bouvines
 battle of, 35
 impact on Flanders, 36, 38, 65

Cambron, abbey of, 70, 76, 77, 119
Charles of Anjou, 53

Cistercian Order, 67, 72–73, 91–92, 93, 100, 102–103
Council of Soissons, 52

Dominican Order
 comital patronage of, 70–71, 95–96, 97
 policy toward property, 107
 role in secular community, 80–81
 stance toward female members, 108–109
Doornzele, abbey of, 79, 119

Eename, abbey of 75, 80, 119
Elizabeth, countess of Vermandois, 26–27
Épinlieu, abbey of, 65, 66, 92, 119

false Baldwin (Bertrand de Rains), 4, 45–48
Ferrand of Portugal
 incarceration of, 35–36, 46–48
 marriage to Jeanne, 3, 29
 Pont-à-Vendun, 29–30
 rebellion and Bouvines, 34–35
Flines, abbey of, 63, 65, 74, 75, 76–78, 87, 92, 111, 119
Fourth Lateran Council, 40
Franciscan Order
 comital patronage of, 94
 role in secular community, 80–81
 stance toward female members, 108–109
Frederick, Holy Roman Emperor, 42

gender
  influence on power, 5, 11, 18, 21, 47, 49, 54–55, 58–59, 113–114
  perceptions based on, 4, 9, 32–34
  versus status, 36
Gregory IX, 51
Guillaume le Breton, 6
Guy of Dampierre, 52, 53–54, 99

heiresses
  position in feudal system, 11, 18, 24–25, 49, 58
  production of, 20–21
Hemelsdale, abbey of, 68–69, 70, 72, 92–93, 119
Henry III, 45
Honorius III, 41, 46
hospitals, 83

Innocent III, 41
Innocent IV, 52
Isabelle of Hainaut, 26

Jacques de Guyse, 7
Jean I of Avesnes, 51, 53–54
Jean of Dampierre, 53–54
Jean of Nesle
  bailliff of Flanders, 3, 38, 42
  membership in Pro-French party, 35–36
  struggles with Jeanne, 43
Jeanne
  consolidation of power, 42–44, 56–57
  death of, 87
  depictions in narrative sources, 7–8
  inheritance of Flanders and Hainaut, 18, 30
  marginalization of, 30–31, 36, 38–39, 49
  marriage to Ferrand of Portugal, 29
  marriage to Thomas of Savoy, 3, 50, 110
  minority of, 3, 25, 28
  patronage of, *see* individual abbeys
John I, 35

literary patronage, 57–58
Loos, abbey of, 75, 119
Louis VIII, 43, 45–46, 47, 58
Louis IX, 47, 51, 53–54, 57

Marchiennes, abbey of, 69, 70, 75, 118
Marguerite
  death of, 87
  depiction in narrative sources, 7–8
  inheritance dispute, 4, 51–54
  marriage to Bouchard of Avesnes, 4, 31–32, 39–40
  marriage to William of Dampierre
  minority of, 3
  patronage of, *see* individual abbeys
Marie of Champagne, 2–3
Marquette, abbey of, 65, 66, 74, 75, 76–78, 87, 92, 111, 119
Matilda of Portugal, 3, 29, 31
Matthew Paris, 7
Messines, abbey of, 75, 118
Michel of Boulers, 43
mills, 76
monasteries, roles of
  asserting comital authority, 67–72
  control of contested land, 64–67
  economic activities, 73–80
  education, 83–84
  pastoralism, 73–74
  social services, 82–83
Mont Blandin, abbey of, 75, 80, 119
Moorsele, abbey of, 79

narrative sources, 5–7
Nieuwenbos, abbey of, 79, 92, 119
Nonnenbossche, abbey of, 69, 118
Notre-Dame des Près, abbey of, 65, 66, 76, 79, 119
Notre-Dame du Val-des-Écoliers, abbey of, 71–72, 89–90, 96, 120

Oosteeklo, abbey of, 68, 79, 120
Oudenbourg, abbey of, 74, 118

INDEX

patrilineage
 definition of, 19
 impact on inheritance, 5, 19–20
Philip II
 consolidation of power, 23, 28–29, 49
 policy towards female rulers, 25, 39, 48–49, 54–56, 59
 struggle with Flanders, 2–3, 25–26, 29, 37–38, 46–47
 use of fief rents, 29
Philip of Alsace, 26–27
Philip of Namur
 Flemish attitude towards, 17–18, 28–29
 regent of Flanders, 3, 17
 treaty of Pont de l'Arche, 17
Philippe Mouskes, 7–8, 41
primogeniture
 definition of, 18–19
 impact on inheritance, 5, 11, 19–20
 implications for women, 20–21, 58
public/private dichotomy, 2, 4, 10–12, 23–25, 56, 84–85, 112–113

Ravensberg, abbey of, 74, 79, 119
reclamation, 77–78
religious patronage
 categorization of, 12–13, 62, 84–85
 donative phrases, 90–91
 meaning of, 12, 14, 61–62, 88–89
 motives behind, 13–14, 44, 63, 89, 91, 111
 pittances, 99–100
 prayer requests, 97–98, 101
Renaud of Dammartin, count of Boulogne, 21, 35, 49
Richard I, 7, 26

Saint-André, abbey of, 80, 119
Saint-Aubert, abbey of, 68, 117
Saint-Bavon, abbey of, 76, 79–80, 119
Saint-Donatien, abbey of, 2, 76
Saint-Martin, abbey of, 69, 70, 117
Saint-Nicholas, abbey of, 68, 117
Sainte-Walburga, abbey of, 70
Siger of Ghent, 35–36
Simon de Montfort, 49–50
Soleilmont, abbey of, 72, 120
Spermalie, abbey of, 1, 2, 61, 77, 93, 120

Ter Doest, abbey of, 78, 119
Ter Duinen, abbey of, 75–76, 78, 119
Ter Hagen, abbey of, 92, 119
Thomas of Savoy, 3, 50, 101
treaty of La Grange, 27
treaty of Melun, 47–48
treaty of Paris, 36, 45, 65
treaty of Péronne, 27–28, 64
treaty of Pont de l'Arche, 17, 25

Verger, abbey of, 65, 120
Victorines (Order of Saint Victor), 83, 96–97, 109
vita apostolica, 80–81, 91, 105–108
Vivier, abbey of, 65

Westkappelle, 53–54
William I of Dampierre, 4, 41, 50, 98–99, 101
William II of Dampierre, 51–52, 98
William II of Holland, Holy Roman emperor, 51–53
Woestine, abbey of, 65, 120
woolen industry, 30, 44, 73–76

Zoetendale, abbey of, 96, 97–98, 117
Zonnebeke, abbey of, 68, 69, 117